INSIGHT GUIDES

Created and Directed by Hans Höfer

Jamaica

Project Editor: Paul Zach
Updated by Ian Randle and Sonia Gordon
Managing Editor: Andrew Eames

Editorial Director: Brian Bell

APA PUBLICATIONS

Jamaica, a vibrant island rich in culture and color in the Caribbean Sea, makes a terrific topic for an equally vibrant and colorful Insight Guide. Hardly surprising, then, that the original edition of this book, edited by **Paul Zach** and **Mike Henry**, became something of a classic amongst visitors and locals. Hardly surprising, too, that there was much to update and revise for the present edition.

Jamaica, with a population of 2½ million people on an island just 146 by 51 miles (235 by 82 km), has made a significant impression on the world's consciousness. Variously famous for piracy, slavery, plantations, cricket, reggae, rastafarians, ganja and, more recently, for Yardies and honeymoon holidays, this has never been a particularly low-key Caribbean island.

In fact, despite its small size, Jamaica is almost a continent in its variety, with mountains reaching 7,402 ft (2,256 meters), with flat agricultural plains, with a huge, sprawling city in Kingston and an inaccessible wilderness in the Cockpit Country, and with some of the best beaches in the Caribbean on the northern coast around the famous resorts of Montego Bay and Ocho Rios. However, all is not all smiles on the island: be careful how you go, don't go alone into unknown locations and be on your guard against unscrupulous salesmen.

Zach

As with the other 188 books in this series, Apa Publications set out to find the best available local talent to assemble *Insight Guide: Jamaica*. Appointed to oversee the project were Paul Zach, a freelance American journalist whose work had spanned the *Washington Post* and US network television, and Mike Henry,

head of Kingston Publishers, who provided many vital local contacts, not least those that enabled Apa photographers to take their cameras to Pocomania rituals.

Apa's team of Jamaican writers was led by the late **Victor Stafford Reid**, a recipient of the coveted Order of Jamaica. Internationally known for his novel *The Leopard*, Reid also wrote books on Jamaica, a biography of Norman Washington Manley, and many short stories. In this volume, Reid contributed "The Jamaicans" and an inside look at Jamaica's vibrant religious life.

Clinton V. Black wrote the in-depth history of this book, surveying Jamaica from Arawak times. Black headed the Government Archives in Spanish Town from 1949 until his recent death. Born in Kingston in 1918, he wrote the standard history text, *The Story of Jamaica*.

The lively travel section, giving readers a new look at popular old attractions as well as opening up new paths and places was largely the work of three contributors: **Olive Senior**, **Dr Ian Sangster** and the late **Ken Maxwell**. For *Insight Guide: Jamaica*, Maxwell traveled throughout much of his homeland in a vintage Rover P4 gathering materials for chapters on South Middlesex, South Cornwall and the Cockpit Country, as well as the feature on language, "Pardon My Patois!"

Senior dissected the sprawling capital city of Kingston and its surrounding region, including Port Royal, Port Antonio, and the Portland and St Thomas parishes. The author of books on Jamaican politics and culture, she took over as editor of the *Jamaica Journal* in 1982.

Sangster researched and produced

Henry

Reid

Black

Sangster

Maxwell

the travel-section chapters about the north coasts of Middlesex and Cornwall counties, including the tourist centers of Ocho Rios and Montego Bay, as well as the Blue Mountains. Sangster was born in Scotland, but emigrated to Jamaica in 1969 to become director of the Sugar Industry Research Institute. He is the author of two books: *Jamaica, A Holiday Guide* and *Sugar and Jamaica*.

Dr Heather Royes is the winner of several awards for her poetry, and holds a PhD from the University of Wisconsin. For this book, she contributed the chapter on arts and provided information for Reid's piece on religion.

Royes

Dermott Hussey teamed with Zach to prepare the feature on "The Red Hot Rhythms of Reggae." His expertise comes from years as a DJ for the Jamaican Broadcasting Company. He was co-author of Kingston Publishers' *Bob Marley, Reggae King of the World*.

Hussey

Apa's resident expert on Jamaican politics was the late **Dr Carl Stone**. A professor of political science at the University of the West Indies, Stone received the National Commander of Distinction award for his contributions to scholarship. The *Daily Gleaner* rated him Jamaica's outstanding newspaper columnist. For this volume, he surveyed "The Political Canvas."

Stone

Barbara Gloudon, one of Jamaica's leading journalists, commentators and playwrights, prepared the chapter on "Dance and Drama: Everybody Is a Star." Formerly features editor for Gleaner Publications and chairperson of the Little Theater Movement, she now leads her own communications agency in Kingston.

Jimmy Carnegie sourced this book's chapter on cricket. Carnegie writes a sports column for the *Sunday Gleaner* and is the author of a biography of cricket legend George Headley.

Jamaican journalist **Lloyd Williams** penned the mandatory piece on the island's infamous ganja trade. Williams has worked for the *Daily Gleaner* for more than 20 years.

Insight Guide: Jamaica owes its superb photography to the work of three principals: Zach, Insight Guides publisher Hans Höfer and **David Stahl**. Stahl, who is based in Sarasota, Florida, spent nearly a month in Jamaica on special assignment for this book. His work has appeared in *National Geographic*.

Jamaican photographers who contributed include **Maria LaYacona**, **Howard Moo Young**, **Dr Owen Minot** and **Anthony DaCosta**. The archives of the National Library at the Institute of Jamaica were invaluable. National Library director **Stepheny Ferguson** opened the drawers of a collection reputed to be the finest on the West Indies.

Those charged with bringing the text and photography fully up-to-date were faced with the challenge of making a good book even better. Further editorial fell to Jamaican-based publisher **Ian Randle** and travel writer **Sonia Gordon**. They checked words and pictures, extensively revising many sections. Gordon also effectively rewrote the crucial practical information section, Travel Tips. A new chapter on the economy ("Education, Migration and Trade") was introduced. The book's overall structure has been changed and maps and pictures have been updated. The final text was proofread and indexed by **John Goulding**.

Carnegie

CONTENTS

Introduction

Jamaica's Attractions 21

History

The Earliest Islanders 26

Spanish Discovery
and Colonization 29

The British Takeover 33

Pirates and Buccaneers 39

The Plantation Era 49

The Transition to
Independence 60

The Political Canvas 65

Migration,
Education and Trade 73

Features

The Jamaicans 85

The Vibrant
Spiritual Spectrum 97

Ganja, the Sacred Weed 102

The Red Hot
Rhythms of Reggae 109

Dance and Drama:
Everybody's a Star 125

Art, from Ghetto to Gallery 129

A Nation of Cricket Lovers 135

Food: Discovering Nyam 141

Pardon my Patois 146

Places

Introduction 157

The County of Surrey 161

Kingston:
The Lively Capital 165

<u>Preceding pages</u>: pineapple; in the shade of a coconut palm.

Port Royal:
Lair of the Buccaneers 184

High in the
Blue Mountains 189

Port Antonio
and Country Comforts 197

The County of
Middlesex 217

Ocho Rios
and Surroundings 218

Spanish Town
and South Middlesex 231

The County of Cornwall 243

Down the way at
Montego Bay 245

Conquering the Cockpit
Country 259

Negril and South
Cornwall 263

Maps

Jamaica 158
Kingston 164
Port Antonio 200
Ocho Rios 219
Spanish Town 231
Montego Bay 244

TRAVEL TIPS

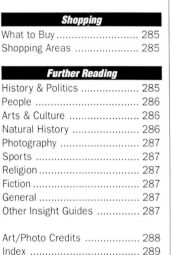

Getting Acquainted

The Place 274
Climate 274
Government 275
Economy 275
Culture & Customs 275

Planning the Trip

What to Wear 275
Entry Regulations 275
Health 275
Money 276
Public Holidays 276
Getting There 276
Specialist Holidays 277
Foreign Investment 277
Useful Addresses 277

Practical Tips

Tipping 277
Business Hours 277
Media 277
Postal Services 278
Telephone & Fax 278
Tourist Information 278
Embassies
& Consulates 278
Emergencies 278

Getting Around

Public Transportation 279
Private Transportation 279

Where to Stay

Accommodation 280
Hotels 280
Villas 282

Eating Out

What to Eat 284
Where to Eat 283

Attractions

Culture 283
Nightlife 284

Sport & Leisure

Participant Sport 284

Shopping

What to Buy 285
Shopping Areas 285

Further Reading

History & Politics 285
People 286
Arts & Culture 286
Natural History 286
Photography 287
Sports 287
Religion 287
Fiction 287
General 287
Other Insight Guides 287

Art/Photo Credits 288
Index 289

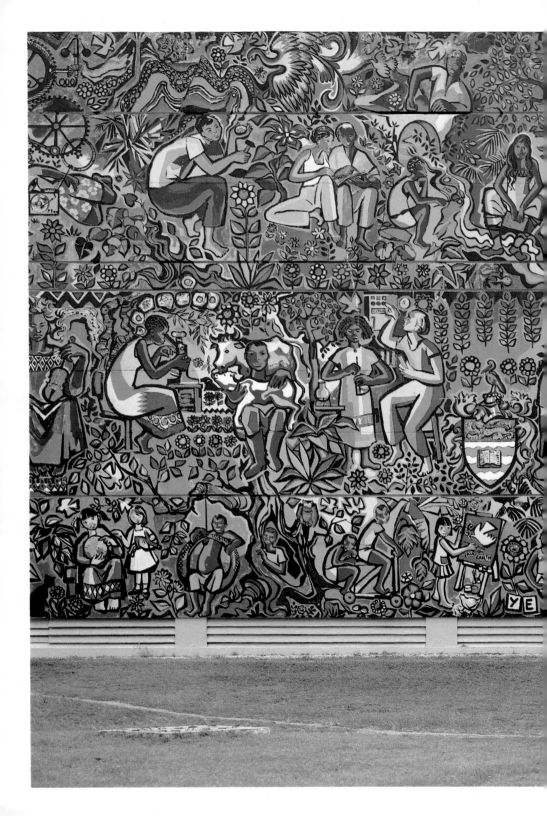

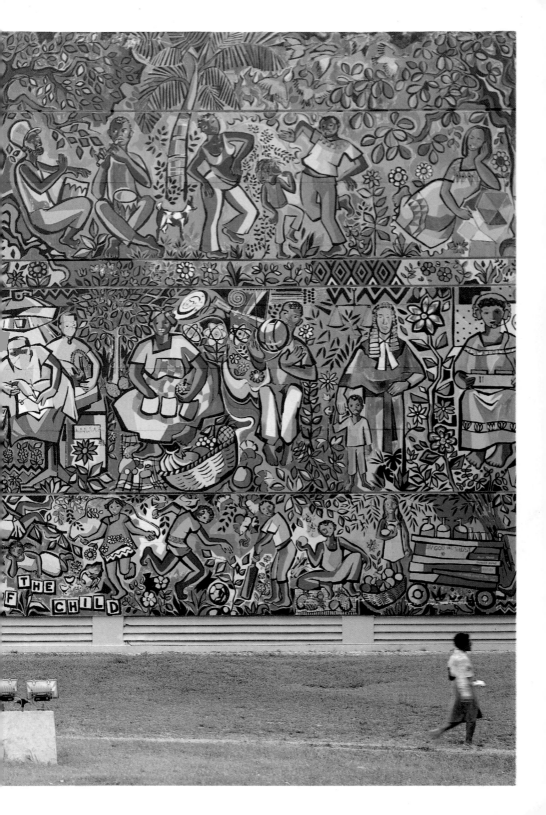

JAMAICA'S ATTRACTIONS

Never had I seen a land so beautiful.
Now I knew where the writers of the Bible
had got their description of Paradise.
They had come here to Jamaica.
– Errol Flynn in *My Wicked, Wicked Ways*

Errol Flynn, the swashbuckling movie idol of the 1940s, literally washed up on the shores of Jamaica in his yacht, *Zaca*, following a hurricane. Flynn, who had a reputation for wooing and winning women, was seduced this time by the siren of the Caribbean Sea. He spent most of the last 13 years of his life on the island.

Jamaica has had the same persuasive effect on mankind for centuries. There's something sensuous in the undulating cut of its contours, in the way the winds tease the palm trees and the seas massage its sands. There's a hypnotic quality to its people's lilting patois and reggae rhythms, to the deafening hush that hangs in the heights of the Blue Mountains, to the hum and whistle of its birds.

So "walk good," but be wary. Once it grabs you, Jamaica might not let go.

Highlands and Cockpits: Few islands or countries of Jamaica's size boast such a diversity of skin tones and facial features, of landscapes and seascapes, of plant and animal life. With a total land area of 4,411 sq. miles (11,424 sq. km), Jamaica is slightly smaller than the American state of Connecticut but somewhat larger than the Middle Eastern country of Lebanon. The island stretches about 146 miles (235 km) east to west from Morant Point to Negril, and bulges to 51 miles (82 km) at its greatest width. About 2.2 million people live here, handsome blends of African, European, Arabic, Chinese and East Indian stock who account for their national motto: "Out of Many, One People."

Jamaica floats in the Caribbean Sea at a latitude 18° north of the Equator. Its reputation has grown around its fine beaches, and most hotels and resorts crowd powdery slivers of sand along the north coast.

Yet rugged highlands dominate the landscape. More than half of Jamaica hovers 1,000 ft (305 meters) above the Caribbean, and 40 square miles rise above the 5,000-ft level. The highest point, Blue Mountain Peak, punctures the clouds at 7,402 ft (2,256 meters), just 10 miles (16 km) from the coastal plain east of Kingston. In the middle of the island sits cool Mandeville on a plateau in the Don Figueroa Mountains, rising 2,000 ft (610 meters) above the checkered agricultural slopes of the countryside.

Jamaica's northwest is pockmarked by the surrealistic karst landscapes of the Cockpit Country – the "Me No Sen, You No Come" land of the free-spirited Maroon people. Sinkholes have settled in the brittle limestone surface, forming a pitted tundra that resembles the inside of an enormous egg carton.

Where the highlands plummet to the sea, spectacular cliffs have been created, like Lovers' Leap on the south coast, where the *duppies* (ghosts) of forlorn sweethearts mingle with the sea mists. Some 120 rivers and streams gush from mountain ravines to carve gashes in the coastal plains. Cloudbursts transform them into torrents that can flood the lowlands; droughts make them into parched ravines clogged with stones.

The evolution of paradise: Geologists believe Jamaica and its neighboring islands in the Caribbean evolved from an arc of volcanos that bubbled up from the seas billions of years ago. Lower lands surrounding the peaks eased out of the waters over 30 million years ago, the legacy of minute skeletons of sea creatures and marine organisms which accumulated on seabeds elevated by volcanic activity. A cap of white limestone, the residue of the skeletons, still covers about two-thirds of the island. This land-building process climaxed about 20 million years ago when the island emerged from the Caribbean.

The Cockpit Country and innumerable cave systems betray the oceanic origins of the country's surface. The limestone fractured and cracked over the eons as rains rutted the surface. Today, rivers like the Tangle River near Maroon Town mysteriously disappear underground, only to reappear in springheads miles away. Cave systems include Twin Sisters on the Hellshire

Coast near Kingston and a series of spectacular chambers called Windsor Cave, nearly two miles long, in the Cockpit Country.

Primeval Jamaica was a rugged, rocky land. Eventually, climate and soil combined to spawn magnificent forests that covered every acre by the 15th century. Its only native fruits when Columbus arrived were guava, pineapple, the sweetsop and possibly the star apple. Virtually everything that blooms today was imported either by the hands of humans or the droppings of birds. Europeans cleared timber from the plains, savannas and some mountain slopes. Then they introduced sugar cane, bananas and citrus. Spanish traders brought coconuts from Malaya in the 17th century. The *ackee* that is the staple of most Jamaican breakfasts came on slave ships from West Africa in 1778. Pimento is a native plant, as is the mahoe, Jamaica's national tree. Other natives include the Santa Maria, cedar, bulletwood, break axe, Spanish elm and ebony. The purple-blossomed *lignum vitae* is the national flower.

Nearly 3,000 varieties of flowering plants have been identified on the island, including 800 species found nowhere else in the world. Indigenous varieties include 200 species of wild orchids, 60 species of bromeliads called "wild pine" by Jamaicans, and about 550 ferns.

This lush, perfumed Eden contains hollows brimming with palm trees, mountains crowned by stunted elfin forests, and dusty plains full of dildo cacti and prickly pear. There are mistletoes called "scorn ground" and "God bush" and an aerial plant called "Old Man's Beard" that drips from power lines in most townships. Bamboo imported from China flourishes throughout the island. Tangles of vines contribute to the exotic scenery; they include a giant pea vine called "cacoon," with huge pods that are stewed and eaten by Maroons.

Bountiful birds: Animal life on the island is limited. There are rats of course, and mongooses introduced by 19th-century plantation owners to combat the rats. The native Jamaican coney closely resembles a large guinea pig, but is a relative of the rat. It lives in burrows in the ground but has become scarce and is rarely seen.

Bats are Jamaica's most numerous animals. About 25 varieties flitter through island belfries. The enormous gentle manatee that inspired tales of mermaids is another mammal still inhabiting lonely waters along the south coast. Whales can sometimes be spotted off the coasts. Jamaica's rapidly dwindling numbers of crocodiles are called alligators. Frogs are called toads, and moths are called bats. The ubiquitous gecko keeps the insect population in check. The comparatively large, ominous-looking ground lizard is common, but Jamaica has few snakes, all of them harmless.

Jamaica's bird population makes up in color and variety what its animals lack. More than 200 species have been spotted on the island, including 25 endemic species. Its national bird, the Doctor Bird, a streamer-tailed hummingbird found only in Jamaica, darts about the island's flower gardens. Bright yellow, orange and green parrots, parakeets and finches sing in the forest. On the ugly side, the John Crow turkey buzzards scavenge garbage and the entrails of dead animals.

Warm breezes: Jamaica's climate has always been its biggest attraction. The warmth that lured its earliest residents now brings hundreds of thousands of sun-worshipping visitors each year. Seasons are non-existent. Rains, averaging 77 inches (196 cm) annually, fall mainly in May and October although mountain trade winds pull down 200 inches (508 cm) a year in parts of the parishes of Portland and St Thomas. Sunshine falls more often. It produces annual average temperatures of 80°F (27°C) on the coast, dropping to the 70s and 60s in higher mountain elevations. Peaks in the Blue Mountains have been known to sustain "frigid" conditions below 50°F (10°C) on rare occasions.

Mostly, the weather is perfect. Cooling trade winds that Jamaicans call the "Doctor Breeze" blow in from the seas to cool the daytime hours. Night brings the "Undertaker's Breeze" from the mountains. Jamaicans used to bundle up against it in fear of catching their deaths of cold. Now they revel in that wind.

As artist-historian Howard Pyle wrote in 1890: "The Air here, notwithstanding the heat, is very healthy. I have known blacks one hundred and twenty years of Age, and one hundred years old is very common amongst Temperate Livers."

Right, hot song stylist Burning Spear lets rip at Reggae Sunsplash.

EXPLANATION

* Sugar Plantations with Water Mill
* Ditto   with Windmills
* Ditto   with Cattle Mills
* Ginger Cotton Coffee & Pimento Plantations &c
⚓ Anchorage for large Vessels
⚓ Anchorage for small Vessels
Roads
Divisions of Parishes
Negro Provinces

SCALE of MILES

When Christopher Columbus "discovered" Jamaica on May 5, 1494, during his second voyage to the New World, he found a thriving colony of Arawak Indians such as he had already met in the neighboring islands of Cuba and Haiti.

From an ancestral home in the Orinoco region of the Guianas and Venezuela, the Arawaks had long before sailed northward in their dugout canoes, settling in each of the islands of the Antilles from Trinidad to Cuba. They probably arrived in Jamaica in two

West Indies in 1492, they had taken the entire Lesser Antilles and were raiding the eastern end of Puerto Rico. They were known and feared in Haiti and from time to time made murderous attacks even on Jamaica. But for the arrival of the Spaniards, the Caribs might have exterminated those first Jamaicans. As it happened, the newcomers from Europe were shortly to complete the work of destruction themselves.

The Arawak Civilization: An estimated 100,000 Arawaks at one time lived on the

waves – the first (the so-called "Redware People") around AD 650, the second between AD 850 and 900.

Some centuries later, the Arawaks' calm and peaceful lives were rudely disturbed by the arrival of another Indian tribe, the fierce man-eating Caribs (from whose name comes the word *cannibal*). Probably also originating in the Guiana region of South America, this warlike people began to spread through the islands in their war canoes, leaving death and destruction in their wake, slaughtering the men and abducting the women.

Farther and farther north they swarmed until by the time Columbus discovered the

island. Aboriginal remains show that they lived in most parts of Jamaica, even as far inland as Ewarton and Moneague and in such upland areas as the Long Mountain and Jack's Hill. The majority of their villages were close to the coast or near rivers, as the Arawaks were seagoing people and lived chiefly off seafood.

An interesting village site, and one of the most accessible, is that at the White Marl, near Central Village, three miles from Spanish Town. On a hill adjacent to the site now stands the Arawak Indian Museum.

The Arawaks were brown-skinned, short and slightly built with straight, coarse black hair, broad faces and flat wide noses. Their only breadstuff, cassava, was doubtlessly introduced by them into the island in their migration from the South American mainland. In addition, they grew sweet potatoes, fruits, vegetables, cotton and tobacco.

Jamaica excelled in the cultivation of cotton. Much of the women's time was spent spinning and weaving. The island supplied hammocks (believed to be an Arawak invention) and cotton cloth to the neighboring islands of Cuba and Haiti, and the conquer-

ing Spaniards themselves had their sailcloth made in Jamaica.

The Jamaican Arawaks were skilled artisans who left their paintings on the walls of many island caves. They were superb stoneworkers and their implements were particularly well shaped, smooth and beautifully finished. They fashioned their dugout canoes from the trunks of cedar and silk cotton trees, hollowing out the trunks first by char-

Preceding pages, an early British map of the island. Left, Columbus meets an Arawak chief. Above, Arawak drawings found in Mountain River Cave near Spanish Town.

ring, then by chipping with their stone axes and chisels. These canoes varied greatly in size: some held one person only, others 50 or more. Columbus supposedly saw one 96 ft long and 8 ft wide (29 by 2.4 meters).

Smoking was both a pastime and a religious ritual with the Arawaks, and the word *tobacco* comes from the name of their pipe. They were a pleasure-loving people and enjoyed dancing, singing, and playing a ball game called *batos*.

As in Cuba, Jamaica's inhabitants divided their island into provinces, each ruled over by a *cacique* assisted by village headmen or sub-chiefs. *Caciques* were much respected; they alone enjoyed the privilege of polygamy, and they occupied the best and biggest houses, in which the family idols and images of spirit deities were kept. If a *cacique* was ill and dying he would be strangled as a mark of special favor.

The Arawaks explained the mysteries of everyday life in their myths. Two supreme gods, Jocuahuma and his female counterpart, were associated with the sun and moon in a myth about the emergence of mankind from a cave. In addition, they worshipped spirits and images called *zemes*. Very few of the original *zemes* survive but three found in a cave in the Carpenter Mountains, Manchester, are now in the British Museum. Five casts of these spirit-gods are in the museum of the Institute of Jamaica. There is also one in the small Arawak museum at Coyaba in Ocho Rios.

The Arawaks were encouraged by their priests to believe that some *zemes* could speak, although this was exposureby the Spaniards as a hoax used by the priests to control the people. The priests were also the medicine men of the tribe and knew a good deal about the medicinal value of herbs. Souls of the departed were believed to go to *coyaba*, a place of ease and rest where there were no droughts, hurricanes or sickness, and time was spent in feasting and dancing.

The Arawaks often buried their dead in caves, placing the head and certain bones of the body in a pottery bowl. Some of the best preserved skulls and the finest examples of their pottery have been found in caves.

CHRISTOPHER COLUMBUS and his SONS DIEGO and FERDINAND.

Wilson sculp.t

From an ancient Spanish Picture in the possession of Edward Home Esq.r
of Bevis Mount near Southampton.

p/21

SPANISH DISCOVERY AND COLONIZATION

"Jamaica, like many other of the West India Islands, is like a woman with a history. She has had her experiences, and has lived her life rapidly. She has enjoyed a fever of prosperity founded upon those incalculable treasures poured into her lap by the old-time buccaneer pirates. She has suffered earthquake, famine, pestilence, fire, and death: and she has been the home of a cruel and merciless slavery. Other countries have taken centuries to grow from their primitive life through the flower and fruit of prosperity into the seed-time of picturesque decrepitude. Jamaica has lived through it all in a few years."

– Howard Pyle, *Jamaica New and Old* in Harper's *New Monthly Magazine*, published in January 1890.

As the 15th century drew to a close, Jamaica was still primitive, its years of hardship and glory still ahead. In Europe, meanwhile, civilized man was entering the Renaissance. One of the most outstanding figures of the age was the Genoese seafarer Christopher Columbus, the man who was to discover the New World.

On August 3, 1492, Columbus – in his flagship the *Santa Maria*, accompanied by two caravels, the *Niña* and *Pinta*, with a total crew of 90 – sailed from Palos de la Frontera, Spain, on his first great voyage. On October 12, he landed on one of the islands of the Bahamas, today's Watling Island. In gratitude to the Lord for bringing him safely to port, Columbus named it San Salvador, or "Holy Saviour."

It was on his second voyage that Columbus discovered Jamaica. He first heard of the island of Xaymaca (an indigenous name of disputed meaning) from the Cuban Indians who described it as "the land of the blessed gold." But Jamaica had no gold. This was a disappointment not only to Columbus but also to those who followed him.

On May 5, 1494, Columbus arrived at St Ann's Bay, and named it Santa Gloria – "on account of the extreme beauty of its coun-

try," according to Columbus' biographer, Samuel Eliot Morison. He thought Jamaica itself "the fairest island that eyes have beheld… all full of valleys and fields and plains." But, finding the Indians hostile, he anchored off the port for the night and sailed down the coast the following day to a harbor "shaped like a horse-shoe."

Here also the Indians were unfriendly, but Columbus was determined to land; he needed wood and water and a chance to repair his vessels. The Indians scattered before the advance of a fierce dog and the Spanish crossbow men, leaving some of their number killed and wounded on the beach. Columbus claimed Jamaica in the name of his patron sovereigns, Ferdinand and Isabella of Spain. He called it "St Jago" or "Santiago" after his country's patron saint. For the rest of the admiral's stay, the Indians supplied him and his men regularly with provisions in exchange for trinkets and other trade goods.

More voyages: On May 9, the fleet sailed westward to Montego Bay – El Golfo de Buen Tiempo, as Columbus called it, "Fair Weather Gulf." He then continued his cruise along the Cuban coast before crossing over again to Jamaica to complete the exploration of this island.

Nine years later, on his fourth voyage, Columbus visited Jamaica again – this time in sad and tragic circumstances. After leaving the American mainland, it became clear that his two battered, worm-eaten caravels were not fit for the Atlantic crossing. He tried to make for Hispaniola but got no farther than St Ann's Bay before the ships were stranded side by side, a bow's shot from the shore. With heavy hearts, the Admiral and his company – including his young son Ferdinand and his brother Bartholomew, watched the vessels fill with water and settle for good in the soft sand of the bay.

Here he was to spend 12 months, beset by hardship, hunger, doubts and sickness, abandoned by the Indians and deserted by many of his followers – some of whom even staged an abortive mutiny.

Eventually, two of his company – Diego Méndez and Bartolomé Fieschi – made the arduous sea journey to Hispaniola, where they managed to charter a small caravel from a Spanish colony. Towards the end of June 1504, the little vessel arrived at St Ann's Bay and the desperate year-long wait was at an end. On the 29th, she left for Hispaniola with Columbus and the survivors of his crew, about 100 in all. In September, Columbus sailed for Spain. He was never to see the New World again.

Serious settlers: It was not until 1510 that colonists arrived in Jamaica, under the island's first Spanish governor, Juan de Esquivel. Sevilla la Nueva, or "New Seville," as they called their settlement on St Ann's Bay, was conceived on a large and not unimpressive scale. It included among the principal buildings a fort, a castle and a church. But the location, close to swamps, proved unhealthy; it was soon abandoned in favor of a new site on the south side of the island in what is now Spanish Town.

Little survives today of New Seville. Finely-carved stone panels, semi-columns, door jambs, friezes and other artifacts found on the site are now in the possession of the Institute of Jamaica.

Spanish Town (the Villa de la Vega of the Spaniards) quickly became a center of activity. With its convenient location – sufficiently near to two harbors and enjoying protection from direct sea attack, and its healthy situation featuring an ample water supply and fertile surroundings, Spanish Town had attracted the colonists' attention.

A number of interesting accounts of the town were written during the Spanish period. A Carmelite missionary, Antonio Vázquez de Espinosa, writing around 1628, says the site was "marvellously attractive... very well built and laid out." An unwelcome English visitor, Captain William Jackson, who plundered Spanish Town 15 years later, thought it a fair town, consisting of 400 or 500 houses, five or six stately churches and chapels, and one monastery of Franciscan friars. Unfortunately, no Spanish buildings still exist, having in time deteriorated beyond repair.

The Spaniards enslaved the native Arawaks and so overworked and ill-treated them that in a short time they had all died out. The process was doubtlessly aided by the introduction of European diseases to which they would have had little or no immunity.

Today our only reminders of these first Jamaicans are their artifacts, found chiefly on their village sites: a small group of words, like barbecue, hurricane, hammock, tobacco and canoe; and a few place names, including Jamaica itself.

Upon the demise of the Arawaks, the Spaniards began to import black slaves from Africa. The first of them arrived in 1517, the earliest ancestors of Jamaica's majority race today.

Jamaica as a Spanish colony was largely a failure. Its main use to Spain was that of a supply base. In the early days of colonization, men, horses, arms and food from here helped in the conquest of Cuba and much of the American mainland. But after that, the island's significance waned until it sank to the position of an unimportant, badly-governed and largely-neglected outpost.

Almost nothing was done to develop the natural resources of Jamaica. The chief trade was the supply of fresh provisions to passing ships and the export of hides and lard to Havana and the mainland. In exchange, the ships that touched here brought supplies of clothing, oil, wine, wheaten flour and a few luxury items.

The colonists devoted themselves chiefly to pastoral and agricultural pursuits. From Spain they brought all the familiar varieties of citrus (except grapefruit). They carried the banana and plantain to Jamaica from the Canary Islands via Hispaniola. They also introduced cattle, horses and swine, which they kept in *hatos*, or ranches, on the open savanna. Chief among the *hatos* were Morante (the name lingers in Morant Bay), Liguanea (in lower St Andrew) and Guanaboa (in St Catherine).

Roads in Spanish times were mostly bridle paths. Settlements, with the exception of the capital, were scarcely better than townships. These included Caguaya (Passage Fort), Oristan (Bluefields), Las Chorreras (near Ocho Rios), Savanna-la-Mar and Puerto Anton (Port Antonio).

Strictly speaking, although the island was under the control of Spain, it was to some extent self-governing. The Spanish governor ruled with the aid of a *cabildo*, a council of nominated members. A strong governor ruled largely by himself; a weak one was controlled by the *cabildo*. A tactless governor quickly ran into trouble with Church authorities.

The Church played an important part in the life of the times. There is still a Red Church Street and a White Church Street in Spanish Town, both named after Spanish chapels, as well as a Monk Street – a reminder of the dark-robed, sandaled figures who were once a familiar feature of the old town.

The end of Spanish control: By the last years of the Spanish occupation, internal strife had weakened the colony. The governors were not properly supported from home, and quarrels with the Church authorities undermined their control.

Frequent attacks by pirates were another corrupting influence in the colony. These were not limited to Jamaica, but formed part

Rivalries among nations in Europe spread to distant lands, and from the mid-1500s to the end of the 18th century, the rich countries of the Caribbean were the scene of international and commercial competition. As early as 1506, French ships appeared in the Caribbean, attacking small Spanish settlements and capturing vessels. In 1555, the Jamaican colonists chased two French ships away. But other Frenchmen followed, as did Dutch, Italian, Portuguese and English, all bent on trade and plunder. In 1596, the Elizabethan adventurer Sir Anthony Shirley raided the island. Other raids by English forces took place in 1603, 1640 and 1643.

These incursions had a demoralizing ef-

of a general effort on the part of certain European nations to loosen Spain's grip on the region. When Columbus discovered the New World, the Pope had issued proclamations neatly dividing the Indies between Spain and Portugal; but it was not long before other European nations began to challenge the justice of this division, "I should like to see the clause of Adam's will that excludes me from a share of the world," declared Francis I, King of France.

Above, King's House in Spanish Town. Virtually the only surviving reminders of the Spanish occupation of Jamaica are place names.

fect on the colonists. They also opened the eyes of more and more people to the attractions and strategic value of the island. During the English raid of 1643, a number of men deserted and had to be left behind. The question was: how long would it be before some foreign power attempted to take and hold Jamaica?

The answer came on May 10, 1655, when a large English expeditionary force sailed into Caguaya (today's Passage Fort). Once again the people of Spanish Town prepared for a marauding raid. But this time the fleet's arrival spelled the end of Spanish rule in Jamaica.

THE BRITISH TAKEOVER

The British expeditionary force which captured Jamaica had been sent out by the Lord Protector, Oliver Cromwell, as part of a plan known as "The Western Design," aimed against the Spanish power and trade monopoly. Cromwell had hastily assembled a fleet under Admiral William Penn and General Robert Venables. He also appointed a council of three commissioners to accompany the important expedition.

But the omens for success were not favorable. "No worse prepared and equipped expedition ever left the English shores," wrote Sir Charles Firth, the Cromwellian scholar, "and the consequences of these initial mistakes and negligences were all aggravated by the mistakes and quarrels of those charged with its command." Ruffians and thieves made up the majority of the troops, with a sprinkling of good soldiers, seasoned and better principled. In short, the crew was a mixture, as one of the captains described it, "of little wine with much water, the one losing its proper strength and vigour, and the other thereby little bettered."

Sailing from Portsmouth at the end of December 1654, the expedition stopped first at Barbados to raise levies from the plantations and take on provisions. In the Leeward Islands, additional recruits were also signed on. Then they sailed for Hispaniola on their great mission to attack the capital city of Santo Domingo.

But there they met disaster. The expedition was roundly defeated, the complete massacre of the forces being averted only by the landing of a party of sailors to cover their flight back to the ships. As it was, a third of their number was left dead or missing.

The assault on Jamaica: Fearful of Cromwell's rage at the failure at Santo Domingo, the British decided to attack some other Spanish settlement. Jamaica, known to be thinly populated and weakly defended, was eventually chosen as the target of invasion.

On May 10, 1655, the fleet of 38 ships and

about 8,000 men anchored off Caguaya, the landing place for Spanish Town, later to be known as Passage Fort. A few shots fired into the little fort dispersed the defenders. Soon the British flag waved above the walls of the fortification. The commanders of the expedition may have hoped to have been able to attack some stronger place from here later; but as it happened, Jamaica was to prove the end of Cromwell's ambitious "Western Design."

An early opportunity of occupying the

capital, Spanish Town itself, was missed. Combined with a further delay by the Spaniards on the plea of considering surrender terms, this gave most of the inhabitants the opportunity to escape with their valuables to the north side of Jamaica and on to Cuba. When the British troops finally marched into the town, they found it empty and bare. In anger and disappointment, they destroyed much of the place, burning the churches and even melting the bells down to make shot.

Confident that they would in time recover the island, the fleeing Spaniards had freed and armed their slaves and left them behind

Left, a portrait of Oliver Cromwell while he was engineering Great Britain's takeover of Jamaica. **Right**, an ancient British cannon that still guards the gates of Spanish Town.

in the trackless interior. According to plan, these freed men would harry the invaders with guerrilla warfare until an army for the Spanish reconquest could be collected. Instead, these people and their descendants later won fame as the redoubtable Maroons.

Although disappointed over the Santo Domingo fiasco, Cromwell decided nevertheless to make the most of the new colony, offering very attractive terms in the way of land grants and other requisites to "such as shall transplant themselves to Jamaica."

The Battle of Jamaica: Meanwhile, under the courageous and determined Governor Cristobal Arnaldo de Ysassi, stout but unsuccessful efforts were made by the dis-

amends for the failure at Santo Domingo. More than 300 Spaniards were killed and valuable supplies of food and arms captured, together with the Spanish royal standard and 10 colors. It was the most important battle ever fought in Jamaica and put an end to Spanish hopes of reconquest, although the war was to drag on for two more years. Ysassi held out in the mountains to which he had escaped, always hoping for the relieving force which never arrived. With his eventual escape by canoe to Cuba, all Spanish influence in Jamaica ended, and the island was officially ceded to the British Crown under the Treaty of Madrid in 1670.

Like the Arawak, the Spaniard has van-

placed Spanish to recapture the island. The decisive battle was fought in June 1658. A large force consisting mainly of Mexican contingents landed at Rio Nuevo and dug in behind a strong fort, armed with cannon, on a cliff near the river's west bank.

The British commander, Colonel Edward D'Oyley, proved equal to the challenge. As soon as news of the landing reached him, he called out 750 of his best officers and men. They sailed around the island to the attack. D'Oyley offered Ysassi honorable surrender terms, but received in reply a jar of sweetmeats and a courteous refusal.

The battle that took place on June 27 made

ished from the Jamaican scene. Apart from the Seville carvings, already mentioned, almost no visible traces of Spanish occupation are left. Only place names, especially river names, survive to remind of past links with Spain.

The defeat of the Spaniards removed the immediate danger of foreign invasion. But in August 1660 the threat of internal rebellion arose in the form of a mutiny of troops led by colonels Raymond and Tyson, the latter having command of one of the regiments quartered at Guanaboa Vale, 9 miles (14 km) from Spanish Town.

The reasons for the mutiny are not clear.

Dislike of Colonel D'Oyley and his iron-handed methods played a part, as did rivalry between those who favored the monarchy and those who preferred the Commonwealth. But the root cause may have been impatience with the continuation of military rule and a longing to settle down as colonists. After all, provisions were now plentiful, trade was increasing, and the general health of the community was improving.

Courtmartial: D'Oyley acted with characteristic promptness to meet this new danger. He tried fair words at first. When these failed, he brought reinforcements into the town and persuaded the troops to hand over their leaders and disperse in exchange for a

It is ironic that D'Oyley's instructions conferred, in effect, the very privileges for which the rebellious colonels had grasped too soon. He was ordered to release the army and encourage planters, merchants and traders. Civil government was established and law courts set up. This was the groundwork that in time would lead Jamaica to become one of the most valuable possessions in the New World.

Under D'Oyley and his successors, Jamaica gradually elevated itself to relative prosperity by the early years of the 18th century. Despite war conditions in the Caribbean and some serious internal difficulties, island-born proprietors rose in power and

complete pardon. A court-martial was quickly convened and the colonels were adjudged to be deserving of death. Without delay, they were executed in sight of both the government and their troops.

News of the restoration of the monarchy in England arrived soon after. Within a year, D'Oyley was appointed governor – the first of more than 60 administrators who were to guide the destiny of the island.

Left, the Union Jack flies over Kingston's King Street during the British colonial era. **Right**, the lifestyle of expatriates, as depicted in an 18th-century cartoon.

wealth. Politics and the island economy were put on a sound footing as sugar production increased rapidly and cattle breeding, logging and coffee cultivation proved more and more profitable.

The British abandoned Spanish Town and shifted their colonial government to the Liguanea Plain with its excellent access to the sea. It was here that they molded Kings Town into a proper English port city. Kingston as it came to be called, saw a spectacular rise in size and importance, with good entertainment enabling a lavish lifestyle for the privileged rich. By 1872, it was the capital of Jamaica.

The Spanish Armada def

ed by Captaine Morgan

Sʳ HEN: MORGAN

Part. 2. Chap. 4.

PIRATES AND BUCCANEERS

Although the war with Spain, sparked by Cromwell's "Western Design," ended with the restoration of King Charles II to the British throne, the fighting never really ceased in the West Indies. Jamaica, as it turned out, was even better situated than Hispaniola for harassing the Spaniards. Early on, official British encouragement was given to the buccaneers – a rough, wild and ruthless collection of sea-rovers – to continue hostilities against Spain's West Indian possessions. They played a role of the first importance in the history of Jamaica and of the Caribbean as a whole.

They were an odd lot, these early rebels. They included runaway bondsmen, castaways, escaped criminals, political and religious refugees, who had gravitated in time towards the small, rocky island of Tortuga off the northern coast of Hispaniola, where they set up a sort of international port. Their early activities were limited to hunting the wild pigs and cattle which roamed the forests of western Hispaniola, to provide meat, hides and tallow. These they bartered to passing ships for ammunition and rough stores. They usually worked in pairs, each man having a partner with whom everything was shared. Armed with knives and long-barreled muskets, they tracked their quarry with the help of dogs. From their method of curing the meat on a wooden frame called a *boucan* (the French adaptation of a Carib Indian word), they earned the name *buccaneer*.

Buccaneers unite: Spain, of course, resented their presence on Spanish soil and hunted them relentlessly from the Hispaniolan forests. Driven to desperation and the realization that survival lay in unity, this scattered, ragged bunch of men banded together as the "Confederacy of the Brethren of the Coast" and took to the sea. At first they used whatever craft that was available – chiefly canoes. But as they captured Spanish ships by surprise attacks, their fleet soon swelled in size. With captured guns and arms, they

fortified Tortuga. Each success brought new recruits, and the stronger and bolder they grew, the farther they raided.

These buccaneers were a hardy breed. Immune or seasoned to the climate and its ills, they were ruthless, fearless and – except in their communal dealings – lawless. As Brethren, they were welded together by a stern code of discipline which accounted for much of their success. They usually sailed under strict articles, the first of which was: "No prey, no pay." All plunder went into a

common pool to be divided according to the share-out scales and disability pensions laid down in the articles. The loss of a finger, for example, rated a payment of 100 pieces-of-eight or one slave, while compensation for the loss of both eyes was 1,000 pieces-of-eight or 10 slaves.

Sir Thomas Modyford began his term as governor of Jamaica in June 1664 by suppressing buccaneering. But the outbreak of the Second Dutch War in March of the following year caused an about-face in policy. The hard-pressed Admiralty could not spare a fleet for the West Indies, the defense of which was placed in the hands of the wild

Preceding pages, Captain Henry Morgan blasts a Spanish armada. **Left,** Morgan, the vaunted governor and buccaneer. **Right,** the execution of pirate Three-Fingered Jack.

Brethren. Historian Edward Long was later to write: "It is to the Bucaniers that we owe the possession of Jamaica at this hour."

In Port Royal, the buccaneers found what they needed most: a ready market for their Spanish loot, facilities for the repair and equipping of their vessels, and ample opportunities for amusing themselves in the ways they liked. They flocked to the Port in ever-growing numbers. "Such of these Pirates," wrote the buccaneer-historian John Esquemeling, "are found who will spend two or three thousand pieces-of-eight in one night… I saw one of them give unto a common strumpet five hundred pieces-of-eight only that he might see her naked."

started humbly enough. Born about 1635, as the son of a Welsh land-owning farmer, he went to Barbados, possibly as an indentured servant, then made his way to Tortuga where he joined the Brethren and became Governor Modyford's strongest ally. The ruthless, resourceful buccaneer leader was the one man who could hold the wild Brethren together and direct their main efforts towards the defense of the island.

The sacking of Puerto Principe (near Camagüey, Cuba), Porto Bello (Panama) and Maracaibo (Venezuela) stand out as incredible milestones in Morgan's equally incredible career. That he was a hater of Spaniards, not averse to extremes of vio-

Nourished by the almost fabulous wealth these corsairs brought in, Port Royal grew and prospered at such a rate that within a decade and a half it had earned the title of the richest – and wickedest – city in the world.

Sir Henry Morgan: It was about this time that a new buccaneer-captain appeared on the scene and instantly claimed the limelight. Under the leadership of Henry Morgan, a tough, thick-set young Welshman, the buccaneers and Port Royal were to reach the pinnacle of their infamy.

Morgan – whose later career was climaxed with a knighthood, the governorship of Jamaica, and other official appointments –

lence and debauchery, is clear in this description by Esquemeling of the sacking of Porto Bello: "Having shut up all the Soldiers and Officers, as prisoners, into one room, they instantly set fire unto the powder (whereof they found great quantity) and blew up the whole Castle into the air, with all the Spaniards that were within. This being done, they pursued the course of their victory, falling upon the City… They fell to eating and drinking, after their usual manner, that is to say, committing in both these things all manner of debauchery and excess. These two vices were immediately followed by many insolent actions of Rape and Adultery committed upon many very honest women, as well married as virgins; who being threatened with the Sword, were constrained to submit their bodies to the violence of these lewd and wicked men..."

Morgan's crowning achievement was the destruction of Spain's supreme New World city of Panama. Peace had previously been sealed between Spain and England by the Treaty of Madrid, and Morgan's exploits – which shattered the treaty – earned both himself and Modyford the deep displeasure of their monarch in England. Eventually, however, the two daring and far-sighted friends were cleared of all disgrace and reunited in Jamaica, Morgan as governor and

Meanwhile the Jamaican government had been cracking down on buccaneering, which had achieved its end and was now going out of fashion. A decision was made to abandon the stricken port and found a new settlement, soon to be known as Kingston, across the harbor. But in spite of the earthquake and later disastrous fires and hurricanes, Port Royal survived to become an important naval station in the following century.

The French invade: As a prelude to 100 years of wars and alarms, the 17th century closed with the only real invasion attempt that Jamaica was to know. Taking advantage of the damage and confu-

Modyford as chief justice.

Although a rich landowner in his own right, Morgan's spiritual home and favorite stomping ground remained Port Royal. His body was entombed here in 1688, and his death presaged the end for Port Royal as a buccaneering port. On June 7, 1692, a violent earthquake broke under the town, plunging the better part of it beneath the sea, together with Morgan's grave.

Left, Calico Jack's "Pirate Princesses," Anne Bonney and Mary Read, take a break from the drudgery of pillaging. <u>Above</u>, Kingston in the 19th century.

sion caused by the Port Royal earthquake, a large French force under Admiral Jean du Casse descended on the eastern part of the island and ravaged the countryside in true and terrible buccaneer fashion. But at Carlisle Bay, Clarendon, where the next landing was made, Jamaica's scanty but gallant forces engaged the invaders and killed 700 of them.

Although the island was saved, it had suffered severely from the attack. About 100 settlers had been killed or wounded, scores of plantations burnt, 50 sugar works destroyed and some 1,300 slaves as well as quantities of loot carted away.

The war dragged to a close in September 1697 with the Treaty of Ryswick. Spain recognized the French claim to the western part of Hispaniola, while they called their part Santo Domingo. Today the island is still shared by two independent states, French-speaking Haiti and the Spanish-speaking Dominican Republic.

The 18th century was only two years old when the War of the Spanish Succession broke out in Europe. England and the Netherlands ranged against France and Spain. Although Europe was the main theater of war, the Caribbean saw some naval activity, including Admiral John Benbow's memorable engagement of a French fleet under the redoubtable Admiral du Casse.

On August 19, Benbow in the 90-gun *Breda* sighted du Casse's squadron off Santa Marta, Colombia. The ensuing six-day battle, though indecisive, was notable for Benbow's obstinate courage in carrying on the running fight in spite of the desertion of four of his captains. At one point, the gallant admiral engaged the entire French squadron single-handed and succeeded in recapturing a British galley previously taken by the French. But at length, with the *Breda* badly damaged, his own right leg shattered by chainshot, and his captains flatly refusing to engage the enemy, Benbow was forced reluctantly to break off the action and return to Port Royal. On arrival he immediately court-martialed the defecting captains, two of whom were sentenced to be shot. He himself died of his wounds at the old port and was buried in the Kingston Parish Church, where his tomb may still be seen.

Slaves and pirates: The war was brought to an end in 1713 by the Treaty of Utrecht. Britain was awarded France's *Asiento*, or contract, for the supply of slaves to Spanish New World settlements. Jamaica quickly became the entrepôt for the trade, the majority of the slaves being shipped from here to Spanish ports in locally owned vessels.

But all was not well with the island. Pursuing its aggressive policy, the House of Assembly was constantly at loggerheads with the governors representing the Crown, especially over money matters. Epidemics raged, violent hurricanes caused grievous loss of life and property, and troubles with the Maroons added to the general confusion.

So did attacks by pirates who were now plaguing the Caribbean in growing numbers. Coastal vessels were constantly molested and isolated plantations plundered. On one occasion Nicholas Brown, the "Grand Pirate," and his companion Christopher Winter burnt down a house near the coast in St Ann with 16 people locked inside. A reward of £500 for his capture was earned by one John Drudge, who captured Brown after a fight on one of the South Cays of Cuba. Brown died of his wounds on the way to Jamaica but Drudge, not to be cheated of the reward, cut off the pirate's head, pickled it in a keg of rum, and produced it in Jamaica in support of his claim.

Among the pirates who flourished at this time was Edward Teach, better known as "Blackbeard," believed by some to have been born in Jamaica. A powerful giant of a man, Teach is said to have struck terror into the hearts of his enemies by going into action with flaming matches plaited into his flowing black beard and hair. He was eventually killed in a sea fight off North Carolina.

Captain Charles Vane, another notorious pirate of this period, was captured after a successful career of robbery and murder and brought to Port Royal, where he was hanged on Gallows Point. But perhaps the most romantic of the lot was Captain Jack

Rackham, called "Calico Jack" because of his penchant for calico underclothes. He started his career as a member of Vane's crew, rising to be its leader.

After terrorizing the Caribbean for more than two years, he made the mistake of lingering longer than a man of his business ought on Jamaica's north coast during November 1720. News of his presence at Ocho Rios was carried to Governor Sir Nicholas Lawes, who immediately dispatched a Captain Barnet and a swift sloop in pursuit. Barnet found Rackham anchored in Negril Bay, enjoying a rum punch party. After a short running fight, he captured the pirate and his crew.

sandy islet still called Rackham's Cay, as a grim warning to other pirates.

The War of Jenkins' Ear: But the pirates, of course, were not the only people raising their pistols on the main. Old rivalries between Britain, Spain and France resulted in almost continuous conflict in the Caribbean.

One of the more notable tiffs of the time was the so-called War of Jenkins' Ear, which broke out in 1739 over the old argument of illegal trade. The stopping of British ships and ill-treatment of their crews by Spanish *guarda costas*, patrol vessels whose captains claimed the right of search, led to reprisals by the Englishmen.

A seaman named Robert Jenkins added

At the trial at the Court of Vice-Admiralty in Spanish Town, the startling discovery was made that two of Rackham's toughest crew members were women. Both Anne Bonney and Mary Read were condemned to death, but Bonney managed to escape punishment and Read died of fever, in prison, before sentence could be carried out. "Calico Jack" was executed. His body was squeezed into an iron frame and hung off Port Royal, on a

Left, Edward Teach, known as "Blackbeard," started his pirate career in Jamaica. **Above**, Sir George Rodney bombards the French fleet on April 12, 1782.

fuel to the fire. He had been captured by a *guarda costa* whose captain, he said, had slashed off one of his ears and told him to take it to England as a warning of the fate awaiting others who broke Spain's trade laws. Jenkins appeared before a committee of the House of Commons in London and waved a shriveled leathery object which he claimed was his ear. Those in the Caribbean who knew Jenkins to be a scallywag insisted that he had both his ears safely under his wig – but the clamor he created in Parliament was more than enough to incite a declaration of war against Spain.

The war itself was not a happy one for the

British. Admiral "Old Grog" Vernon, so named because he ordered the sailors' rum diluted in an effort to reduce drunkenness among the crew, mounted one disastrous campaign after another from Jamaica, costing the lives of some 20,000 men.

The peace which followed the Treaty of Aix-la-Chapelle in 1748 was a fragile one. By 1756, the old rivals found themselves embroiled in the Seven Years War. In the West Indies, almost every French island fell to the British by the time the war ended in 1763 with the Treaty of Paris.

Tensions were running high in Jamaica in the late 18th century. The famous bandit Three-Fingered Jack caused alarm every-

where. Fires and hurricanes ravaged the island, taking a heavy toll on life and property. A storm in October 1780 completely destroyed the town of Savanna-la-Mar, capital of Westmoreland parish.

Of more long-term effect was the American War of Independence, which started in April 1775 with the historic skirmish at Lexington Green near Boston. Britain's West Indies colonies did not sympathise with the motherland over this war. In fact, the Jamaica House of Assembly made its sentiments clear in a petition to the King, justifying the actions of the American colonists. France and Spain, meanwhile, were anxious to avenge their past losses in the Caribbean while Britain was preoccupied elsewhere.

In 1781, British forces surrendered to American General George Washington at Yorktown. By the following year, their status in the Caribbean was exceedingly low. Only Jamaica, Barbados and Antigua remained in British hands.

Rodney saves the day: The Count de Grasse, Admiral of France, joined forces with the Spanish and launched an invasion of Jamaica in April 1782. But they were intercepted by Admiral George Rodney on April 9 off the island of Dominica. In a three-day running engagement, Rodney masterfully manoeuvered his 36-ship fleet to break the enemy lines near the tiny Iles des Saintes between Dominica and Guadeloupe. To this day, the conflict is remembered as "The Battle of the Saints."

When the victorious Admiral Rodney sailed into Kingston harbor with his prizes of war in tow, the island went wild with jubilation. The splendid French flagship *Ville de Paris*, with the count himself aboard as prisoner, was in British hands. Rodney was honored by the Crown with a barony and a pension of £2,000 a year. Today a monumental statue of Rodney, sculpted by John Bacon, dominates the square in Jamaica's Spanish Town. The statue is flanked by two of De Grasse's cannons.

Toward the end of the 18th century, the youthful Horatio Nelson visited Jamaica. While awaiting the arrival of his ship, the *Hinchinbrooke*, he was put in command of the batteries at Port Royal's Fort Charles in preparation for a threatened French invasion which never materialized. Later he led an expedition from Jamaica to Nicaragua; it failed when yellow fever wiped out two-thirds of his forces.

But Nelson went on to become one of the greatest of all British naval commanders, and his residence in Jamaica is commemorated by a marble tablet fixed to the wall of Fort Charles. It reads:

IN THIS PLACE DWELT HORATIO NELSON
You who tread his footprints
Remember his glory.

Left, British Commander Lord Horatio Nelson. **Right**, France's Admiral Count de Grasse surrenders to British Admiral Sir George Rodney (left) in an 18th-century engraving.

Hamilton delin.

Thornton sculp.

The French Admiral COUNT De GRASSE Delivering his Sword to ADMIRAL (now LORD) RODNEY, (Being a more Exact Representation of that Memorable Event than is given in any other Work of this kind) On Board the Ville de Paris, after being Defeated by that Gallant Commander on the Glorious 12.th of April 1782 —— in the West Indies ——

JOHNNY NEW-COME in the ISLAND of JAMAICA.

JOHNNY NEWCOME IN LOVE IN THE WEST INDIES.

Consulting Old Mimbo Jumbo the Oby Man, how to get Possession of the charming Mimbo Wampo

"Let me alone for dat Massa."

Delicately declaring his Love to the amiable Mimbo Wampo, while she is picking his Cocoes

"You lub me Massa! eh! eh! ?

Smitten with the charms of Mimbo Wampo, a sable Venus, daughter of Wampo Wampo, King of the Silver Sand Hills in Congo.

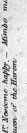

A few of the Hopeful young Newcomes

1	2	3
4	5	6
7	8	9

Mr Newcome taking leave of his Ladies & Pickcaneenees, previous to his departure from Prying Pan Island, to graze a title in his Native Land.

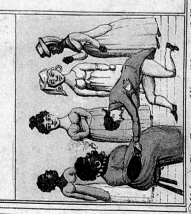

Mr Newcome happy. — Mimbo made Queen of the Harem.

1. Lucretia Diana Newcome, a delicate Girl very much like her Mother; only that she has a great antipathy to a pipe, and cannot bear the smell of Rum. — 2 Penelope Mimbo Newcome. — 3 Quaw Dash Newcome prodigiously like his Father. — 4. Cuffy Cato Newcome. — 5. Caesar Cudjoe Newcome. — 6.Hebus Quashebah Newcome. — 7. Aristides Juba Newcome. — 8. Hector Sammy Newcome. — 9. Hanibal Pompo Wimbo Newcome.

Published April.1808. by William Holland, Cockspur Street, London.

47

TO BE SOLD & LET

BY PUBLIC AUCTION,

On MONDAY the 18th of MAY, 1829,

UNDER THE TREES.

FOR SALE,

THE THREE FOLLOWING

SLAVES,

VIZ.

HANNIBAL, about 30 Years old, an excellent House Servant, of Good Character.
WILLIAM, about 35 Years old, a Labourer.
NANCY, an excellent House Servant and Nurse.

The MEN Belonging to "LEECH'S" Estate, and the WOMAN to Mrs. D. SMIT

TO BE LET,

On the usual conditions of the Hirer finding them in Food, Clothing and Medical ance,

THE FOLLOWING

MALE and FEMALE

SLAVES,

OF GOOD CHARACTERS.

ROBERT BAGLEY, about 20 Years old, a good House Servant.
WILLIAM BAGLEY, about 18 Years old, a Labourer.
JOHN ARMS, about 18 Years old.
JACK ANTONIA, about 40 Years old, a Labourer.
PHILIP, an Excellent Fisherman.
HARRY, about 27 Years old, a good House Servant.
LUCY, a Young Woman of good Character, used to House Work and the Nursery.
ELIZA, an Excellent Washerwoman.
CLARA, an Excellent Washerwoman.
FANNY, about 14 Years old, House Servant.
SARAH, about 14 Years old, House Servant.

Also for Sale, at Eleven o'Clock,

Fine Rice, Gram, Paddy, Books, Muslins, Needles, Pins, Ribbons, &c. &c.

AT ONE O'CLOCK, THAT CELEBRATED ENGLISH HORSE

BLUCHER,

CKDAW NO. 12 THE SLAVE TRADE AND ITS ABOLITION

ADDISON PRINTER GOVERNMENT OFFICE.

PRINTED IN GREAT BRITAIN

Within a year of the English takeover of Jamaica in 1658, one of the commissioners – Major-General Robert Sedgwick – predicted that the Maroons would become "a thorn in the sides of the English." His words proved truer than perhaps even he himself expected. These former slaves who had escaped to the wild mountain country and earned the name *cimarrón*, Spanish for "wild" or "untamed," entrenched themselves for centuries, even developing a culture of their own.

As the island became more settled and English plantations spread farther inland, the Maroons found it easier to swoop from the hills at night, set fire to the fields, and steal cattle and other stock. Runaway slaves from the new plantations swelled their numbers and gave them greater confidence. In 1663, they ignored an offer of land and full freedom to every Maroon who surrendered to authorities; and for the next 76 years, irregular warfare resulted in a government expenditure of nearly £250,000 and the passing of some 44 Acts of the Assembly.

In time, the original Maroons settled chiefly in the eastern and northern parts of the island. In 1690, however, the Clarendon slaves – consisting mainly of Coromantees, an extremely brave and warlike people from Africa's Gold Coast – rebelled and escaped into the woods. Led by a general named Cudjoe, they joined forces with the Maroons and launched a campaign known to history as the First Maroon War. Cudjoe's brothers, Accompong and Johnny, carried the war in the west, and sub-chiefs Quao and Cuffee controlled affairs in the east.

The First Maroon war: Concentrated on the northern slopes of the Blue Mountains and in the forested interior, including the weird and trackless Cockpit Country, the Maroons developed guerilla warfare. Skilled in woodcraft and familiar with the untracked forests, they avoided open fights. Instead, disguised from head to foot with leaves and tree boughs, they preferred ambush. What's more, it was

almost impossible to surprise them in their settlements. Keen-eyed lookouts spotted approaching forces hours before their arrival, and spread the warning by means of an *abeng*, a cow's horn bugle.

British troops, unaccustomed to the country and climate, suffered heavily in their early clashes with the Maroons. But as more and more troops were thrown into the campaign, including Mosquito Coast Indians, tracker dogs, and companies of *mestizos* and free blacks, the tide began to turn. The piv-

otal point may have come with the successful storming of Nanny Town, the stronghold of Queen Nanny and her Windward Maroons high in the vast wilderness of the Blue Mountains. The town was destroyed and never rebuilt, and to this day the site is believed to be haunted by the ghosts of those who died in the bloody engagement.

Pressed on all sides and faced with starvation, as most of their provision grounds had been systematically destroyed, the Maroons agreed to listen to surrender terms. The English commissioned a Colonel Guthrie to seek out the great old warrior Cudjoe in his Cockpit Country hideout and conclude a

Preceding pages, William Holland's biting Johnny Newcome cartoons of 1800. **Left**, a sign typical of pre-emancipation Jamaica. **Right**, Maroon Chief Cudjoe makes peace.

treaty of peace. Formalities were carried out on March 1, 1739, under a cotton tree amidst a cluster of Maroon huts at the entrance of the passage to Petty River Bottom Cockpit.

Under the terms of the treaty, the Maroons were guaranteed full freedom and liberty, and were allotted 1,500 acres of land between Trelawny Town and the Cockpits. Cudjoe was appointed chief commander in Trelawny Town, and his successors were named in order, beginning with his two brothers, Accompong and Johnny. The chief was empowered to impose any punishment he regarded as fitting for crimes committed by his own people, except those requiring the death sentence; these cases had to be referred concerned themselves with tropical crops which could easily be sold in Europe or North America. Tobacco, indigo and cocoa all achieved modest success, but sugar turned out to be the most profitable of all.

The sugar era: A large labor force was required for sugar production, and it was from this need that the African slave trade to the West Indies grew. At the same time, the small cultivator disappeared from the fabric of the islands' social structure, phased out as ever-larger areas of land came into the hands of a few powerful sugar planters with their armies of slaves.

The English first started the systematic cultivation of sugar cane in Barbados in

to a government judge. Two white men, named by the governor, were to live permanently with the Maroons to maintain friendly contact. The Maroons, on their part, were to cease all hostilities against the British. They were to reject asylum pleas from runaway slaves, helping instead to recapture them in exchange for a reward. And they were to assist the government as necessary in suppressing local uprisings or foreign invasions.

A similar treaty was concluded with Quao, chief of the Maroons left in the Blue Mountains. The First Maroon War was ended, and more than 50 years of peace were to follow.

The first settlers in the West Indies had 1640. So profitable was the crop that within 10 years, the wealth of the planters had multiplied 20-fold and the slave population had risen to more than 20,000.

The capture of Jamaica opened up a piece of land more than 26 times that of Barbados. Governor Modyford, upon his appointment in 1664, promptly set about establishing a sound footing for Jamaica's sugar industry. It grew prodigiously. By 1673, there were 57 estates. Another 66 years later, the island had 430 estates. Jamaica was on its way to becoming the world's single largest producer of sugar.

During their 18th-century heyday, the West

Indies "sugar colonies" were extremely valuable. They were fiercely fought over in every war and fiercely bargained for at every peace conference. Their importance was out of all proportion to their size; for a while, the British West Indies had more political influence with the Crown than did all 13 of the American mainland colonies.

The large Jamaican sugar estates were villages in themselves. They consisted of the overseer's house and offices; the sugar works and mill; the boiling house, curing houses and still house; the stables which housed the grinding cattle; lodging for the white bookkeepers; workshops for the blacksmiths, carpenters and coopers; and streets of houses for

cares and troubles of management to paid attorneys and overseers. Generous, hospitable and hearty, the planters liked to make a great show of their riches, especially in Europe. Such displays strengthened the belief in the great wealth of the sugar colonies.

Slaves strike back: Despite this ostentation, a specter of fear walked the sugar estates day and night. 18th-century plantation life was founded on force, and despite the tyranny which held him in bondage, the slave did not accept his lot without a struggle. Whenever he saw a way, the slave rebelled, killing his white masters and destroying their hated plantations. Many African blacks did not even wait until they had arrived in the new

the slaves. On rising ground – usually some distance from the sugar works themselves – the planters built their Great Houses. Constructed of finely-cut stone blocks and seasoned timber, with handsome carved woodwork and highly-polished floors, they set the elegant style of the day.

The ambition of most planters was to live in Europe as absentee proprietors, luxuriating off their estate profits and leaving the

<u>Left</u>, **Maroons demonstrate guerilla tactics as they prepare for an ambush on the Dromilly estate in Trelawny in 1796.** <u>Above</u>, **slaves toiling on a West Indies sugar plantation.**

land to start their resistance: slave-trading voyages often ended in failure because of an uprising among the slaves.

In the early days of the slave trade, Africans shipped to the West Indies were mainly prisoners of war or criminals, bought from local chiefs in exchange for European goods. But as the slave traffic increased, other means had to be found to maintain the supply. African tribal wars were stirred up, for no other reason than to replenish the supply of prisoners who could later be sold as slaves. Stragglers were captured from neighboring villages for the same purpose, and regular man-hunting raids were organized by tribes with the help of white hunters. Slaves so taken were usually chained to one another and brutally driven to the coast, where they were stored in "factories" – large fortified castles built especially for the purpose – until the slave ships arrived for the dreaded "middle passage" to the West Indies.

Lasting from six to 12 weeks, the middle passage was perhaps the most dreadful of all experiences a slave endured. On arrival, he was put ashore, exhibited and auctioned to planters and local dealers. The price range normally varied from £25 to £75. Of the tens of thousands of black Africans imported into Jamaica during the 18th century, about 5,000 were retained each year as slaves. The rest

ice was generally much lighter than field labor under the driver's lash, and domestic slaves dreaded being transferred to the fields more than anything else.

Punishment was a regular part of estate life. A planter could do pretty much as he liked with his slaves. In time, a revision of slave laws brought the master under stricter control, but the early slave code was very brutal. One reason for its severity was a belief that only by terrorism and tight discipline could slaves be prevented from rising and killing their masters, whom they greatly outnumbered.

The slaves were given provision grounds on which to grow their own yams, potatoes,

were re-exported.

Those days are still very much a part of the Jamaican consciousness. Reggae superstar Bob Marley spoke of it in "Redemption Song," the last track on the final album (*Uprising*) released before his death:

Old pirates, yes they rob I
Sold I to the merchants ships
Minutes after they took I from the
bottomless pit …

Life on the plantation: The majority of plantation slaves were *predial* (field workers). Many more did domestic duties in the great house and overseer's residence as cooks, maids, butlers and grooms. Domestic serv-

plantains and other foodstuffs. They worked their grounds in the few free hours allowed them daily, producing almost all the food they needed to subsist. They sold their surplus produce in Sunday markets, thereby earning a little extra money which they hoped in time might be sufficient to buy their freedom. If a slave's owner wished, he could set his subject free, either in his own lifetime or by his will.

The lot of a slave, dependent as it was on the whims and fancies of others, could be terrible indeed. But he wasn't always alone in his struggle for rights. Among his friends were the early church missionaries – first the

Moravians and later the Wesleyan Methodists and the Baptists. They taught the slave Christianity, did what they could to protect him from cruelty, and later took part in the struggle for the abolition of slavery itself.

Slaves had few opportunities for recreation, but they learned to make the most of them. During the Christmas and New Year holidays, colorful John Canoe bands roamed the streets, and teams of pretty Set Girls dressed in the rich clothes and jewelry of their mistresses to compete with one another in the lavishness of their costumes. And once a week, there was the Sunday Market. A carnival atmosphere prevailed as thousands of people came to sell or trade pigs, goats and

and its many wonders; stories of longing and despair, and stories of hope.

Rebellion: In 1760, the most serious slave revolt in the island's history broke out. The government called upon the Maroons' assistance, as provided for in their 1739 treaty.

Known as Tacky's Rebellion, the revolt began in the parish of St Mary but spread throughout most of the country. Tacky, its leader, was a Coromantee slave who had been a chief in Africa. He gathered a small party of trusted followers, mostly Coromantees like himself from the Frontier and Trinity plantations, and laid his plans in secrecy and with great care.

Before daybreak on Easter Monday, Tacky

fowls; yams and other vegetables; small homemade articles like mats, baskets, bark ropes and jars; and delicacies like grapes, melons and strawberries from the high, cool St Andrew mountains.

There were nightly gatherings outside the huts when the day's work was over. Then there was singing, dancing, and the telling of stories – stories of Anansi, the cunning Spiderman, of gods and animals of Africa

Left, a typical "Negro Market in the West Indies" in 1806. **Above**, a British emancipation society revealed this view of slaves being tortured in "A Jamaica House of Correction."

and his band stole down to Port Maria, murdered the fort's drowsy storekeeper, and made off with a supply of muskets, powder and shot. By dawn, hundreds of slaves had joined Tacky. They moved inland according to plan, overrunning the estates and killing the surprised or sleeping white settlers.

Meanwhile, a slave from the overrun Esher plantation slipped away and spread the alarm. The governor in Spanish Town, as soon as he received the news by overland express, promptly dispatched two companies of regular troops and called out the Maroons from their Scott's Hall settlement.

The engagements that followed were

fought with great skill and daring by the slaves. But as the conflict wore on, the prospects of success grew dim, and a number of slaves lost heart and returned to their plantations. Not so Tacky: he and a band of about 25 men held out until overwhelmed by greater numbers, whereupon they fought free and took to the woods. They were pursued by the Maroons, one of whom – a sharpshooter named Davy – caught up with Tacky. Both were running at full speed when Davy raised his rifle and shot the rebel leader dead. The rest of Tacky's band were later found in a cave. They had committed suicide rather than be captured.

By this time, slave revolts were breaking

conflict which gave rise to the black republic of Haiti out of the colony of St Domingue, provided inspiration for the disaffected. From the time it began in 1789, there was fear in Jamaica that the spirit of subversion might spread to the slaves. European refugees poured into the islands, bringing slaves who carried the news of what was taking place on Hispaniola, only 100 miles away. This flow of refugees, and later of French prisoners of war, was a danger to Jamaica's security: it gave spies and agents of the revolution an opportunity to enter and create disorder.

The events also caused alarm to the Spanish government in Santo Domingo, which shared a common border with St. Domingue.

out in parishes throughout the island. An uprising of Coromantees in Westmoreland proved almost as serious as Tacky's Rebellion, and again Maroons were called upon to help suppress it. Other conspiracies, a number of which were discovered and quelled before real trouble started, flared up in St Thomas-in-the-East, St James and Kingston. Months passed before peace returned to the island.

Inspiration from abroad: In the late 18th century, two events of worldwide importance began to be felt in Jamaica: the French Revolution and the anti-slavery movement in England.

The revolution in France, and the ensuing

In 1793, when Spain and England both went to war with revolutionary France, they sent separate expeditions to invade St Domingue. The British succeeded in capturing Port-au-Prince in March 1794. They hung onto the city for four years, but the invasion eventually collapsed, decimated by yellow fever and by the superior numbers and military skill of Toussaint l'Ouverture, the first of a remarkable series of black Haitian leaders.

Jamaica was unable to send assistance to the British troops in Haiti. There were problems enough at home. In 1795, the Second Maroon War broke out, encouraged by the example of the French islands and – said

54

some – promoted by actual French agents.

The immediate cause of the Maroon War is said to have been the flogging in Montego Bay of two Trelawnys for pig-stealing. But it was well-known that trouble had been brewing among the Trelawny Town Maroons for some time. The flogging, carried out under sentence of court, was not objected to; in fact, the men would have been far more severely dealt with by their own people for such an offense.

The real rub was that the work-house driver who wielded the whip, and most of the prisoners who were allowed to look on and mock, were runaway slaves whom the Maroons themselves had previously captured.

This was a harsh blow to Maroon pride. When word of the incident reached Trelawny Town, there was an instant uproar, and wild threats of vengeance were voiced against the people of Montego Bay. Alarmed by this reaction, magistrates asked for troops to reinforce the local militia – and thus were the first tragic steps taken.

The Earl of Balcarres, who had recently arrived as Jamaican governor, treated the matter most seriously. A veteran of the

American War of Independence, he believed in strong measures. The Earl declared martial law, took command of all forces, and set up headquarters at Montego Bay.

One of his first moves was to send a detachment of men inland to destroy the Trelawny Town provision grounds. But when the detachment reached its destination, it found the grounds already razed and the Maroons vanished. But not for long – for on the return march to Montego Bay, the detachment was caught in a devastating Maroon ambush. The colonel and a number of officers and other men were killed or wounded, and the survivors fled in disorder.

With this skirmish, the Second Maroon War began in earnest. For the next five months, a mere 300 or so hardy, determined mountain men held out against 1,500 chosen European troops and more than twice that number of local militia. As the war dragged on, the whole island was disrupted. Jamaica, in the words of a writer of the time, seemed "more like a garrison... than a country of commerce and agriculture."

It became increasingly clear to the Earl of Balcarres that no one could search out a Maroon but another Maroon. So the governor and his council decided on the use of dogs. A shipload of 100 terrifying beasts was imported from Cuba, where they were in common use for hunting runaway slaves and robbers, together with 40 handlers called *chasseurs*, strong men accustomed to great exertion and hardship.

The news of the dogs' arrival caused panic among the Maroons. In the wild and uncharted Cockpit Country, the Maroons had shown that they could elude almost any number of troops sent against them; but there was no escape from savage bloodhounds that tracked by scent. Before the dogs were released, the Trelawnys sued for peace.

One of the terms of surrender was that the Maroons would not be transported from the island. But using a slim technical pretext as a loophole, the determined Balcarres secured the transportation of some 600 Trelawnys to Nova Scotia, from where they were later removed to Sierra Leone. Trelawny Town was turned over to a detachment of British troops, for whom a barrack was built on the site. The Maroon menace had been laid aside forever.

An end to slavery: The end of the 18th century saw the beginning of the end of the system of plantation slavery. In Great Britain, changes in the industrial and commercial life were causing doubts about the soundness of supporting the West Indies' slave-based economy. More important, a wave of humanitarian reform was sweeping Britain, part of a new demand for liberty being voiced throughout Europe.

A movement led by William Wilberforce secured the abolition of the slave trade in 1807, and complete emancipation from slavery in 1838. In Jamaica, abolitionists found valuable allies in the missionaries of non-conformist churches, by now well-established and making heartening Christian progress

among the black population. It was another matter, however, with the planter-dominated House of Assembly and with the majority of slave owners. They fiercely opposed the measures, seeing in them nought but disaster and ruin.

In the end, the planters defeated themselves by exhausting the patience of the British Parliament. It only required one more slave uprising to hurry the day of freedom.

As it turned out, that final uprising was the most serious in the island's history. It broke out during the 1831 Christmas holidays, and its influence was felt far and wide. Disorder was centered in St James. "Daddy" Sam

Sharpe, a Baptist leader who sparked the revolt, is now regarded as a national hero. He was hanged in the Montego Bay square that today bears his name. So slavery came to an end in Jamaica.

With emancipation, sugar production fell sharply. The old plantation economy slowly died and estates were sold for whatever they would fetch. An attempt was made in the 1840s to provide labor with indentured workers from East India, with poor results.

Although the original white planter class had gradually given way to a new class of owners – chiefly mixed-bloods and Jews – the old oligarchic system of government remained unchanged. The legislature of the island was still elected by a handful of voters who met qualifications of property and income. The magistrates did the will of those in power, and the black peasantry was left to manage as best it could. To add to the distress of the latter, the American Civil War had cut off supplies of their staple foods, while severe droughts at home ruined their own crops. In addition to these, Edward John Eyre, who became governor in 1862, had little sympathy with the poorer classes and did almost nothing to assist them.

Matters came to a head in October 1865 with an uprising in St Thomas-in-the-East. Known as the Morant Bay Rebellion and led by Paul Bogle, it resulted in the killing of a number of whites. The uprising was put down by Governor Eyre with great severity. More than 430 persons were executed or shot, hundreds more were flogged, and 1,000 dwellings were destroyed.

Bogle and George William Gordon, a prominent mulatto legislator of the day, were hanged. Gordon was blamed by Eyre for the trouble; in retrospect, he appears to have been a scapegoat. A century later, both were declared national heroes. A statue of Bogle by sculptress Edna Manley now dominates the courthouse square where the rebellion started.

Eyre's handling of the uprising caused an outcry in Britain that led to his eventual recall. But before leaving Jamaica, he got the frightened members of the Assembly to surrender their constitution in exchange for the Crown Colony form of government.

Left, Paul Bogle. Right, a statue of Bogle by artist Edna Manley in Morant Bay's town square.

Throughout the last decades of the 19th century and the first decades of the 20th century, Jamaica's governor wielded wide powers under the Crown Colony system. Sir John Peter Grant in the 1870s was particularly successful in pushing through reforms and improvements of far-reaching importance, and island leaders who followed Grant continued his brisk pace.

Local government was reorganized. The judicial system was completely overhauled and an up-to-date police system was formed.

earthquake in January 1907. On each occasion, it was rebuilt.

The outbreak of World War I brought this era of Jamaica's history to an end, and by the 1930s, the island was headed for another crisis. There were many contributing factors. Discontent at the slow pace of political advance was coupled with fallout from the worldwide Great Depression, resulting in falling sugar prices. Growing unemployment was aggravated by the curtailment of emigration opportunities. Panama disease ruined

Education, health and social services saw major progress. Among the government agencies created was one for the protection of East Indian immigrant laborers. An island-wide savings-bank system was organized. A public works department was established and roads, bridges and railways were built. Cable communication with Europe was created. The banana trade, which was to be key to the economy throughout the 20th century, got under way.

The capital was transferred from Spanish Town to Kingston in 1872, prompting massive urbanisation of the latter. The city weathered several major fires and a violent

the banana industry, and the population growth rate was steeply rising. Dissatisfaction came to a head in 1938 with widespread violence and rioting, especially at Frome in Westmoreland.

Out of these disorders came the island's first lasting labor unions and the formation of associated political parties. A nationalist lawyer and the island's foremost barrister named Norman Washington Manley helped found the socialist People's National Party (PNP) in 1938. He hoped that it would lead his people to independent rule over a society free of class and economic distinctions. The PNP was later to be closely linked with the Trade

Unions Congress (TUC) and the National Workers' Union. The Jamaica Labor Party (JLP) evolved soon afterward from the Bustamante Industrial Trade Union (BITU), established by a tall, charismatic leader named Sir William Alexander Bustamante.

The rise of labor to political power was a new and dramatic development. Its leaders pressed not only for increased wages and working conditions, but for political reform as well. One result of this was the new Constitution of 1944, based on full adult

to see colonial ties severed. He felt that Jamaica had more to gain from British paternalism and economic aid than from a sudden plunge toward independence. Only reluctantly did he change his mind and support Manley in the 1950s.

The divergent political philosophies of these two national heroes were seen in Jamaica's choice of design for a national flag. The result incorporates a piece of the personality of both leaders. It has the black color of Jamaica's majority race, as well as the green

suffrage. This brought the Crown Colony period to an end and placed the island securely on the road to self-government.

All in the family: From the beginning, the parties and their leaders were at odds with each other. Manley respected the British and their traditions but wished to see an early end to colonial rule. He and his party spearheaded the movement for self-government. Bustamante, by contrast, was not as anxious

Preceding pages, Jamaicans spill into the streets of Kingston for pre-independence celebrations. **Left**, Coke Chapel crumbles during the 1907 earthquake. **Above**, King Street in 1920.

(of the land) and gold (of the sun), and a diagonal cross reminiscent of the British banner. Despite their differences, Bustamante and Manley were cousins. In fact, three of Jamaica's first five prime ministers – Bustamante, Michael Manley (Norman's son) and Hugh Shearer – hailed from the same family.

Towards independence: Further constitutional advances followed in 1953 and 1957, the latter providing for cabinet government. By 1959, the island was self-governing with only defense and international relations referred to the Crown.

The years that brought these rapid constitutional advances to Jamaica also saw the development of natural resources, notably in the field of bauxite mining for the production of aluminum; industrialization; the expansion of the tourist trade; and the growth of nationalism.

An experiment in closer association with other units of the British Caribbean led to establishment of the West Indies Federation in 1958. But the Federation was beset by problems from the start. Its collapse commenced in May 1960 when Bustamante declared his party's opposition to Jamaica's membership. Manley, whose party was then in power, put the issue to the Jamaican people for a referendum vote that resulted in

secession. The British government offered no objection.

By February 1962, agreement had been reached. A new Constitution had been approved, and Jamaica's Independence Day was set for August 6, 1962. General elections held on April 10 resulted in a victory for Bustamante's Jamaica Labor Party. Two weeks of celebration and rejoicing, such as Jamaica had never seen before, preceded the first session of the new Parliament on August 7. Princess Margaret, standing in for her sister, Queen Elizabeth II, presented the Prime Minister with the constitutional instruments of independence.

Jamaica moved smoothly into its new sovereignty. Institutions vital to independence were operating efficiently – the administration of justice, the civil service establishment, development corporations and the central bank. In short, the tried and tested machinery was there, backed by a well-developed political maturity.

The political parties provided the major means of integrating the society. They cut across racial and class lines, bringing together coalitions of different interest groups. More importantly, they represented the centerpiece of the political power structure in the country, replacing the traditional structure headed by planters and merchants in the 1930s and 1940s.

Bustamante stepped easily into the role of director of the island's political affairs. There were new initiatives in a number of areas, including agriculture, and by July 1963 a Five-Year Development Plan went to Parliament. It was prepared by 32-year-old Edward Seaga, a Harvard-trained social scientist, then Minister of Development of Welfare. Seaga proved even more successful as Minister of Finance and Planning in the JLP's second five-year term, and he succeeded to the prime ministership himself in 1980.

Jamaica became the 109th member of the United Nations. The government's ideological stand was enunciated by Bustamante in his declaration: "I am for the West. I am against Communism."

Bustamante retired shortly before the JLP's next general election victory in 1967. He was succeeded by Donald Sangster, whose sudden death brought Hugh Shearer, a prominent trade unionist, into power as prime minister.

The expansion of industry, bauxite, oil-refining, cement-making and clothing manufacture all contributed to the island's growth during this period. But there were serious impediments to the profound spread of prosperity, notably a rapidly increasing national population. For a time, emigration to Britain helped relieve the pressure; but as the 1970s dawned, the island was still grappling with unemployment and the problem of balancing its books.

Above, JLP leader Alexander Bustamante rides into Kingston. **Right**, key issue of Kingston's *Daily Gleaner* newspaper.

INSTITUTE OF JAMAICA
WEST INDIA REFERENCE LIBRARY

The Daily Gleaner

LARGEST CIRCULATION   ESTABLISHED 1834   Price: THREEPENCE

Vol. CXXVIII No. 186.   KINGSTON, JAMAICA, W. I., WEDNESDAY, AUGUST 8, 1962.   THIRTYTWO PAGES

JAMAICA CELEBRATES INDEPENDENCE
Princess opens first Parliament

HER ROYAL HIGHNESS the Princess Margaret at Gordon House, reads the Throne Speech with which she declared open Jamaica's first Parliament, yesterday morning. On the dais with her are His Excellency the Governor-

General, Sir Kenneth Blackburne; the Earl of Snowdon; the Governor Sir Kenneth Blackburne, with members of the Royal party among those standing behind by front of the dais at right are the bewigged Speaker of the House of Representatives, the Hon. Tacius Golding, and the President of the Senate, the Hon. Senator G. J. Campbell to right and left are clerks of the Legislature, and at right, members of the Parliamentary Opposition.

'...News received with satisfaction...'
Khrush's telegram to Busta

MOSCOW Aug. 8 (Reuter)—Mr. Khrushchev has sent a message to Sir Alexander Bustamante, Prime Minister of Jamaica, congratulating the people of Jamaica on attaining independence, the Soviet news agency Tass reported last night.

At the same time the Soviet Government has declared its recognition of Jamaica as an independent and sovereign state and has expressed its readiness to establish diplomatic relations with it, the agency said.

Mr. Khrushchev's telegram said: "Abiding by the great principles of equality and self-determination of the peoples the Soviet Government has hereby announced its satisfaction news of the proclamation of the independence of the Jamaica people."

From China

TOKYO, Aug. 8 (AP)—Both Nationalist and Communist China announced Tuesday their recognition of Jamaica which becomes independent today.

President Chiang Kai-shek sent congratulations to Sir Kenneth Blackburne, then Governor of Jamaica and named Councellor Yu Tsing to be the Nationalist Envoy in Lima, Peru, as special envoy to attend the Independence Day ceremonies.

Foreign Minister Chen Yi of China's Communist regime declared

Her Royal Highness in Throne speech:
UK and Jamaica wish to maintain bonds of friendship

THE FIRST PARLIAMENT of the independent Jamaica, summoned to a joint sitting by proclamation of Her Majesty the Queen, was opened in state at Gordon House yesterday morning by the Queen's sister, Her Royal Highness the Princess Margaret.

Queen's message:
I warmly welcome Jamaica to Commonwealth

Multi-coloured

Plea for UN membership

Jamaica plans to seek admittance to the United Nations. Independence Day announced was made by the Prime Minister.

Busta on taxes:
Those who can pay will have to pay more

That taxation is likely to be increased among people in the higher income brackets was indicated at the Prime Minister's Press conference yesterday afternoon at Irvine Hall, University of the West Indies.

In answer to a question from a foreign correspondent about the "haves" and "havenots" and a reported plan of the Government to tax the rich in order to help the poor, Sir Alexander replied: "Let me be very frank with you. Those who can pay will have to pay a little bit more."

Ashenheim Ambassador to Washington

Mr. Neville N. Ashenheim, C.M.G., is to be the first Jamaican Ambassador to Washington. It was announced last Saturday from the Premier's Office.

MARILYN MONROE FOUND DEAD
Sleeping pills nearby

HOLLYWOOD, August 7 (AP)—Blonde and beautiful Marilyn Monroe, a glamorous symbol of the gay swirling life of Hollywood, died tragically Sunday.

Midnight...then bonfires, fireworks...
Down the Union Jack, up the Black, Gold and Green

With pomp and ceremony, and in an atmosphere of general rejoicing, the country, Jamaica became an independent nation at midnight Sunday.

More than 30,000 people provided the National Stadium Sunday night to see the Union Jack hauled down and the Jamaica National Flag hoisted in its place to the top of the flagstaff while eager thousands.

From Macmillan—
Jamaica equal partner with UK

Sharing the spotlight of attention was the Hon. Sir Alexander Bustamante, who became the first Prime Minister of Jamaica, and twice the second Minister of External Affairs and Minister of Defence as well; and the Leader of the Opposition, the Hon. Norman Washington Manley.

Prime Minister's message:
I know you will respond to the challenge

Sir Alexander Bustamante Prime Minister of Jamaica, in a special message to the people of Jamaica on the occasion of the island's attainment of Independence, said yesterday, that he spoke with pride and courage.

"I speak to Jamaicans, both at home and overseas, as Prime Minister of the Government of Jamaica on this historic moment when we attain our independence.

LAUGH IT OFF

THE POLITICAL CANVAS

The political machinery tooled by the parties of Manley and Bustamante still looks somewhat British. One has only to attend a session of Parliament at Gordon House and watch as the meeting is called to order by a Speaker whose black face is incongruously framed in a white wig. He sits above a desk containing a silver tea service, a table of books of constitutional law and a gold sceptre.

This bicameral Parliament consists of a 60-member House of Representatives freely elected by a plurality of voters from the country's 14 parishes. All parishes are run by parish councils elected by voters. Every citizen aged 18 or over is eligible to vote.

Technically, Jamaica is still a member of the British Commonwealth and a constitutional monarchy; thus, the Queen of England is titular head of state. As a result, another ceremonial throw-back is the Queen's appointment of a governor general as her local representative. But the "GG", as Jamaicans call him, is a Jamaican recommended by the prime minister. Real power remains vested in the leader of the ruling party, who is appointed prime minister. He or she appoints a variable number of cabinet ministers and recommends the appointment of 13 members of the 21-seat Senate. The governor-general appoints the remaining members on the advice of the leader of the opposition.

The Senate was originally supposed to function like the British House of Lords, as a chamber in which distinguished citizens, businessmen and outstanding professionals outside the hurly-burly of party politics could be appointed to bring expertise and objectivity to governmental deliberations. This has not happened. The Senate has instead become dominated by retired and aspiring politicians who provide a mere echo of the partisan debates in the lower house.

Representatives are elected to the 60 single-member constituencies of Parliament. The constitution makes the House dominant, giving it control over finances and the power to override the Senate. However, its actions are influenced considerably by the executive branch, which controls voting through strong party loyalties and discipline, and by determination of the House's agenda of activities.

Joshua and the promised land: Despite a decade of slow progress under the JLP following independence, the People's National Party (PNP) under the persuasive leadership of Michael Manley – an economist, seasoned trade unionist and son of Norman – swept to victory in the 1972 elections, winning 37 seats to the JLP's 16. With its youthful image, the PNP had stressed "time for a change," promising social and economic reform. Under Prime Minister Manley, Jamaica's political culture became even more issue-oriented and polarized than it had been in the days of Norman Manley and Bustamante. "Change" proved to be a move to the left which Manley described as "democratic socialism."

A graduate of London University, Manley entered politics after a stint as a labor union negotiator. His movie-star looks and commanding presence endeared him to women and awed men. People traveled hundreds of miles just to hear him speak. Manley even visited Ethiopia and had an audience with former Emperor Haile Selassie, winning him points among the traditionally apolitical Rastafarian subculture. He received a staff from Selassie, a "rod of correction" which he said he would wave to right wrongs and transform the country's deteriorating social fabric. The PNP then promoted Manley as a modern-day "Joshua" who would lead the people to the Promised Land.

Notwithstanding his penchant for showmanship, Manley initiated important changes in a social structure sharply divided between rich and poor. Among them were the passing of a minimum wage law, new labor legislation recognizing workers' rights, an attempt at land reform and increased construction of low-income housing. He imposed a levy on multinational bauxite companies which gave Jamaica a bigger, more deserved chunk of the earnings from its most important natural resource. Poor farmers also received a fairer share of fertile lands previously concentrated in the hands of property barons.

Unfortunately, many of Manley's policies

Left, Sir Alexander Bustamante and Princess Margaret celebrating Independence Day, 1962.

were instituted with little regard for their economic consequences. For example, major utilities were nationalized, but the government's lack of foreign exchange for the purchase of machinery led to the deterioration of electric plants and water purification and pumping stations.

The sharp swing toward socialism gained momentum after the party was returned to power in 1976. But it couldn't solve the nation's economic difficulties. Aggravated by the drastic increase in world oil prices, hardship dominated the economy. Growing unemployment, severe shortages of even basic necessities, dwindling foreign exchange reserves and successive years of negative growth bred a sense of despair. This led to the flight of much needed capital and the migration of many skilled and professional Jamaicans to the comparative security of the United States and Canada.

Manley's foreign interests leaned increasingly toward Cuba and the Soviet Union, and he became a popular spokesman for Third World "have-not" countries. Consequently, the US aid upon which Jamaica had been dependent began to dwindle.

As the 1970s drew to a close, the JLP, reorganized, refreshed and led by Edward Seaga, laid down its challenge for leadership. Its main political theme was "deliverance" – especially from economic mismanagement and the threat of an alien political system. Seaga placed greater emphasis on private enterprise and promised closer links with the US. He stood staunchly against Cuba and Communism. These differences between two ambitious men led to Jamaica's most explosive elections in 1976 and 1980.

The politics of polarization: the political traditions of Jamaica differ markedly from those of liberal democracies in Europe and North America. Party feelings are more intense and militant and JLP and PNP supporters tend to be hostile toward each other. There is a strong territorial sense of party loyalty at the local community level, and skirmishes between adjacent communities are frequent and often violent, particularly during election campaigns. High levels of unemployment and significant urban and rural poverty makes party followers dependent upon favors granted by their respective parties. Consequently these inter-party hostilities often boil over into personal abuse, attacks on political

meetings, even murder, as followers fight to elect their party in hopes of reaping material rewards such as jobs, contracts, housing, government land and other benefits.

But, as the Jamaica Tourist Board points out, trouble has rarely spilled out of certain constituencies in urban Kingston and visitors have remained virtually untouched.

In other developing countries, the military often plays a major role in running political parties, if not the government itself. However, the Jamaica Defence Force (JDF) has generally maintained its independence from political parties. This highly trained group of about 2,000 men and women is not large by Caribbean standards. It is an offshoot of the

crack West India Regiment which distinguished itself in Great Britain's World War II campaigns in Egypt, Europe and Africa.

Possibly as an alternative to controlling the military, Jamaica's political parties enlisted their own gun-toting gangs to try to scare voters to their side during the 1970s. Charges of Cuban assistance and counter-charges of CIA interference were slung around by both sides. Party violence became serious as voters prepared to go to the polls in December 1976.

Even the beloved reggae superstar Bob Marley became a target. A gang of gunmen burst into his home, now the Bob Marley

Museum, and machine-gunned Marley, his road manager and others, two days before a scheduled free "Smile Jamaica" concert which Marley hoped would help cool the over-heated political climate. Marley later wrote about the attack in his song "Ambush in the Night". He bandaged his wounds and went through with the concert, albeit reluctantly, and Manley later met Seaga to sign a "Pledge of Peace." But the truce proved temporary. The stakes were much too high.

In an attempt to restore order, Manley declared a state of emergency. Earlier, he had toughened criminal laws under a new Ministry of National Security Act which spawned the sinister, barbed-wire Gun Court,

a prison and non-jury court for crimes committed with guns. This court speeded up trials, eliminated bail, and dealt severe life-sentence penalties. These measures were strongly criticised, in judicial circles, as a violation of basic human rights. Nonetheless, a lull in violence resulted and the people of Jamaica apparently saw nothing wrong in the actions of the Manley government. The PNP won the 1976 elections in a landslide.

The euphoria of the huge election mandate

Left, Norman Manley, People's National Party founder, in a reflective mood. Above, former PNP leader and Prime Minister, Michael Manley.

soon gave way to harsh reality. One month after the vote, Manley announced that Jamaica had entered a state of economic crisis. The International Monetary Fund (IMF) agreed to bail out the country with a loan, but Manley balked at the strings that were attached. The IMF wanted a 40 percent devaluation of the Jamaican dollar and a boost in tax benefits that appeared weighted in favor of the rich. Manley finally accepted the terms and the loan when he found his country teetering on the brink of bankruptcy.

The prime minister's flirtation with left-leaning countries of the Third World, however, led to a continuing erosion of confidence among Jamaica's traditional Western allies. He became a spokesman for the Non-aligned Movement, and paid visits to Cuba and Moscow.

The exodus of the middle and upper-class turned into a flood. Even leaders in education and technology began leaving the country. Manley angrily told them if they did not like his policies they should leave. Businesses shut down and the lack of skilled workers led to a deterioration in maintenance of public utilities.

By 1979, Manley's government found itself $150 million in debt. Seaga and the JLP started their next campaign early.

Silencing the guns: By 1978, clashes between supporters of the PNP and JLP were again on the increase. Marley, now an international musical superstar, again tried to intervene. He staged a "One Love" concert in April to commemorate the 12th anniversary of the 1966 visit to Jamaica by Haile Selassie, the Messiah of his Rastafarian creed. More than 25,000 Jamaicans watched Marley call JLP leader Seaga and Prime Minister Manley to the stage, lock hands with both in a raised pyramid, and sing:

One Love, One heart
Let's get together and
feel all right.

Again, the Marley magic silenced the guns. Again, the truce proved temporary. That election year saw an unprecedented political bloodbath that made international headlines. More than 514 people died. Frightened tourists stayed away.

London's *Guardian* newspaper summed up the ugly air that hung over this beautiful island as election day 1980 neared: "As the elections approach in October, violence and terror have become the permanent preoccupation of the 700,000 citizens of this hot unruly city. Soldiers and police point their guns at crowded pavements from their Toyota land cruisers, helicopters rattle overhead at night, shining searchlights in dark side streets, gunfire wakes you in the small hours. Nightlife has dwindled with two cinemas closing this week…"

On October 30, 1980, more than 85 percent of Jamaica's registered electorate bravely left their locked-and-barred domiciles to exercise their right to vote. Seaga's rejuvenated JLP won 51 of Parliament's 60 seats, the biggest margin of victory since 1944. Michael Manley conceded defeat before all

the island. The Cuban Embassy was closed and its officials expelled from Jamaica. Seaga also set about returning hotels and other government enterprises to private hands.

These newsmaking foreign-policy shifts played an important part in Seaga's main priority – rebuilding Jamaica's shattered economy. The policies had an immediate impact on the economy. Western investors interpreted them as an invitation to begin returning. In little more than a year, Seaga halted the negative slide of the nation's economic indicators and boosted them back into the plus column. Jamaica registered a modest two percent increase in its rate of economic growth in 1981, better than many

the votes had been cast.

A new start: The resounding victory of the JLP in 1980 triggered tidal waves of optimism in Jamaica. Seaga set about trying to mend the rifts in Jamaican society. But he did not stray from his platform. One of his first official acts as prime minister was clearly to signal his foreign policy preference. He became the first head of state to pay a visit to the newly inaugurated US President, Ronald Reagan, who had been elected only a few days after Seaga's own victory. Reagan later repaid the visit with an overnight stop in Jamaica in April 1982, becoming the first reigning American president to set foot on

developed countries. Inflation declined dramatically from 29 percent in 1980 to just six percent in 1981. Soaring unemployment leveled off and even decreased slightly. The government also recorded its first balance of payments surplus in seven years.

After this promising beginning, the economic and political fortunes of Seaga's government tumbled. Decline in hard currency earnings combined with increased imports, encouraged by government policies, triggered a deterioration of the country's balance of payments problems. This escalated to crisis proportions due to adverse world market conditions for bauxite and alumina.

Tight monetary policies and a big devaluation of the Jamaican dollar, designed to ease pressure on the balance of payments, had some adverse effects. Cut-backs in public spending affected educational and health services, as well as maintenance of the infrastructure. Lay-offs, severe cost of living increases, and declining consumption and purchasing power visited hardships on the population.

After winning an election in 1983 in which Manley refused to take part, due to a dispute over voter registration, the popularity of Seaga's JLP fell considerably.

Hurricane strikes: Hurricane Gilbert, which tore through the Caribbean in September

Kingston, the bloody clashes that marked the 1980 elections were absent. Manley entered the battle with a more moderate platform than before. Although he stood by his position as a social democrat and announced his intention to re-establish ties with Cuba, he assured Jamaican voters and United States officials that he would not restore the intense relationship with Havana which he encouraged in the past. He abandoned ideas of nationalization and announced his intention to promote entrepreneurship by discouraging the import of luxury items, and encouraging investment in agriculture by offering incentives such as tax breaks for farmers.

Although Edward Seaga's policies had

1988, was the first to strike Jamaica directly in 37 years. It was one of the worst disasters in the nation's history. Roughly one quarter of the country's population was left homeless, damage to property exceeded $300 million, and the country's banana and coffee crops and poultry industry were destroyed.

In 1989, elections brought the two political rivals together again. This time, although scattered violence erupted, predictably in

Left, Michael Manley, Reggae star Bob Marley and JLP leader Edward Seaga at the 1978 "One Love" concert. Above, Edward Seaga and cabinet at the tomb of Sir Alexander Bustamante.

saved a floundering economy, little of the gains filtered down to the poor of Jamaica who make up the majority of the nation's 2½ million people. On February 9, 1989, in the wake of the hurricane disaster, Jamaicans voted Michael Manley into office again. They remembered his social programs and voted for the candidate they believed would try to protect their interests.

Two years into his third term, deteriorating health forced Manley to hand over office to his deputy, P.J. Patterson, and to resign from active politics. The Acting Prime Minister stayed the course set by Manley and, in 1993, he led the PNP to election victory.

The past 50-odd years have seen tremendous changes in Jamaica and its people, not least of which has been the astonishing growth of the population. In the 1940s the total population was estimated at just over a million; today there are 2½ million resident Jamaicans, and another estimated 2 million in various countries overseas. To understand modern-day Jamaica and the motivations of its society it is necessary to back-track briefly.

The colonial legacy: The labor force, by the time of emancipation in 1838, already outnumbered its white masters who were responsible for the administration of the country and its businesses. A century later Jamaica was still a British colony and the structure of the society could be compared to a pyramid. At the very top were the white administrators, mostly foreign, while in the middle was a very thin band of middle-class Jamaicans. These were the independent business people, mostly traders of middle-eastern and oriental extraction, a sprinkling of professionals of mixed ethnic backgrounds and a few blacks.

The largest wedge at the base of the pyramid was reserved for the largely black population, descendants of the emancipated slaves. They had minimal education and formed a huge pool of unskilled labor and peasant farmers. The colonisers saw to it that the labor force could read, write and do simple arithmetic but beyond that, learning was not encouraged. Cheap labor was still needed for the agrarian-based economy and too much education would have depleted the ranks of readily available workers.

One result of this attitude was that it bred in the minds of the Jamaican laboring class an association of inferior status and lack of dignity with most forms of manual or menial work. It also bred a determination to beat the system. Despite being free people, they were only free to aspire to whatever their colonial masters allowed. Another result is that every poor Jamaican who was able to, struggled to

Preceding pages: many rural areas are still very poor. Left, education has long been the path to emigration. Right, raking a path of beans for the local coffee industry.

educate his or her children to enable them to escape from the shackles of this new type of slavery.

Migration was one route to self-betterment and before the turn of the century many Jamaicans were seeking opportunities abroad: to Panama to help build the canal, to Costa Rica, Honduras and later Cuba. The largest wave of migrants before World War II went to the United States, primarily to the East Coast cities. It is estimated that approximately 400,000 people in Boston, New York,

Philadelphia and other major Eastern cities are of Jamaican origin.

After the war when the United States restricted immigration, Jamaicans went to Canada and the mother country, England. Between 1950 and 1960, a quarter of a million migrated to England and, subsequently, they sent for their family members to join them. They settled principally in London, Manchester, Liverpool and Birmingham. Eventually, the UK was forced to tighten immigration rules and for a while the numbers of people migrating declined.

Them and us: Back in Jamaica the middle class had already achieved a large measure of self determination and the future of their descendants was more or less assured. Here, population growth was slower than on the lower rungs of the economic ladder. With the assistance of the churches, the middle classes founded schools for their children and saw to it that they were educated to the highest standards. Those who could afford it sent their children to colleges and universities overseas; if the children were bright enough it was the Ivy League universities of the States, as well as the hallowed halls of Oxford and Cambridge in England.

In general, the middle class were as patronising and contemptuous of their darker skinned or less fortunate countrymen as were

"prestige" professions: medicine, law, banking, engineering and the like. Only a white collar job would do and it was a point of pride to be able to say about one's child: "My son the doctor," or "My son the lawyer (or) the engineer" – whatever. As long as it could not be said of him: "Dat wutless bwoy. Him tun laborer!" in tones of utmost disgust.

The emphasis was on educating the sons of the family. It was not widely thought that girls needed to aspire to anything beyond being efficient housekeepers in order to make some lucky man a good wife and mother of his children.

With the dawn of the 1960s, the complexion of middle-class Jamaica, particularly in

the ruling white plantocracy, if not more so. In time, the mass of impoverished and struggling Jamaicans came to view any other Jamaican of lighter skin tone and greater material wealth as having taken the place of their former colonial masters.

With the break away from English dominion to full independence in 1962, a surge of renewed hope and a feeling of rejuvenation overtook the population who, for the first time, felt that this was truly *their* country and they had a vested interest in making it work for them.

For a long time, the only jobs which were considered worth having were the traditional

the business place, began to change. Slowly. No longer was it an occasion for comment to see black bank clerks and lawyers; it was becoming the norm. This younger generation of Jamaicans had not had to endure the turbulence of the birth of a new nation. They had enjoyed the first-fruits and led, for the most part, privileged lives. Their attitude, outlook and expectations were therefore radically different from those of their parents' generation. These were the baby-boomers who, because of the sacrifices of their families, were able to step into teaching and other professions, or to go into business for themselves.

The country continued to drift further away from an agrarian-based economy towards a more industrial base. Newer and more technology was needed and an educated workforce became more important. Tourism was a dynamic new growth industry as was bauxite, both of which were beginning to replace the income earning potential of the more traditional exports of bananas and sugar. For the decades of the 1950s and 1960s, Jamaica underwent a period of relative prosperity and stability. The Jamaican currency was strong and was trading at US$1.20 to J$1.00. Crime was negligible and was largely confined to pick-pockets and occasional housebreaking in the major towns.

influx of American popular music. Sound systems appeared on street corners blaring out the latest hits, with many small Jamaican studios producing mostly cover versions of popular songs.

Kingston in the 1950s and 1960s was a major port of call for cruise ships and Victoria Pier at the end of King Street was a lively bustling port. The craft market on the pier, a luxury hotel (the Myrtle Bank) and well-stocked shops lining the major thoroughfares were vibrant with "the good life." Or so it seemed to the rural poor. They flocked to the capital city with its burgeoning music and entertainment industry and its promise of a better life. All attempts by the govern-

Country comes to town: With prosperity came easier access to radio, television and travel. Television was a somewhat late arrival – in the early 1960s – and with its content being almost 100 percent American, it was natural that the population would be influenced by American lifestyles and values. The desire to escape all reminders of colonial life and attitudes no doubt assisted the enthusiastic embrace of things American. Even Jamaica's folk music roots began to give way to the

Left, the sugar cane industry is important to the island's economy. **Above**, country people come to town to read the news and sell their produce.

ment to persuade the rural population to remain down on the farm proved futile. The continuing influx of people from country to city placed unplanned-for demands on essential services and housing. It fell to the government of the day to try and cope with the demands and needs of the larger mass of people, a task with which it has been struggling ever since.

In the wake of this migration disillusionment was swift and tragic. There was not enough work for unskilled labor; unemployment grew as did the incidence of crime. Within 20 years the population in the capital doubled, from 376,000 in 1960 to more than

700,000. Most gravitated to traditional residential neighborhoods west and east of the city center and these older communities have become sprawling slums of poverty in the Kingston of today.

Survival of the fittest: Commerce moved uptown to New Kingston, a cluster of highrise buildings housing head offices of banks, embassies and modern shopping plazas. The better-heeled citizens moved north into luxurious suburbs such as Norbrook and Cherry Gardens. The streets remain the preserve of the less prosperous and are where real city life is played out in the main streets of downtown Kingston. The pavements and arcades are the domain of street vendors

selling everything from clothing to fruit. The old city seethes with life and it is clear why the rural folk continue to flock to Kingston. Here they have a chance to earn something.

The struggle to provide education to keep pace with the population growth has been defeated, in part, by the aversion of the lower income level population to any form of birth control. Attempts by successive governments to encourage birth control were viewed with hostility and interpreted as "a plot to kill black people".

Since the debt crisis of the 1970s and during the 1980s, government spending on education has been drastically cut. The re-sults are overcrowded classrooms and a lack, in some cases, of even basic facilities. Poor working conditions and low salaries have forced a considerable proportion of teachers to leave the profession, to emigrate, or to supplement their earnings by working in the private sector.

The distribution of wealth has become increasingly inequitable since independence with the greatest poverty being in the rural interior and in the slum districts of the large towns. Most dwellings in these areas have neither electricity nor running water. Successive years of self-serving, corrupt and inept government led to problems which were exacerbated by the worldwide oil crisis of the 1970s. While governments flirted with shifting the economy to an industrial base, more cautious voices which suggested building up and maintaining Jamaica's agricultural base were largely ignored.

The IMF approved a policy of retrenchment, beginning in the 1970s. This, coupled with enormous increases in the cost of living ever since and a continually depreciating currency, have created a barely suppressed anger in the population.

It is felt that the only way out of Jamaica's current economic problems is for the country to produce and export more of its goods; the domestic market is too small and impoverished to sustain non-export development. This is a common problem with the other Caribbean islands and attempts are being made to develop regional trade tariffs through Caricom, the Caribbean trading association. As far back as the 1950s the idea of a Federated West Indies was mooted but was defeated at the polls due to nationalism and self-interest. With the rest of the world forming powerful trade blocs, the wisdom of a Caribbean trading bloc is belatedly being forced on these island nations.

It is also obvious that with the dismantling of the Soviet Union, the spread of Communism is no longer a threat. The Caribbean, therefore, is no longer a foreign policy priority for any US administration and it would be foolish to base the economy of the region on Washington's continued support.

Jamaica, like many of its Caribbean neighbors, is on its own.

Drugs of sorts: <u>Left</u>, pharmacy worker in Kingston. <u>Right</u>, marijuana is a popular local crop.

81

The story of Jamaica's unique ethnic evolution began when Mongoloid peoples crossed the Siberian land-bridge into Alaska many millennia ago. They worked their way down the frost-free McKenzie Valley into the warm south, crossed the Central American isthmus into South America, and subsequently voyaged into the Caribbean, pausing to drop off several cultures, including the Aztec and Mayan civilizations. As they continued south and east, some members of the march broke off the long hike, took to the sea and became Canoe People.

The Canoe People evolved into distinct groups – Ciboneys, Arawaks and Caribs – and sailed into the Caribbean on a deadly chase: the Ciboneys fleeing the Arawaks, the Arawaks fleeing the Caribs. The Caribs, who brought up the rear, were fierce unneighborly man-eaters. The Ciboneys, along with a few stray Arawaks, found shelter on the island of Cuba. The balance of the Arawaks settled in Jamaica. Christopher Columbus ran into them when he was searching for a new route to India, so he assumed they were all Indians.

Of the first Indians, the Arawaks, only traces remained by the time of the 17th-century English conquest. All had been killed off by enslavement, murder and disease during the Spanish years. But great effort was made to see that all died Christians.

The Spaniards, with regard for their conquistador image, had been horseback colonists who needed foot-servants for gold digging, wild-pig hunting, and breaking wild horses for sale to passing expeditions. The gentle Arawaks had been unable to cope with these rough adventurers after a settled life. The Canoe People had met the Spanish Boat People, to the Indians' lament.

The demise of the Indians meant that new attendants were urgently needed by the "dons", who prized their siestas. So the Spanish brought in a second group of Boat People. Unlike the first, the Africans came not by choice or chance but by chain. Some British

whites were later brought in as "almost slaves" or indentured workers. The indentured whites were treated worse than the black slaves, since they were only on lease and if worked to death could be replaced at no cost.

Black slavery under the Spaniards was not the squalid, somber savagery that is usually depicted. The blacks saw to that. Soon after their arrival, they discovered the mountains.

Jamaica has a great backbone of mountains which runs the length of the island. The spectacular scenery owes much of its beauty

to the thick foliage cover – just the kind ideal for harboring guerilla fighters.

So when the black slaves struck their blows for freedom, they naturally took to the mountains. Their African forebears had been good fighting people: Akim, Ashanti, Fanti, Coromantyn, Mandigo and Angola. In any case, it was a fairly easy relationship until the English conquest. Then the remaining blacks were set free as the Spanish fled. They moved to the mountains and entered island annals as the Maroons.

Maroons of the Cockpit Country: Up in Maroon country it gets dark early in the winter months, and the evening turns cool and fragrant with pimento and jasmine and the night-blooming cereus. There is a grand throating of frogs, the nighthawk's *gi'e-me-me-bit*, whistling toads, and the eerie "Creech Owl." But on the eve of Cudjoe Day, there is little dark in Accompong, one of the ancient fortress towns of the Maroon people. The great Maroon chief, Cudjoe, harried the English army from here and from other strongholds for 50 years after the day in 1690 when he walked away from a slave plantation at a place called Suttons.

Every year on January 6, Accompong Maroons gather to celebrate The Day. They come from home or abroad, wherever they have followed the Money Fly. Maroons will

each other, located in the wildest heights of the island in an area today known as the Cockpit Country. But when Cudjoe was into his guerilla campaign, working his variants of ambush and attrition, the nervous English soldiers named the district "The Land of Look Behind."

At daybreak on Cudjoe Day, the drums commence. The drumming is complex, the rhythms twisting and changing as intricately as the carvings on the instruments. The singing is a series of surging harmonies fitted for the stomping march. In probably the most important event of the day, the Maroons make a traditional pilgrimage to Old Town, Accompong's burial place, and to the Treaty

tell you that the Money Fly is a shiny, bluish insect that is seldom seen unless it's on its way out of the window. But if it lands on your hand, *wayah-O*! That is bankable! Jamaicans have followed the Money Fly to Panama to build the Panama canal; to New York to help settle Harlem before the 1920s; to Cuba to ensure the success of the sugar industry in the early 20th century; to Britain to run the buses and hospitals and even to soldier in its wars, from the guns of Morro Castle and the War of 1812 (where old Stonewall Jackson personally commended their battle quality) to World War Two.

Accompong and Cudjoe Town are close to

Place. Here, under a silk cotton tree, on March 1, 1739, after the English had sued for peace, the First Maroon War ended. The Second Maroon War came 50 years later. Many skirmishes kept the mountains alight for one and a half centuries.

After the pilgrimage come the ceremonies of unveiling the monument to Cudjoe and the ancient Maroon fighters, put up by the National Trust. The Trust, which is state-funded, has established a series of monuments around the country to mark the sites of "folk" struggles ignored in the older history books written by English scholars.

The Windward Maroons: One hundred miles

to the east, in the Blue Mountains, the Windward Maroons – descendants of the Nanny Town fighters – also have their government monument. It honors the legendary Nanny of the Maroons, a warrior priestess who, like Cudjoe, waged her own great war against the English. She is now a national heroine with the rather touching title, "The Right Excellent Nanny."

The Windward Maroons set up strongholds in 1658 during the English conquest, before any of the other Maroon companies. As Spanish loyalists under elected leader, Juan de Serras, they went into the Blue Mountains, the Sierras de Bastidas, to establish a base from which to attack the English.

retain traditions as proud as the mountain peaks around them. But their isolation has been eroded by the advent of television and motor roads.

Many Jamaican Maroons went to war overseas for the same British forces they were harassing at home. Among their legitimate battle honors were expeditions in the Napoleonic Wars, the capture of Cuba and Haiti, and sackings of Campeche, Porto Bello, Panama, Santo Domingo, Cartagena and Nicaragua. They had a "no-go" from Britain when they volunteered for service in the Boer War against white South Africans rebelling against English rule. But they were welcomed by Britain in the other African

For the next 100 years they did so. Then they too, like the Accompongs in the west, were petitioned by the British government to make peace. The Maroons became virtually an independent nation within a nation. They remain so today with their own governmental subdivisions that are headed by colonels.

The Maroons still live in their towns today. No longer the "untamed ones" – the name derived from the Spanish *cimarrón* – they

Left, a resident of Jamaica's German community in Seaford Town holds up portraits of her children. **Above**, Colonel C. L. G. Harris, former leader of the Western Maroons.

wars waged against black Ashantis fighting colonization. Late in the 18th century, the Jamaican fighters were drawn into a regular army and named the West India Regiment. The present Jamaica Defence Force is an offshoot of this regiment, and its famous band has become the Jamaica Military Band which still parades at state functions in Zouave uniforms.

Until emancipation in 1838, Africa and England had been the two ancestral lands of nearly all Jamaicans, except for a sprinkling of Spanish and Portuguese Jews. But white landowners, correctly fearing that after emancipation the blacks would desert the planta-

tions for the free hills, began importing hundreds of white laborers from Germany, Scotland and Ireland. Surprisingly, thousands of blacks immigrated from Africa about the same time.

The Germans of Westmoreland: The white migration never amounted to much, but it left a few rural pockets with English and German names. The most noted of racially German locations, Seaford Town in the parish of Westmoreland, still exists today – although migration in recent years has depleted its population.

Moreover nearly a century of in-breeding has sadly had a degenerative effect on the population of 200 or so residents, nearly all of whom have one of four family names: Somers, Eldermeyer, Wedermeyer or Kameka. Their ancestors had immigrated to Jamaica at the beckoning of a Prussian doctor, William Lemonius, settling on land provided by Lord Seaford. Those Germans who began intermarrying with Jamaican blacks in the 1930s contributed to a dilution of the number of whites living in the area.

Other evidence of the German influence are contemporary Jamaican place-names like Hanover, Blenheim, Berlin, Potsdam, Saxony and Bohemia. Along the south coast in the parish of St. Elizabeth, many residents' coffee-colored hues, Caucasian features, blue eyes and lilting accents betray the coming of Scottish and Irish immigrants. As with all living things in this zestfully fecund land, however, they have been blended into the rich racial landscape.

The last of the African immigrants came as indentured plantation workers. And Indians from India continued a migration that began about 1838. Chinese arrived, starting in 1860. The "Syrians" came as itinerant peddlers and shopkeepers. Most came from the country now called Lebanon, but all Arabs are known as "Syrians" in Jamaica.

Within a few generations, they had accomplished by love what governments in some "enlightened" lands had outlawed. For here, the land began filling up with velvety skins in exciting colors ranging from ash-black to "Jamaica" white. It was a blending of stock that has produced beauties who include three Miss Worlds, athletic stars who have cap-

tured many Olympic gold medals, Rhodes scholars, poets, painters, novelists, and musicians so original that thousands of tourists jet in for their reggae festivals. But the mix also produced trouble. There was an easy relationship between blacks and whites in Spanish Jamaica. It was not so easy in English Jamaica – and this uneasiness fanned the flames in paradise.

Quadroons, Quintroons, fustee and mustee: Harsh laws studded the lives of blacks and half-breeds in English Jamaica. A rainbow of new "races" was catalogued according to infusion – Quadroon, Quintroon and Octoroon, better known as *fustee*, *mustee* and *dustee* in rumshop jollity. This new terminology was applicable to children of both races; but, curiously, the British only used the classifications to deride blacks.

As a result, the new practice of "passing for white" became common in the Americas. To block the spread of the *rungus*, cheating, among the often undetectable Octoroons, a new color entered the kaleidoscope: every free non-white in Jamaica had to wear a blue cross sewn on the shoulder, besides carrying a pass.

When Jamaican slaves were emancipated in 1838, 27 years before their counterparts in the United States, plantation owners received total compensation of £6.15 million sterling. But that did little to help the average planter *bakkras*. They owed more than that in mortgages and loans held by English bankers. Within a year, they were rattling the tin cup.

No sooner had Queen Victoria signed the emancipation papers at Frogmore, Windsor, before the ex-slaves lit out for the mountains. Their ancestors had done so in centuries past when they "bushed-up" for guerilla war against the English; this time, the war was of passive resistance and fully legal.

The mid-19th century blacks went into the mountains for psychological and economic reasons. Year after year, prior to emancipation, they had been involved in many bloody revolts as they fought valiantly against superior weapons and trained soldiers. Most of their leaders had been caught and executed – among them, Tacky, Mansong, and "Daddy" Sharpe, whose Christmas Rebellion had started out as a strike call, the Caribbean territory's first labor union-style action.

Now, with the end of slavery, the blacks had unpleasant memories of existence on the

Left, a "pure" Jamaican – German and African parents – with a warm smile.

slave savannas where they were ridiculed as "bell people" by the free people in the mountains. The plantation bell had dictated when to rise, eat, retire or appear for punishment. They intended to put a distance between themselves and the bell-ringers.

The slaves' former owners had refused to sell them lands, hoping to tie them to the plantations as low-wage workers. Instead, many blacks went into private enterprise, escaping up the mountain to grow yams, and to raise small stock like pigs and goats. Others fled to "free villages" founded by themselves and their friends, many of whom were valiant abolitionist white Baptist preachers who suffered physical assaults for preach-

eral dutifully saw to their mothers' declining years, even if afterwards they sought to cut all links with their heritage. They often accomplished this by "lifting" their color – marrying someone of a lighter shade. A Quadroon would look for a Quintroon and so forth. Only God and Einstein may fathom the permutations.

It seems unfair to saddle the *mestizos* (mixed race) with the rough ride their darker-skinned brothers undoubtedly had. But their woes were many. For example, George William Gordon, the mulatto leader of peasants who rescued his impoverished white father by saving his tiny estate from the hammer, was framed and hanged as a scape-

ing about a God who was the father of all, both black and white.

Most mixed-bloods stayed on the savannas, where they were crushingly called "Red Ibos" – in a knock at what blacks considered a sellout of the motherstock. "Red" man is the pejorative for a "white" man in Jamaica. But the mixed-bloods could hardly be blamed for electing to dig in where their chances for advancement were better. In fact, many Ibos were being looked after by their owners – who were also their fathers. Many a fair-skinned "outside *pikni*" was sent to England for education. To their credit, once they had acquired a profession or an inheritance, sev-

goat by the English governor in the 1865 Morant Bay rebellion. At independence, his countrymen made him a national hero.

While the English perfidy of giving favors to the Maroons kept the non-whites divided, Gordon was the first in a line of mixed-bloods to whom Jamaicans know they owe a debt for more than 100 years of political leadership: all the way from Assemblyman Gordon to the national heroes of recent decades, Sir Alexander Bustamante and Norman Manley.

Left, "ebony and ivory" skins of the Jamaica Defense Forces.

Color-coded society: But something took the "par" out of "paradise." A bias in tint did it – and not only back then. Up into the 1950s, black pressure groups were demonstrating for the employment of black girls in downtown offices and the education of black kids in whites-only schools. It is not hard to see where the trouble began.

The depressed economy of the sugar estates after emancipation meant that drastic cuts in expenses were necessary. The costly importation of English overseers was out; the planters had to look elsewhere for top help. But where?

Then they noticed the "outside *piknis*," (pale-skinned usually illegitimate children of whites and blacks) right in their own stables. They had the right color, or at least a close approximation, and this was the first requirement for authority in the color-coded society. Secondly, their loyalty would be assured. Indeed, to stay upwardly mobile, they could be counted upon to make tougher demands on blacks to work longer days for their pay. In short, these cabin children were godsend to dad. This was all well and good for keeping the rum punch cold (ice was brought south on sailing vessels from the US or Canada), but it certainly heated up the Jamaicans of darker hue.

The English-descendant planters and their city cousins, the white and Jewish merchants, did nothing to ease the growing tensions. These merchants had made fortunes selling flour and salted cod, the enduringly popular "sal'fish" which had been issued to the slave quarters since the Days of Obedience until the blacks grew sensibly fond of it. To divide and rule was a tried and proven rule in empire building, a certain path to wealth and power. The policy had failed in America because the Westminster chaps forgot they were dealing with their own kind; but in Jamaica, the color-related decisions on job and social privileges stuck.

It seemed that accounts, for example, were kept better by men of light cast. In the stores, blacks were best at lifting bales; but it took a mulatto to cut the cloth. The "brown boy" network also worked in schools and churches; an unwritten clause obeyed by teachers and pastors ensured that the front pews and available school places were reserved for whites and "high-browns." Fifty years after 1838, only 10 percent of blacks were literate. Not that it did them much good. Up into the 1950s, a black girl in a bank teller's cage drew crowds of gapers to the door.

The police force was officered by ex-constables of the Irish Constabulary, poorly trained by English standards. A few were only functionally literate.

The state church was Anglican. Even if he had doctorates oozing like canticles at matins, a black priest never rose above archdeacon, an honorary post usually conferred just before quitting time. The Catholics ran a similar course. Rapture engulfed the Jamaican blacks one day in 1950 when "the most educated man in Jamaica," a priest named Gladstone Wilson, was elevated to monsignor. This title of honor fell far short of a bishopric, but it *was* going up.

In their days of hardship, the Jews had been drawn to the blacks by their mutual disadvantages. As usual, they were the objects of ancient accusations that in other races would be considered clever business. As the 18th-century English historian Edward Long wrote: "The rascally tricks, for which both ancient and modern Jews have always been distinguished, served to embitter the popular hatred against them." Now they were playing it quietly. Pogroms were still in the race memory.

The color curtain was everywhere. Hotels, owned by white and foreign interests and catering mostly to Americans, were believed to be very hung up on the matter; they subtly indicated that the color bar was up, contrary to front desk declarations. The slogans fooled no locals, but visitors were straight-facedly assured they were disembarking in a happy land where "blacks and whites are in harmony like black and white piano keys." Embarrassing signs of discord, such as the throngs rushing out of paradise to wash up or carry baggage in other lands, in order to feed their families back home, was put down to the "love of travel in our people." Oddly, only the blacks among "our people" were bitten by this travel bug.

One day, the black editor of a news magazine, tired of the pretense, dove into the swimming pool of Kingston's exclusive Myrtle Bank Hotel. The splash was heard throughout Jamaica's three counties, and white outrage was exceeded by mulatto indignation.

Little wonder that at independence, when

the national motto – "Out of Many, One People" – was chosen, one young black scholar caustically proposed that if a new dispensation was truly ahead, it should read: "Out of Many, One BLACK People."

In the way of the conquered everywhere, some blacks scrupulously avoided criticizing the system, in the quietly desperate hope that they would someday be called up for their "passin' papers." This class of individuals was tagged "roast breadfruits" by their countrymen. The breadfruit, a beloved entrée of Jamaican country cuisine, has a black skin when roasted but the "heart" remains white. It was introduced to the island by Captain Bligh of *Bounty* fame as a cheap staple food for the slaves.

Jamaica had been founded on the guest house system and had never provided for its barefoot staff beyond bed-and-breakfast. The city-born, street-wise fellow worked at the hotel pool and plucked lead guitar in the *mento* band. In spite of two jobs, he still couldn't make ends meet. He was queueing at the American Embassy, hoping for a green-card permit to try the American plan of full-board. In the way of the young and sardonic, he was making a wry joke of his tamarind season – the hard dry times when only the tart, mouth-puckering tamarind will fruit.

A green card or landed-immigrant visa to the US is money in the bank to many Jamaicans. Nevertheless, the rate of recidivism back to "The Rock" is high. When the US government makes cushy social security pension payments through the local embassy, "The Rock" is not so tough.

In a sense, a love of high living is the reason which impels so many Jamaicans to leave. Under the Union Jack, the Caribbean was neatly divided into sugar-cane fields, timber lands, cotton fields, spice islands, and so forth. Each separate territory was dependent upon and acquired a taste for imported foods. Rice, flour, salted cod and tinned fish are still the main constituents in Jamaican shopping bags.

When the overloaded economy sank under the weight of oil prices in the mid-1970s, and with the consequent increase in import prices, there was a great outcry at the cutting off of imported corn flakes. On an island ripe with oranges, pineapples, bananas, mangoes, avocados and the like, many a person will pay high prices for low-grade American apples.

Today, harsh economic realities are forcing Jamaicans to retrench and rediscover their own. This includes the fantastic success of "roots" music; the entrance of traditional songs and ceremonies into the repertoire of the National Dance Theatre Company and the Jamaica Folk Singers; the powerful work of visual and literary artists, "self-taught" or schooled through the government's Cultural Training Centre; an exciting re-birth of fashion design, and an increasing number of excruciatingly attractive children who have made "baby-watching" a widespread contemplative activity.

Tales of Anansi: The English rovers who contested these seas were not of the caliber of conquistadors. Plain men at best, rogues at worst, they left law books and forts but no art of architecture, save a few small, exquisite churches and some Georgian houses. The island is now on the job, writing its own score out of many rhythms.

One of the most powerful of these rhythms is the *Anansi* myth, firmly rooted in Jamaican folklore. The tales of Anansi the Spiderman were brought from the west coast of Africa by the first slaves, and went into business as the only therapy for three centuries of hideousness. He took on the trappings of the tribal oral historian, with an interpretive addition.

Bra 'Nansi filled the role of storyteller, hero or villain. He was great at disguises, omniscient but nonetheless willing to be defeated to help prove a moral point. He was something to everyone: his indestructability, knowledge and wit were an investment in hope. The stories were frequently satirical and cynical. They never had a live-happily-ever-after ending. Anansi's devotees were always on the lookout for the unexpected; everywhere were challenges that must be faced, or otherwise they come in at the back of the neck.

Anansi's presence in politics is sequential, a bridge across the gulf that pre-election rhetoric creates. Anansi is used to woo voters, and after the elections it becomes an art that wins over the loser even as it acclaims the victor.

Right, Keeping the spirit of Anansi, the Spiderman, alive in stories told while fence-sitting, a popular pastime throughout the Jamaican countryside.

THE VIBRANT SPIRITUAL SPECTRUM

It is Sunday in Jamaica. The opaque sunlight of morning falls upon little girls in bright dresses and white hats as they skip down the mountain roads and village streets of the island. Some hold the hands of their brothers, who look cranky and uncomfortable in tiny suits and ties. Old men in dark double-breasted suits with baggy pants clutch their Bibles. Big coal-skinned women dressed in flamboyant satins and lace stumble through stony lanes and fields in their best shoes. Throughout the country, stone churches begin to fill with these people, their fingers tapping out staccato rhythms on tambourines and their voices echoing across the hills.

Here, as in most of the Caribbean, Christianity prevails and thrives. More than 80 percent of the population profess to belong to one form of Christianity or another, the legacy of centuries of European rule and influence. Yet recent years have seen increasing numbers of Jamaicans looking to their ancestral African home for spiritual inspiration. And even within the framework of Christianity, the seductive spirits of Africa have reached out across the centuries and the seas.

Zemes and Saints: A curious footnote to the Caribbean's reputation as a cradle of Christianity in the West is found in the name Jamaica. Historians generally claim that the name comes from the Arawak word *Xaymaca*, purported to mean "land of wood and water." But in Josephus' time there was a district in Palestine called Jamaica. And since Josephus wrote in the 1st century AD, it seems reasonable to assume he had not met the Arawaks. The theory that the name was chosen for its connection to the Holy Land is plausible, given the piety of the Spaniards who scattered saints' names all around their American conquests – including the ultimate Christian appellation, San Salvador.

A scant six years after Columbus left the Caribbean for the final time, the first three abbacies had been created, one of them on Jamaica's north coast near today's resort town of Ocho Rios. From there, the Span-

iards went about wiping out every other religion and massacring its adherents in the name of God. The Arawaks, like any other careful farming folk, had guardedly scattered their piety among various *zemes* (spirits) headed by the god Jocuahuma and his wife. But in a fury to plant the "true cross" in every nook and cranny of the New World, the incoming Christians put the Indians to the sword, often en masse, and after Absolution had shrived their heathen souls. Those who managed to survive were enslaved and

thereafter worked to death.

A Dominican priest named Bartolomé de Las Casas, appalled by the unholy scene, led the call for reform. Las Casas was not of the Old Country Inquisitors. His father had been with Columbus on the earlier voyages; he himself went to the Indies as a young fellow with Nicholas de Ovando, Governor of Hispaniola, in 1502. He was the first priest ordained in the West Indies in 1523. His personal liking for the Arawaks, whom he saw dying off before his eyes, moved him to suggest that to save those left, the stronger, tougher Africans should be brought in. He knew the black men well. They had lived in

Preceding pages, **Christians line up for a baptism at Gunboat Beach.** **Left**, a girl in Sunday dress in Porus. **Right**, a female minister in Kingston.

Spain for many centuries, both as slaves and freed men.

It was of course a Jesuitic solution. After surviving in the tropics for an age, fighting off or staying ahead of the Caribs in their ocean-going canoes, the Arawaks were suddenly (in Fray Bartolo's eyes) incapable of standing the heat and in need of removal from the hearth. In truth, Las Casas was commendably soft on Arawaks. But that left him hard on blacks.

Las Casas' father had taken an Arawak back to Spain. The young Bartolo had taken a shine to him and his people. As a rule, they were gentle – but not much so when sufficiently riled.

myal cult were important components of its ceremonies. Practitioners used potions and entered trances to counteract the influences of *obeah*, the island's peculiar brand of witchcraft and sorcery. Its influence peaked in the mid-1800s, but it is still practiced today.

The *kumina* ceremony is also practiced in modern Jamaica on rare occasions. *Kimbanda* and *kyas* drums beat out hypnotic rhythms. A queen or priestess sprinkles the drums with white rum, then fills her mouth with the liquid, spitting sheets of alcohol over the participants. The smell of white rum, cigarettes and sometimes ganja hangs over the scene. The queen calls and sings in quavering shrills mixed with ancient African words.

The blacks who came to the west from Africa brought their Islamic and animistic religions with them. Animism is an intellectually powerfully doctrine burdened with a title which at first glance suggests something akin to animal worship, but which actually comes from the Latin word *anima* for "soul." It is a doctrine that encompasses the spirituality of the world's great religions, holding that life comes from a spiritual source, a soul, as distinct from matter. Like Christianity, it states that life is everywhere.

White rum and goat's blood: In early Jamaica, one manifestation of Animism was *kumina*. The music and dance of the African

Then a goat is hugged and petted before an executioner severs its head in sacrifice. Blood gushes out of the goat's trembling body. It is mixed with rum and fed to the participants.

For obvious reasons, early *kumina* rituals somewhat frightened the European conquerors of the island. British historian Edward Long wrote in 1774: "Some of these execrable wretches in Jamaica introduced what they called the '*myal* dance' and established a kind of society into which they initiated all they could. The lure hung out was that every negro initiated into the *myal* society would be invulnerable to the white man; and, although they might in appearance be slain, the *obeah* man could at his pleasure, restore the body to life."

Forced into accommodation with Spanish Catholicism, these early forms of African worship found no real difficulty. The incense, chantings, robes and candles were not unlike the formalities of their own priests, the so-called "witch doctors." Like them, the Christians also conjured up spirits, called saints, and threatened death as a penalty for disobedience. The plaster statues in the alcoves compared favorably with their own stone and clay "dolls." It all made for a swinging, rollicking wedlock between both beliefs, and no serious damage to either.

The marvelously evocative result of this

Bent, sprung and coiled into wondrously rhythmical shapes, they lift the old standards into a compelling tempo. What emerges is a Rock of Ages that really rocks, *te deums* without tedium.

In the ritual of ascent into total purity, Pocomania worshippers exalt God by placating the whole self, body and soul. After being purified by powerful surging, singing and chanting prayers and a "tromp" or shuffling match around the table, the faithful are capable of entering a state of grace, or trance, that lasts for several hours. Like today's "new" charismatics, healing and speaking in "unknown tongues" is in the liturgy.

The Spanish Catholics gave way to the

union came to be called Pocomania (from the Spanish *poco* meaning little, *mania* meaning madness). In this hybrid faith, the Christian altar has become a *poco* table of a length determined by the size of the congregation. Covered with a piece of white cloth, the African color for solemnity and mourning, the table is laid with bowls of cooked white rice, white dove-shaped breads, and plucked white-feathered chickens. White-turbaned priests sing white Christian hymns, the tunes all but unidentifiable in their *poco* state.

Left, interdenominational mass at Kingston Parish Church. Above, church in the country.

English Protestants in 1655 and the Protestants gave way to the English Catholics at the time of the Restoration that brought Charles II to the English throne. Nevertheless freedom of worship has long been established in English-speaking Jamaica. The only exceptions were short periods of persecution of Baptists and Jews, the former for being soft on slaves, the latter when they became so rich the gentiles remembered that they had killed Christ.

In the dominant Christian sphere, analysis reveals almost equal percentages of Anglicans, Baptists and members of the Church of God. Other groups include Seventh Day

Adventists, Methodists, the United Church of Christ and Pentecostals. There is also a healthy smattering of Roman Catholics, mainly among the Chinese, Lebanese and East Indian communities whose ancestors came around the turn of the 20th century.

Recent years have marked the rise of the fundamentalists – handclapping, gospel shouting sects led by voluble aggressive preachers. American-oriented, American-supported, they have made dramatic incursions. There are also members of the Revival Zion sect, cousins of those who shuffle through Pocomania, yet clingers to beliefs in Christian dogma.

Nowadays, except for a handful of devotees, "jumping *poco*" is a dwindling religious art form. The drive to identify a cultural origin unentwined with and independent of white Christianity, turned the search elsewhere. And out of this search for a Deity, whose best strokes would be in the interests of his different folks, has come the most potent socio-religious political happening since Columbus waded ashore: Rastafarianism.

It took a while for a solution to the problem to gel. The belief that all things, including man, were an extension of and fused with the God spirit – the principle of the African religion – had been lost under the intentional cultural destruction wrought by the slave system. Ethnic and family dislocation effectively destroyed the historic connections.

Marcus Garvey and Ras Tafari: What happened was bizarre, as sudden as it was shocking. A handful of "crazy men" appeared in the 1930s, making absurd claims about the Emperor of Abyssinia being the Messiah: Ras Tafari, afterwards crowned as Haile Selassie, which translated means "the Power of the Trinity."

Few suspected then the profound effect the movement would have on Jamaican society. Rastafarians were long-haired and bearded long before the advent of hippy fashions. If their interpretations of the Bible were outrageous, they quoted with conviction, and were ready to suffer for their beliefs.

The movement arrived closely on the heels

Left, a Pocomania table deep in the Clarendon parish countryside. **Right**, the man who inspired African pride, Marcus Garvey, also inspired the "Back-to-Africa" Rastafarian religion.

of another whose impact was just winding down on the world's blacks. Founded and led by a Jamaican, Marcus Mosiah Garvey, the Universal Negro Improvement Association (UNIA) sought to gather ancestral Africans from a diaspora unmatched save by the scattering of the Jews.

Garvey was born at St Ann's Bay on August 17, 1887. He was working as a printer when he founded his little organization with the grandiose name. The label turned out to be prophetic. Garvey's group did become universal. He soon found the island too small for his ideas and after visits to some Central Americans countries, he moved to the United States. The UNIA soon became a monolith.

Garvey called for self-reliance among "Africans at home and abroad." He advocated a "back-to-Africa" cause. He awakened a black consciousness and pride that aroused the hostility of whites as it stirred the ideas of such young black Africans as Nwamdi "Zik" Azikiwe of Nigeria, Kwame Nkrumah of Ghana, and Jomo Kenyatta of Kenya, each of whom would one day lead his country to independence.

In the United States, Garvey's work led inevitably to the defiant Montgomery bus ride that signaled the start of the civil rights movement and to the canonization of Martin Luther King Jr. He also attempted to estab-

GANJA, THE SACRED WEED

In spite of its contemporary synonymity with Jamaica, *cannabis sativa* – the botanical term for ganja – is not native. Ganja came to Jamaica in the satchels of the indentured laborers imported from India in the middle of the 19th Century. Like the Rastas and Coptics of modern-day Jamaican, Hindus of those times revered this so-called Indian hemp as a "holy plant."

Sugar-estate plantation owners soon determined that the use of ganja diminished the productivity of their laborers. Thus, the first legislation introduced in Jamaica to outlaw the use of marijuana stemmed from capitalistic con-

cern about productivity and profits.

Still, the use of ganja grew slowly as the numbers of East Indians increased. The birth of the Rastafarian movement in the 1930s provided another boost in its use in Jamaica. But ganja did not become a major influence until the "Greening of America" in the 1960s brought the "reefer" out of the ghettos of Harlem and into the mainstream of life in the United States.

Mexico served as the first primary source of supply for the surging American market. But stringent border inspections instituted by US law enforcement agencies forced American dealers to turn to alternative sources for ganja. Jamaica, only two hours' flying time or an easy sail from

the Florida peninsula, topped their shopping lists. By 1974, about 70 percent of the ganja grown in Jamaica wound up in the United States.

Most farmers harvest their own crop to maximize profits and eliminate Jamaican middlemen. As one prospering grower explained, "In this business you can spend a year and set your family right. You can build a house, buy a car. You can live a comfortable life. I have seen guys who couldn't change their pants and since this ganja business, they can change dozens of pants now. It has helped a lot of people in Jamaica." Many Jamaicans call ganja "the poor man's friend."

In a country of high unemployment, low wages and a lack of job alternatives for the under-educated, the temptation to get rich off ganja is strong. Parliament continues to resist calls to legalize or ease penalties against ganja, but legalization in Jamaica, in concert with similar moves in the United States, would make ganja just another crop. Its price would plummet and the huge profits would evaporate.

It is virtually impossible to envision a unilateral move by the Jamaican government to lessen or abolish its ganja laws without the blessing of the United States, and this seems very unlikely. Jamaica is in a difficult position. The legal ramifications are many when dealing with a drug that a significant number of the population considers a sacrament or at least a medicinal godsend, while an equally significant number rely on its cultivation for economic livelihood.

Certainly, visitors to Jamaica find the plant in ample supply. It's usually available at resort areas from young men who stand for hours outside hotel gates and even from hotel employees trying to make some money on the side. Even deep in the rugged interior, wanderers may be flagged down by youths toting a flour sack full of ganja.

But ganja users must always bear in mind the official penalties. The Dangerous Drugs Act states that for the possession of ganja, a first offense carries a stiff fine or imprisonment for "a term not exceeding three years or both such fine and imprisonment." For subsequent convictions the fine and length of imprisonment are increased. Sentences for cultivating, selling, or otherwise dealing in ganja can bring up to 10 years' imprisonment. Offenders under the act are every person who manufactures, sells or otherwise deals in prepared ganja. It's an offense to have ganja in one's possession, or to occupy premises used for preparing, smoking or selling ganja. It is likewise an offense to carry smoking paraphernalia. ■

lish a steamship company, the Black Star Line, an understandable corollary to a return of exiles but also a strong plank in his self-reliance platform. His steamships floundered on what is believed to have been an old-fashioned legal sting prepared for awkward blacks in ugliest America.

Garvey's honesty and integrity has never been in doubt, even among his detractors. He died in obscurity in London in 1940, but his body was brought home in pomp and ceremony to his native island for burial in a mausoleum befitting a man who, posthumously, has been made a national hero.

Locks, beards and Bibles: As widely powerful overseas as Garvey's UNIA was, its local

hope to any suffering godchild who was kidnapped from the Old Country. At the last, there is the ineluctable conviction of the Return from Exile – to Ethiopia.

Rastafarianism's contemplative and meditative nature, assisted by sacramental ganja smoking, drumming, Bible reading and chanting, has imbued the best of its followers with an ability to accommodate a religious, abstract-political, non-racist racialism. They have also acquired a capacity to culture ideas through music, costume, physical exercises, art, poetry and indigenous "cottage" industries like broom-making.

Reggae music developed in the rasta "yards" and produced superstars like the late

influence has been no match for Rastafarianism. A doctrine that pre-dated Black Power by two decades, it had settled into its cadence well before the tramp of Black Muslims was heard in Detroit.

Its strength is in the spiritual power it exerts, not only through its teachings, but by asserting a root-continuity of the African race through history. Its adherents are regarded as children of the *Negus*, a title of the Ethiopian kings in their descent from King Solomon and the Queen of Sheba. It is a mind-sweep warranted to steady and give

Left, the sacred weed. **Above**, zealously biblical.

Bob Marley. Politicians are so conscious of Rasta influence among Jamaica's youthful majority that as Marley lay dying of cancer in a Miami hospital, he was awarded the Jamaican Order of Merit, equivalent to a peerage in the old British Empire.

The true Rastafarian trains to desire nothing above the essentials in food and materials, to stand fit and feisty, afraid of no loss save his beard and Bible. The beard is a sign of his pact with Jah and the Bible his source of knowledge, especially the prophecies of the Old Testament which he believes speak of Haile Selassie and Ethiopia. At the core of his faith is an absolute belief in the divinity of Ras Tafari – which substantiates a belief in his own divinity as a child of Jah, Jehovah, God. Selassie's physical death did not kill belief in Ras Tafari. The crucification at Calvary did not kill Christianity.

I-and-I and Ras Tafar-I: The earliest Rasta-farians developed a heroic spiritual strength that withstood ridicule, physical assault, discrimination, and imprisonment for ignoring the "Babylonian Law" against the smoking of the sacramental herb, ganja (marijuana). The appearance of Rastafarianism has been largely attributed to three mystics. Separately and unknown to each other, aided by Holy Writ and working *inwards to the I*, the inner divinity, the id – or, as expressed in Rasta liturgy, the *I-and-I* – these mystics arrived at the conclusion that the King of Ethiopia was the Messiah. His imperial titles included King of Kings, Lion of Judah, Elect of God.

The scriptures refer to Ethiopia and its people more than 40 times. They provided a rich lode of information and interpretation for the Rastas – as they have for the many adversary readings that have set denominations at each other's throats since the Tower of Babel.

Selassie's visit to Jamaica in 1966 drew larger airport crowds than Queen Elizabeth's and incomparably more emotion. An estimated 100,000 followers braved a downpour. Skeptics of the faith delight in recalling that the Ethiopian emperor, appalled at the dreadlocked legions that swarmed around his plane, refused to exit until Jamaican authorities convinced him he would not be harmed. Rastas, in contrast, say Selassie wept at the overwhelming reception.

Selassie's title, Lion of Judah, has inspired Rastafarians to adopt the lion's image as their own. Indeed, the animal's mane has inspired some of the most elaborate of the dreadlock hairstyles. The locks also hark back to Africa, the hairstyles of Masai and Galla tribesmen, and even the biblical story of the power of Samson's hair.

The doctrine has spread worldwide, wherever blacks live, and has attracted a growing minority of young whites. But the movement has also become a cover for criminals who adopt the hairstyle of their reggae idols. Rascality is not a Rasta trait. The brethren are too deeply spiritual to doubt that Jah the Father, the inner I, will provide for all needs. That includes the sweetest smoking *sinsemilla* (ganja) this side of Eden.

The trappings of Rasta: Three major sects of Rastafarians have evolved into their own Jamaican subcultures. The older, more traditional communities of Rasta prophet Prince Emmanuel live in the hills of Bull Bay, east of Kingston. They occasionally can be seen around town, with their hair rolled into turbans, selling brooms and booklets. The Twelve Tribes sect has attracted more of the young political Rastas. Bob Marley, who took the tribal name Joseph, belonged to this group. Their headquarters are near the offices of Marley's Tuff Gong studio in Kingston. And the third sect, the Ethiopian Zion Coptic Church, an entrepreneurial spin-off, has run into problems because of its dealings in ganja.

Indeed, the practice of smoking the sacred ganja sacrament continues to be one of the most controversial aspects of the Rastafarian movement. Not all members use the herb, however. Those who do, usually smoke it in a pipe, called a "chalice," made of cow or goat horn or bamboo. The ritual of preparing the chalice with water, mixing the tobacco with "herbs," and lighting it is a sacred one, accompanied by the recitation of prayers, psalms and benedictions.

The Rastafarian religion has established a working code against greed and dishonesty, sexual envy, exploitation and aberration. Yet it has also accommodated the arts and a competitive edge in job efficiency, sports and games – while maintaining a strong pride in black history.

The dedication of Rasta men and women has fired the imagination of the young Jamaican. The shoulder-length ringlets, the usual mark of a "dreadlock," now bob about everywhere – at international tennis tournaments, in the national soccer squad, or decently held under a Rasta-knit turban at important desks in commercial and government offices. The red, green and gold colors of the Ethiopian flag now adorn Jamaican clothes. The "Dread," the true Rasta, is a peaceful, careful, preferably self-employed achiever who stays within the law – save for his sacramental smoke.

Right, In 1981, the Ethiopian Orthodox Church conducted funeral rites for reggae superstar Bob Marley, a Rastafarian.

THE RED HOT RHYTHMS OF REGGAE

What's that music playin' on the radio?
What's that music playin' everywhere I go?
I don't think I've ever heard
A sweeter feelin' in the whole wide world
Than that music playin' in my heart...
       – Gil Scott-Heron in *Storm Music*

So sings poet-songwriter Scott-Heron in homage to reggae, the hot, raw recipe of rhythm and syncopation that is as synonymous with Jamaica as is jazz with New Orleans, salsa with Puerto Rico, soul with Detroit, and blues with Chicago.

In little more than a decade, the rugged sound of reggae fought its way up from cheap amplifiers fronting shabby record stores in the slums of Kingston to the sophisticated sound systems of the First, Second and Third World elite. Its influence has been widely felt: reggae has left its mark on the compositions of Paul McCartney, the Rolling Stones, Paul Simon, Eric Clapton, Elton John and Stevie Wonder. And it carried a tough, streetwise kid named Bob Marley from the ghetto to international stardom.

Reggae music has crossed language barriers, broken down race and class lines, patched up political schisms and dissolved religious differences. It has displayed a remarkable ability to drain hostilities and peel away peoples' prejudices. Its narcotic beat rarely fails to stir the most somnolent of cardiovascular systems.

The universal appeal and acceptance of Jamaica's unique reggae sound has turned the island into what one writer called "The Third World Nashville." Recording studios and record shops abound. Two of the largest studios are Tuff Gong International, a legacy of the late Bob Marley which is now headed by his wife, Rita; and Dynamic Sounds, operated by Byron Lee when he is not performing with his legendary Dragonaires. These and dozens of other studios crank out hundreds of new titles each month in an attempt to satisfy the voracious appetite of Jamaica's listening public. New singers,

bands and studios appear and disappear almost overnight.

Despite the diversification, reggae music is the elixir that keeps Jamaica's recording industry healthy, much as country-and-western music fuels the studios of Nashville. The story of the evolution of that music is a fascinating journey through Jamaica's colorful musical history.

Origins of reggae: The story starts with a myth that still prevails in some circles – that an import from Trinidad called calypso is Jamaica's music. There are two possible reasons why.

The first was a talented Jamaican singer named Harry Belafonte. Belafonte recorded folksy commercial tunes like "The Banana Boat Song," "Jamaica Farewell" and "Island in the Sun." The albums on which these hits appeared also served up a healthy portion of songs with a calypso flavor. The American recording company that turned Belafonte into an international star apparently saw little difference between two tiny islands in the Caribbean, let alone differences in their music or even in their dark-skinned inhabitants.

In reality, Jamaica did have a brand of popular music of its own – mento. Mento descended from the music and dance that slaves from Africa used to enliven the drudgery of life on Jamaican plantations. Cruel masters often tried to beat the vestiges of African culture out of the souls of their slaves, but some cultural traditions inevitably persisted. Their music survived even after the authorities discovered that rebellious slaves used drumming to communicate with other pockets of dissidents on the island. University of West Indies historian Edward Brathwaite noted in a study of Creole society in Jamaica: "It was this drumming, which the authorities and the missionaries tried unsuccessfully to eradicate by legislation and persuasion, respectively, which retained and transmitted important and distinctive elements of African/folk culture into the period after Emancipation."

The slaves also took a decidedly African approach to the fashionable Spanish, French and English salon and court dances of the 19th century. Traces of the Parisian Qua-

Drawn after Nature & on Stone by J. M. Belisario.   Printed by A. Duperly.

BAND of th. JAW—BONE JOHN—CANOE.

Kingston Jamaica — Aug. 1837.

drille can still be recognized in contemporary Jamaican folk dances.

At first, mento was essentially music that accompanied a dance believed by some to have been sired by the quadrille. It called for a slow, undulating hip movement and close body contact below the waist that is commonly called "dubbing." So, to assume that mento is merely a Jamaican version of calypso is not accurate. Both forms acted as vehicles for social commentary, and even protest, but calypso embraced amoral and malicious themes that grew out of the slanderous *mauvaise* language of Trinidad and the more genteel, but barbed, linguistic traditions of *picong*, while mento leaned toward

fade under an assault of popular music transmitted from the United States. The lack of recording facilities in Jamaica at the time, which might otherwise have preserved and popularized mento, hastened its demise. Yet it had already firmly established itself in the island's musical evolution. According to folk-music researcher Marjorie Whylie, "In the context of popular Jamaican music, mento could well be regarded as the matrix."

The Dukes of sound: Jamaica's first radio station, an amateur effort called ZQI, turned itself on in 1939. It broadcast live and taped programs of European classical music and American pop, and smaller servings of Jamaican folk and classical tunes. Radio Ja-

more playful, almost pornographic lyrics.

Mento gained its foothold in rural areas where crowds flocked to lively *brams* dances in pre-transistor radio days. The country bands consisted of a rhumba box (an adaptation of the African thumb piano), bongo drums, guitar and shakers. Even aristocrats sought mento bands to add spice to their high society dances.

But by the early 1950s, mento began to

maica replaced ZQI in 1950, but continued to feed the island a diet heavy on mainstream American music. Meanwhile many islanders had begun tuning in to powerful stations in the southern United States that pumped out the exciting, danceable beat of rhythm-and-blues. Louis Jordan, Fats Domino, Amos Milburn and Roscoe Gordon became the rage in Jamaica.

Rhythm-and-blues put stress on the second and fourth beat of the musical measure – the afterbeat – not unlike mento. R&B groups also pioneered the electrification of the guitar and organ, and later the bass. These instruments were to become fundamental in

Left, Isaac Mendes Belisario's light look at a Jamaican musical combo of the mid-19th century. Above, an old musical history shows the African influence on island music.

the development of popular Jamaican music.

In addition to its marked similarity to local rhythms, R&B also soared in popularity on the crest of a Jamaican phenomenon called the "sound system," a prototype of the disco. "Sound system men" trucked outsized speakers fed by powerful amplifiers to hired halls and beer gardens in every nook of Jamaica. People packed the halls when "the systems" thundered to the latest rhythm-and-blues recordings from New York and Miami.

Rivalries erupted between the systems men of the 1950s. Two of the greatest were the glittering Duke Reid and Clement Dodd, who disc-jockeyed under the *nom de guerre* Sir Coxonne.

Michael Thomas graphically described Reid's style in an article in *Rolling Stone* magazine: "Reid used to arrive at his dances in flowing ermine, a mighty golden crown on his head, a .45 in a cowboy holster, a shotgun over his shoulder, and a cartridge belt across his chest. He was gorgeous, gold rings on every finger and thumb, the perfect gaudy image-melt of Hollywood gangster and high camp aristocrat. He'd have himself carried through the throng to his turntables, and then he'd let one go, the latest Lloyd Price, a rare old Joe Turner, and while the record played, Duke would get on a mike and start DJing, going 'Wake-it-Up, Wake-it-Up' and 'Good God' and 'Jump shake-a leg'."

The success of Reid and Coxonne spawned more competing systems – Nick's, Tom the Great Sebastian, each promising systems that challenged the sound barrier and "exclusive" singles. Reid and Coxonne regularly flew to New York to sniff out new music, and Jamaican artists began to take a cue from American rhythm-and-blues. Early vocalists like Laurel Aitken, Derrick Morgan and Owen Gray cut records strongly influenced by the New Orleans R & B sound. At first intended mainly for the systems market, their recordings found their way into the hands of the public. So Reid and Coxonne exchanged their sound systems for recording studios. By 1959, a record industry weaned on rhythm and blues and a modicum of calypso/mento began producing music that wasn't quite either, but which was very Jamaican.

Local talent: Jamaica's early musicians often developed their skills in military bands. One group at Alpha Boys' School proved particularly fertile ground. Established in the 1890s by the Sisters of Mercy order of Roman Catholic nuns, Alpha catered to underprivileged youths and orphans. They included trombone players Rico Rodriguez and Don Drummond, tenor sax players Tommy McCook and Roland Alphanso, alto saxman Lester Sterling, trumpeter Johnny Moore, lead guitarists Jah Jerry and Ernest Ranglin, drummer Lloyd Knibbs and Drumbago, bass players Lloyd Brevette and Cluet Johnson and pianists Jackie Mittoo, Gladstone Anderson and Theophilus Beckford. These giants of Jamaican musical history graduated to jobs in dance bands or north coast hotels until Reid, Coxonne and another systems man-turned-producer named Prince Buster

coaxed them into the recording studio.

While this pool of talent was experimenting in the studio, the government's Jamaica Broadcasting Corporation (JBC) took to the air waves in 1959. Its programmers showed a sensitivity for indigenous music that had been missing on local radio. In fact, the JBC played a milestone tune into prominence.

Beckford's "Easy Snappin" walked the line between rhythm-and-blues and boogie-woogie. In the process, it stumbled upon a new musical style. Beckford nimbly poked out a steady boogie-woogie riff on his piano in the first and second beat. So did Jah Jerry's guitar, prior to his solo. Cluet Johnson walked his bass on a straight four while Papa Son's brushwork accented the first and second beat. The horns of Alphanso, Rodriguez and Ossie Scott, meanwhile, laid back behind the beat in the best jazz tradition. Vocalizing was kept to a minimum, allowing the musicians more room to play. The cumulative effect proved several degrees cooler than steamy R & B. Beckford had officiated at the birth of ska.

The onomatopoeic sound of the piano comp – *ska-ska-ska-ska* – gave this newborn musical form its name. The island's musicians suddenly found themselves with a music of their own to play, explore and cultivate.

The rise and fall of the Skatalites: Sir Coxonne succeeded in corraling Alpha's band of iconoclastic musicians; as a result, his Studio One amassed a catalog that is a veritable thesaurus of Jamaican music. From its ranks rose the Skatalites, comprised of McCook,

blues melodies, melancholy, and a kind of non-verbal protest, an expression of his own deteriorating mental state. It was this rebelliousness in Drummond's music, and his conversion to the Rastafarian faith, that ultimately had a tremendous impact on the aspiring young musicians of his day.

Ras Tafari, with its spiritual godhead in Ethiopian Emperor Haile Selassie and its other African cultural inspirations, redefined the folk rhythms of *kumina* and *burru* beginning with the 1959 Ffolkes Brothers hit, "Oh Carolina." That song introduced the legendary drumming of Count Ozzie, a musical guru and an ardent follower of Ras Tafari who had a major influence on the music of

Alphanso, Moore, Drummond, Mitto, Jerry, Brevette, Sterling and Knibbs. Although short-lived, the group left Jamaica a lively, largely instrumental musical form that fostered its own peculiar dance movement – a bobbing torso which was seemingly powered by a piston-like arm movement. Dancers grunted – *uh, uh, uh,* – virtually echoing the horns and guitar.

Trombonist Drummond dominated ska in much the same way that Bob Marley came to dominate reggae. Drummond developed a highly personal instrumental style that successors have yet to surpass. A significant number of his compositions reflected minor

The evolution of contemporary Jamaican music as depicted in album covers: Left, the legendary Don Drummond. Above, the Skatalites and "Toots" Hibbert.

the Skatalites. But ska peaked in popularity by 1966. Drummond, its most eloquent exponent, murdered his sweetheart and was committed to a mental asylum where he died in 1969. The Skatalites disbanded.

Thereafter singers began to encroach upon the music that had once been dominated by instrumentalists, articulating what the horn men had only hinted at. Musicians soon took a back seat to the vocalists. "Rock steady" had arrived.

Renting a tile: Perhaps as a result of the pensive "What do we do now?" period that followed the euphoria of independence, the tempo of Jamaican music slowed down. More emphasis was put on syncopation. The drop of the drum, characteristic of mento's rhythmic structure, became more pronounced. The guitar strum of rock steady also harked back to mento. The style freed the bass from timekeeping and gave it an infinitely more melodic role, again a possible throwback to the manner in which mento bands used the rhumba box. As its name implies, dance strongly motivated rock steady. But it was slower and more languid than the high-energy exercises sparked by ska. Dancers swayed to Delroy Wilson's "Dancin' Mood" and Alton Ellis' "Rock Steady" as if glued to one spot, keeping all their frustrations in that little space – "renting a tile."

The lyrics of some of these new tunes mirrored the poets' attitudes toward their people's place in Jamaican society. They did not always like what they saw. Consider Bob Andy's "I've Got to Go Back Home":

I've got to go back home
This couldn't be my home
It must be somewhere else
Can't get no food to eat
Can't get a job to get bread
That's why I've got to go back home...

As the lyrics became even angrier, rock steady gave way to reggae. This new emphasis on what songs had to say opened the door for a flood of Jamaican vocalists. Ironically, the best had begun their careers during the heyday of instrument-oriented ska. One of the most successful was Jimmy Cliff, a skinny teenager with a soothing voice.

Born in Somerton, a small town on the outskirts of Montego Bay, Cliff left home for the lights and lures of Kingston. There he lived in its gaping pits of poverty singing and recording several rhythm-and-blues-type numbers for sound systems men who balked at playing them. But in 1962, the precocious 14-year-old Cliff persuaded Beverly Records producer and owner Leslie Kong to give him a break. Kong did and never regretted it. Among Cliff's biggest hits for Kong's label was the 1964 story of a storm, "Hurricane Hattie." That same year Cliff migrated to Great Britain.

England's swelling population of Jamaicans re-adapted ska and called it "bluebeat." Cliff signed with Island Records in London in 1965 and scored with hits including "Many Rivers to Cross," a brooding ballad about his own hard times and struggles to survive. After winning a Brazilian song contest in 1968, Cliff returned to Jamaica where he immediately cut his first international hit for Leslie Kong, entitled "Wonderful World, Beautiful People."

Cliff's biggest break came when producer-director Perry Henzel cast him in the lead role of a movie, *The Harder They Come*. Cliff portrayed Ivan O Martin, a singing, gun-slinging tragic hero, whose story (to a point) paralleled Jimmy's own life. The film became a cult classic and is credited with properly launching reggae music into the world limelight.

Cliff did not fare quite as well as his music, however. His subsequent conversion from a rebel singer into a clean cut Muslim apparently lost him many of the fiery young fans looking for anti-establishment heroes. Ironically, these fans turned to another Jamaican singer that Cliff had introduced to Kong, a

man who wore his snaking locks like a crown and claimed the throne of the king of reggae. His name was Robert Nesta Marley.

Cliff has remained original and philosophical about his unfairly diminished role in the development and popularization of reggae. "My role has been as the shepherd who opens the gate. Now we're going into a different pasture," he said. With Marley gone, Cliff may get another much-deserved crack at the title. His international stature has continued to grow steadily, if not dramatically, and he commands massive international followings.

Whatever happens to Cliff, he has still fared better than the man who apparently gave Jamaica the word reggae, if not the music itself. Frederick "Toots" Hibbert recorded his first single the year before Cliff burst into prominence. Fame has eluded Toots despite a powerful voice that he used in the best traditions of American gospel music. Toots' style was inspired by Ray Charles and Otis Redding.

His trio, Toots and the Maytals, survived every twist in popular Jamaican music up until the 1980s. Clement Dodd produced the group's first hit, "Six and Seven Books," in 1962. For Prince Buster's label, they produced several top sellers including "Pain in my Belly." After serving time in prison on charges of dealing ganja, Toots bounced out in 1966 with a song based on his experience called "5446 Was My Number." He followed it up with the timeless reggae anthem, "Pressure Drop."

the realm of all-out social protest as restlessness increased among Jamaica's poor majority and rivalries intensified between the two political parties that promised salvation. Many groups even added militant touches to their songs. This marked the era of the "Rude Bwoys," as the word "boys" come out sounding when spoken in emphatic patois.

Birth of the Wailers: In the midst of this rapidly changing music and social scene of the mid-1960s, behind walls of corrugated tin and plywood in West Kingston's tough Trench Town, four youths named Junior Brathwaite, Peter (Tosh) MacIntosh, Bunny Livingston and Bob Marley began rehearsing. When Clement Dodd opened his Ja-

In Stephen Davis' definitive book, *Reggae Bloodlines*, Toots boasted: "I invented reggae. Wrote a song called 'Do the Reggay' in 196- I don't remember when, but I wrote it anyway. It's true. Reggae just mean comin' from the people... So all our music, our Jamaican rythmn, comin' from the majority. Everyday t'ing that people use like food; we just put music to it and mek a dance out of it...When you say reggae you mean regular, majority. And when you say reggae it mean poverty, suffering, Ras Tafari, everything. Ghetto. It's music from the rebels, people who don't have what they want."

Regardless of its literary origins, reggae, as the music came to be called about 1968, took the mild protests of the steady poets into

maica Recording and Publishing studios in 1964, the group was just one of many that came knocking on his door.

"When they first came in, they were like most other groups just starting out – young, inexperienced and willing to learn," Dodd recalled. "I coached them, worked on their songwriting. I had an album from the States by all the top soul artists. Bob Marley liked the Impressions, the Tams and the Moonglows the most. You can hear the influence on some of his early songs." That influence is most apparent in some of the group's slow, romantic songs like "It Hurts to Be Alone." Faster ska hits like "Simmer Down" featured superlative backing by the Skatalites.

As the gangs of tough, unemployed "Rude Bwoys" began roaming the streets of Jamaica, they protested their poverty by loot-

<u>Left</u>, Jimmy Cliff, as he appeared on a record sleeve. <u>Above</u>, an irresistible beat.

ing, shooting and defying the police. The music of Bob Marley's group echoed the times. They took the name Wailing Rude Bwoys before shortening it to the Wailers.

Derrick Morgan, the Clarendonians and Desmond Dekker of "Poor Me, Israelites" fame, also took up the tenor of the times. But it was the Wailers who prevailed. With a major assist from producer Lee Perry, they transformed reggae into its best-known form. Others claim to have created the style. Clement Dodd said he patented the sound when experimenting with an echo unit when his guitar began strumming the now-familiar *chaka-chaka-chaka* rhythm. But as one writer put it: "Reggae is not just a music, it is more a philosophy, with the advice handed out to a danceable beat."

In an interview with *Rockers* magazine, Bunny Livingston Wailer offered another description of reggae in perfect patois:

"Well mek me tell you little history about Africa and reggae. Africa a one nickname; Ethiopia is the real name fe the whole a dat place. Reggae means the *Kings* music from the latin *Regis* e.g. like Regal. Now Ethiopia (Africa) is a place with plenty King so they have to be entertained with the King's music. So from you a play reggae with the heavy emphasis pon bass and drums, you a mingle with the spirit of Africa. The rhythm is connected to the heartbeat…"

Bob Marley understood that. His metaphysical imagery, his embrace of Rastafarianism and its inseparable association with the music, made reggae a musical style to be reckoned with.

Stir it up, rub it in: Embittered by the token pay that producers offered Jamaican artists of the times, the Wailers disbanded in 1967. Marley went to live with his mother in Wilmington, Delaware. But after a few months he returned to Jamaica, where he reorganized the Wailers.

This time, the group formed its own label called Wailin' Soul. Despite a string of hits including "Bend Down Low," "Stir It Up" and "Nice Time," they still failed to turn a profit. To add to the misfortunes, Bunny Livingston was jailed for nearly a year on ganja charges.

The restive Marley left Kingston again, this time for the parish of St Ann, where he had been born in the village of Rhoden Hall in 1945. He tried planting corn instead of

singing. But a black American singer named Johnny Nash came to Jamaica in search of talent. Story has it that when Nash saw Marley performing on television, he immediately set out for the country to find him.

The Wailers agreed to record an album for Nash's production company. Nash's own version of Marley's "Stir It Up" climbed into the Top Ten in many countries. Marley also collaborated on a film score with Nash in Sweden and penned the popular "Guava Jelly" with its immortal refrain: "You've got to rub it on my belly like guava jelly."

Meanwhile, Lee Perry had put together one of the great reggae studio bands, the Upsetters, for his new record label of the same name. Led by brothers Aston and Carlton Barrett, the Upsetters released several instrumental hits named for Italian spaghetti westerns, "The Return of Django" and "The Liquidator."

Before these records could fill the void left by Marley's departure, however, he returned from overseas. The Wailers teamed up with Perry to produce some of their finest work: two classic reggae albums, *Soul Revolution Part Two* and *Soul Rebel*. One featured a song called "Duppy Conqueror" that firmly established Marley as a powerful songwriter with its description of his release from a prison stint.

Yes me friend
Dem set me free again
Yes me friend
Me dey pon street again.

Marley's melodies also broke new ground. The timing and the manner in which the importance of the instruments was apportioned just sounded different. It embraced all the popular musical forms that preceded it, but Marley's brand of rhythm struck original notes that have come to symbolize reggae.

The money finally began trickling in. The Wailers used it to form their own company, Tuff Gong, in 1970. Late the next year, they exploded their biggest hit to that date, "Trench Town Rock."

In 1972, Marley's group joined forces with the Upsetters. Bob did lead vocals and played rhythm guitar, Tosh sang and also strummed guitar, Bunny sang and handled percussion, Eral Wire Lindo controlled the keyboards, Aston "Family Man" Barrett played bass, and Carlton Barrett pounded drums. The new incarnation of the Wailers rocketed to international fame under the tutelage of a part-Jamaican producing genius named Chris Blackwell.

Blackwell and Marley catch fire: The London-born Blackwell had come to Jamaica as a youth with his Irish father and Jamaican mother. He led a privileged childhood between a palatial Kingston home that has since been turned into the Terra Nova Hotel and a country estate in St Mary.

The versatile Blackwell worked as an aide-de-camp to two British governors of Jamaica, Sir Hugh Foot and Sir Kenneth Blackburne. He was also a real-estate salesman, a scooter hirer and a water-ski instructor in Montego Bay before a cousin per-

suaded him to try his hand at the recording business. Blackwell first hit the top of the charts with his production of Laurel Aitken's "Little Sheila." Pioneer singers Owen Gray and Jackie Edwards also joined his stable of talented artists.

In 1959, Blackwell joined with Leslie Kong and two others to establish Island Records, the label that helped make Jimmy Cliff an international star. It established headquarters in a looming house on Hope Road that

Above, a young fan of reggae and the Rastafarian religion that inspires much of the music takes a turn on stage at Reggae Sunsplash.

subsequently became Tuff Gong's offices. Rapidly growing sales of Island's records in Britain prompted Blackwell to migrate there. In 1962, his cover version of Millie Small's "My Boy Lollipop" became the international hit that clinched his reputation as a successful producer of early British rock as well as Jamaican music.

The Blackwell-Marley association spawned the Wailers' first internationally acclaimed album, *Catch A Fire*. Critics in the United States and Great Britain praised it as the advent of a new wave in rock music. Similar applause greeted the release of the follow-up, *Burnin'*.

But the sweetness of success soon soured. Bob Marley's overwhelming stage presence and voice singled him out as the soul of the group. Tosh and Bunny left in 1975 to launch solo careers of their own. Tosh developed his own international following with albums like *Legalize It* and *Bush Doctor*. Bunny (Livingston) Wailer turned elusively inward and unpredictable after several stunning efforts, led by *Blackheart Man*.

Acclaim for a musical messiah: Bob Marley became a solo act in essence, too, but beefed up his act with an expanded version of the Wailers and a set of soulful back-up singers called the I-Threes. They consisted of his wife Rita, Marcia Griffiths and Judy Mowatt. With their backing, Marley danced, stomped, sang and shook his shaggy mane to greater success beginning with the release of *Natty Dread* in 1975. Albums like *Rastaman Vibration*, *Exodus* and *Survival* followed. They included such enduring singles as "Natural Mystic," "Jammin" and "Positive Vibration."

The Third World gave Marley his warmest receptions. He hailed the transformation of Rhodesia into Zimbabwe with a song and a triumphant concert at the Independence Day celebrations in Salisbury on April 17, 1980. The Zimbabweans hailed him as a musical messiah. His own government in Jamaica awarded him the nation's third highest civil honor, the Order of Merit. That made him the Honorable Robert Nesta Marley, O.M. Marley became fabulously wealthy. Still, he never forgot his roots as he sang in one of his most poignant songs, "No Woman, No Cry":

Said I remember when we used to sit
In the government yard in Trench Town
Observing all the hypocrites
Mingle with the good people we meet ...

And then Georgie would make the fire light,
I seh, log would burnin' thru the nights
Then we would cook cornmeal porridge,
Of which I'd share with you ...

By 1981, most of the world had acclaimed Marley as an international superstar and a major influence on contemporary music. Only the stubborn, stagnating studios in the United States resisted this Third World upstart. But at the same time, they made hits of Marley's compositions recorded by others – like Eric Clapton's version of Marley's "I Shot the Sheriff."

Ironically, it was during a tour that Marley hoped would finally make his mark on America that his meteoric rise to fame sud-

them the prime minister and government officials.

The next day, Marley was eulogized at a funeral ceremony conducted by members of the Ethiopian Orthodox Church. His wife, five of his children and his mother celebrated him with some of his own songs. Then his body was driven to a gravesite in the hills of the parish of St Ann near his birthplace. The funeral procession stretched for 55 miles.

Reggae without Marley: Ironically, now that Marley is gone, Americans have finally acknowledged his music. On January 19, 1994, Marley was inducted into the Rock & Roll Hall of Fame before an audience of 1,500 at the Waldorf Astoria Hotel. The posthumous

denly ended. At the age of 36, at the height of his popularity, Marley died of brain cancer in Miami's Cedars of Lebanon Hospital on May 11, 1981.

Jamaica showered its fallen hero with a funeral the likes of which only Jamaicans could stage. Marley lay in state at the National Arena in Kingston from 8am to 7.30pm on May 20. His body was dressed in a blue denim suit, a Bible propped in his right hand, his guitar in his left. A tam in the red, green and gold colors of the Ethiopian flag covered his head, and his locks were neatly arranged on his shoulders. An estimated 24,000 people filed passed his casket that day, among

award was accepted by his widow, Rita, his mother Cedella Booker, and several of his children. The 13 years since Bob's death have seen the Marley family battling for the rights to the huge fortune left by Bob, who died without making a will.

Four of his children, meanwhile, formed their own successful group, The Melody Makers, led by Ziggy Marley who is backed by his siblings Sharon, Cedella and Stephen. Reggae is still performed by accomplished groups such as Third World who continue to experiment with the genre.

Full circle: From Argentina to Japan, reggae spans the globe. Its influence can be seen in the music of performers such as Paul McCartney, Stevie Wonder, Paul Simon and Eric Clapton, who have borrowed reggae and added their own twist.

The rise of foreign reggae artists and groups has also paid tribute to the Jamaican music. Among the most successful have been British groups such as Steel Pulse, UB40, Maxi Priest, and London-born Shinehead; all are in the vanguard of a new generation of practitioners of reggae. In a return to roots, as it were, from Africa have come Alpha Blondie and Lucky Dube, the latter sounding eerily like Peter Tosh.

Sunsplash: Jamaica's own annual orgy of music, Reggae Sunsplash, has also become a

time to time, black, brown, white and yellow join hands in the middle of the night. They sing, smile and sway in unison. Reggae music has brought them together.

Still, many wonder whether Jamaica's unique brand of contemporary music is continuing to evolve, or whether it is beginning to stagnate without its most famous practitioner. In the absence of any new direction, the local scene has undergone a revival of the "dub" and DJ forms of reggae. This has spawned a new breed of dub poets, notably Mutabaruka, and DJ or Dancehall artists such as Shabba Ranks, Buju Banton and Tiger have shot to international stardom.

Shabba Ranks exploded on to the interna-

sellout event both at home and on tours abroad. 1993 saw the event moved from its traditional home in Montego Bay to a new venue in Kingston. An increasing legion of fans (over 200,000 each year) make the summer pilgrimage to hear the latest sounds Jamaica has to offer.

For four days, bands and soloists parade across the stage from late night to well past dawn. Rastafarian hawkers peddle vegetarian I-tal food and *sinsemilla* (ganja). From

Left, a poster on a Kingston wall invites all to one of the city's frequent reggae extravaganzas. **Above**, welcoming the dawn at Sunsplash.

tional music scene in 1989. Since then this Grammy Award winner has brought his own brand of hardcore Dancehall to homes all over Europe and the United States. His albums contain a diversity of music styles including soul and rap which have brought him popular acclaim, success in the mainstream charts and recognition by the music industry.

Back to basics: What used to be called DJ music has adopted a new name – Dancehall – and created an entirely new craze in fashion and dance. The lyrics of Dancehall music are direct and often controversial; the delivery is harsh and frequently aggressive. Outsize speakers and powerful amplifiers once again hold center stage in the streets as well as in halls and beer gardens. Unlike the days when a few "sound system" men like Duke Reid and Clement Dodd set the tenor and tone of the music, a seemingly endless succession of DJ artists rule the night and the Dancehall scene.

Dancehall style: The fashions in hair and dress for patrons of these sessions have likewise undergone radical changes. Men, or "dons," strut their stuff like peacocks in gaudily colored clothing, bedecked with massive gold chains and jewelry known colloquially as "cargo." Bart Simpson type hairstyles, or elaborately sculpted hair patterns

are in vogue; very dark sunglasses are obligatory, regardless of the time of day. The women, or "queens," not to be outdone, wear complex hairstyles dyed in multi-colors, or adorn themselves in wigs and elaborate hairpieces. Their clothing ranges from suggestive to downright X-rated; competition for the most attention-grabbing outfit is fierce. In fact, a whole new growth industry devoted exclusively to the designing and making of Dancehall outfits has emerged. The music and the fashions have been successfully exported to the United States and Great Britain.

The undisputed "queen" of the Dancehall scene is Carlene, a girl of middle-class ori-

gins who has parlayed Dancehall into a lucrative business of fashion shows, television ads and appearances at home and abroad.

Uptown/downtown: If Dancehall is the vehicle of expression of "downtown," then *soca*, imported from Trinidad, is the adopted mode of expression of "uptown." This fusion of soul and calypso (so-ca) is the essence of Trinidad's annual carnival celebrations. It was brought to Jamaica over 18 years ago by a group of friends who regularly made the annual pilgrimage to Trinidad's carnival, returning with the hits of that year. "Orange Carnival," which they started as a private fete, grew to an annual commercial event for local and overseas fans.

Byron Lee and The Dragonaires, one of Jamaica's most enduringly popular bands, have been regular participants in Trinidad's carnival over the years. Four years ago, Byron Lee took Jamaica Carnival to the people with costumed street parades and invited artists from Trinidad performing together with Lee's own band, The Dragonaires. The carnival scene has since exploded outside of the corporate area into resort towns across the island. In the process, a number of individual events with fruity names like "Mangerine Carnival" and "Grapefruit Carnival" were born. Back in Kingston, the Oakridge Carnival and Downtown Carnival have joined the burgeoning festivities which take place in Easter week.

Between reggae's offshoot (Dancehall), and the importation of soca, there is a void which has been filled by a return to the "golden oldies." A resurgence in popularity of tunes of yesteryear, all the way from the 1940s to the 1980s, is noticeable on the local radio stations and by the frequency of public "Oldies" sessions. Veterans of the music industry, Winston Blake and Bunny Goodison are in great demand both for their knowledge of the music and for their extensive collection of records.

Contemporary artists still maintain the prophetic tradition of reggae music made popular by stars like Bob Marley and Dennis Brown. Luciano is just one such artist producing "nouveau roots" and "culture" music. The evolution of the music into its next phase is still waiting in the wings.

Left, vintage sounds at the Country Club in Kensington. **Right**, Byron Lee and the Dragonaires.

Drawn from Life, and Lithd. by J.M. Belisario.

"KOO, KOO, OR ACTOR-BOY."

Kingston, Jamaica.

Printed by A. Duperly.

DANCE AND DRAMA: EVERYBODY'S A STAR

Jamaicans pride themselves on their sense of rhythm, their love of laughter, their loose-limbed style. It's not peculiarly Jamaican, of course. It's Caribbean. It's African. It's a reflection of the many cultures blended into one unique style, a marriage between the Old World and the New.

In such a society, those who entertain on stage must sweep and soar and rise on every occasion to satisfy the demanding audiences. Jamaican audiences can be cruel in their detachment, sitting on their hands until those onstage have earned their approval. But when the performers do gain that respect, the Jamaican audience embraces them.

Regrettably, Jamaica's cultural image has long been linked with contortionist limbo dancers, kerosene-guzzling fire eaters, and calypso dancers who gyrate to endless reprisals of "The Banana Boat Song" and "Island in the Sun." Island tour companies would do well to exploit the sophistication of many modern travelers arriving on the north coast by mounting bus tours to Kingston to showcase what Jamaica really has to offer in the realm of dance and theater.

Dance to prominence: Even novice travelers would enjoy a performance of the National Dance Theater Company of Jamaica, popularly known as the NDTC. It vividly embodies the rich tapestry of expression that draws its inspiration from the island's diverse ethnic influences. The company is based in Kingston. Its annual season runs from mid-July to mid-August, but there is also a mini-season in November and December. Special performances include a sampler of religious works from the Company's extensive repertoire, held at the Little Theater at dawn on Easter Sunday every year. It's definitely worth rising with the sun to see.

The National Dance Theater Company is an ensemble of dancers, musicians and singers which started out in 1962 as an offshoot of that year's independence celebrations. Two young men, Rex Nettleford and Eddy Thomas, were the catalysts.

The Jamaican Company has been acclaimed in concerts from Mexico City to Moscow, from Adelaide to Atlanta, and points in between. Elected heads of government and blood royalty have thrilled to performances of the NDTC. And the dancers have triumphed in spite of the thin air of Mexico City and bouts of jet lag incurred by jaunts from Jamaica to Australia.

They have been cheered by homesick Jamaican immigrants and expatriates in Brooklyn and Toronto, Cardiff and London. Young Muscovites have tried to barter company members right out of their blue jeans, and Canadian parliamentarians in black tie surprised the Jamaicans by turning up unannounced at an early overseas performance in a small Canadian town.

Ballets of the spirit: The repertoire of Jamaica's dance companies incorporates eclectic dance forms ranging from the indigenous to classical to modern, reflecting the island's decades of exposure to external influences. The Jamaica School of Dance, one of the schools of The Cultural Arts Center, has helped foster the growth and development of dance in Jamaica. In the past 15 to 20 years, other talented dance companies have emerged and gone on to win national and international acclaim. Two such are L'Accadco and Tony Wilson's Company.

The Jamaican government has traditionally thrown its support behind the island's artistic movements, a fact that has undoubtedly contributed to Jamaica's preeminence in Caribbean-wide artistic and cultural circles. Yet, neither the NDTC or any other performing group has ever received financial aid from any central governmental source. They flourish strictly on the willingness of company members to excel and attract throngs of paying customers.

Festival!: Dance is only a small part of the cultural fruits that bloom throughout the island in mid-summer each year. The weeks leading up to the annual Independence Day celebrations on August 6 have simply been designated "Festival!" – with an exclamation point. Painters, public speakers, singers, woodcarvers, sculptors, musicians, photographers, even chefs roll out their best work and most polished performances in competition for prizes and plaudits.

Festival! merged from old Jamaican community traditions of Christmas morning concerts, "tea-meetings" of songs and dances and recitations, and church fund-raising rallies. It also provides an outlet for the Jamaican flair for "showing off." In the 1950s, the Jamaican government began organizing this hodgepodge of events into a single, massive outpouring of talent. Now a formal Festival Movement meanders through the countryside each year encouraging competition in various artistic endeavors, village by village and town by town. Finals are held during Independence Week in Kingston. Many are nationally televised.

Obviously, Trinidad's internationally famous Carnival celebrations provided a spark for Jamaica's Festival! Gate receipts and business sponsorships have added a touch of commercialization to the festivities. But the importance of Festival! surfaces in the deep involvement of schools throughout the island. They seize the opportunity to motivate their students to maintain and further develop island traditions.

Pantomime in patois: An old Jamaican phrase advises that "we tek bad sinting mek joke." Roughly translated, this means that the speaker tempers potential tragedy with humor. Nowhere is this Jamaican characteristic more in evidence than in the distinctive 140-year-old tradition called the National Pantomime.

Although the word pantomime evokes visions of a performance without words, Jamaicans adapted the word to describe a fast-moving musical comedy with plenty of dialogues in the local patois. Far from being a silent show, this delicious concoction produces a potent piece of theater alive with wisecracks, send-ups of peculiarly local situations, and lampoons of historic events. Pantomime "makes sport" of grave matters, and mimics the foibles, the heartbreaks and the joys of Jamaican life. The pantomime audience in turn responds with continuous peals of laughter and even joins in repartee with the performers, becoming an integral part of the show itself.

The pantomime tradition dates back to the years when Jamaica's Little Theater Movement, the Caribbean's oldest theatrical ensemble, staged traditional versions of the English pantomimes that were based on fairy tales. Actors and actresses performed in standard formulas: a Dame, for example, always appeared in a comic, exaggerated manner so that there was no confusion about the actual male identity of the performer. A Principal Boy and a Principal Girl routinely added romantic interest and a villain provided the conflict in the story line. "Beauty and the Beast," "Sleeping Beauty," and "Pandora's Box" were among these early British favorites.

But as Jamaicans always do, they soon transformed English tradition into their own thing. They added characters from Jamaican folklore like Anansi, the West African

Spiderman, and his innumerable prodigy – Brer Tacoma, Brer Tiger and others. Soon playwrights brought in their caricatures of public figures like politicians and police chiefs. English music-hall songs gave way to indigenous rhythms, including the drumming frenzies of Pocomania and the beat of Christmas time's John Canoe (Junkanoo) dances. Contemporary rhythms like ska and reggae eventually found their way into pantomime scripts like that of "Johnny Reggae." "Carib Gold" in 1960 and "Banana Boy" in 1961 saw the introduction of sophisticated dance movements, ushering in the establishment of the NDTC in 1962.

The island's finest designers of costumes and stage settings, leading composers and musicians, playwrights and directors regard it as an honor to be part of the pantomime team each year. Major actors, actresses, dancers and singers donate their time and talent. Miss Lou and the late Ranny Williams led the headliners for many years. And the pantomime has made household names of performers like Charles Hyatt, Oliver Samuels, Lois Kelly Miller and Leonie Forbes.

The pantomime opens its season at 6 pm on Boxing Day each year.

Local productions: The National Pantomime, NDTC and Festival! are only the most visible manifestations of Jamaica's rich tapestry of

the villages and towns of the island where they reach an even greater, more appreciative audience. It's not uncommon in Kingston to find as many as six new plays or revivals, and a dance performance or two, all of them running together at one time.

Since 1976, the Little Theater Movement has also operated a national School of Drama as part of the Institute of Jamaica's Cultural Training Center. Some have bemoaned the introduction of "drama education" as unnecessary in an island so full of natural talent. Nevertheless, the school systematically trains students in all aspects of the theater from stage acting to developing light and sound systems.

performing arts. Tucked in unexpected corners of Kingston and even small villages in the countryside are small theaters where amateurs perform like professionals. Major nationally-known playwrights like Dennis Scott, Barry Reckord, Louis Marriott, Sam Hillary, Trevor Rhone and Gloria Lannamann regularly unveil new works at these intimate local venues.

Such smaller productions have a built-in advantage. They can be taken on tour through

Left, Louise Bennett in the pantomime "Queenie's Daughter". **Right**, company members of the Jamaican National Dance Theater in concert.

There is also more Jamaican music – beyond the steady beats served up by discos, sound systems and reggae concerts. Music on the island is not just reggae – which is dealt with in more detail elsewhere in this book. The Jamaica Folk Singers, led by Olive Llewin, have earned an international following for performances that weave music and movement into an educational form of entertainment. In addition, the National Chorale offers folk and classics.

The full spectrum of Jamaica's performing arts – dance, drama and music – adds up to an island that is one vibrant, glowing stage, even after the curtain has fallen.

ART, FROM GHETTO TO GALLERY

Tivoli Gardens grows from the rubble of West Kingston. The street pavement is cracked and potholed; the vacant lots are indiscriminately littered. Poverty glares at the people of Tivoli Gardens. But it has not blinded their visual appreciation or stripped them of their self-esteem.

In defiance of the destitution that surrounds them, these people have transformed blockhouse architecture into an artistic wonderland. Tivoli Gardens' residents have painted the walls of their flats – not just in solid shocks of color, but with individualized works of art. There are red, green and gold tributes to former Ethiopian emperor Haile Selassie, who is revered by the country's Rastafarians. There are pastel, pop-style pastiches that have now been made famous by reggae record album covers. A flowery paean bids visitors: "Welcome to our New City."

Mostly, there are pristine landscapes and florals that remind residents of the natural beauty that lies only a few minutes away from the ghettos of West Kingston. A mother and daughter, arm in arm, look out at a lake while father romps with a dog. These images are bold statements that prove rampant poverty has not robbed the Jamaican spirit of its richness .

The walls of Tivoli constitute only one example of the island's colorful tradition of "yard art."

Surprising strokes from the painters' brush decorate the island – from cliffside villages in the Blue Mountains to makeshift cafes in Negril. Even the execution, symmetry and poetry of the reams of political graffiti scrawled on every inch of unadorned island space in the run up to general elections underline the Jamaican's drive to express themselves, to create.

Unfortunately, honest, unpretentious "yard art" has inevitably "inspired" rows of banal woodcarvings, baskets, beads and paintings that gather dust on the shelves of the souvenir stands on Ocho Rios, Fern Gully, Montego Bay and other tourist hubs. This commercialization of genuine artistic values, mass-produced with little care or pride, is aimed at earning an easy buck from the indifferent visitor bent on bringing home a sample of "native art" bought at the airport on the way out to wave under the nostrils of envious neighbors and to fill the gap on the mantelpiece between the Niagara Falls souvenir plate and the bowling trophies.

More satisfying – and worthy of the praise,

attention and higher prices it commands – has been the work of the self-taught, intuitive artists, who have emerged from the masses of yard artists. Many actually hailed from the Tivoli Gardens and the Trench Towns of Jamaica.

John Dunkley, for instance, was a humble Kingston barber. Born in 1881, Dunkley had limited schooling. But he followed many other young Jamaican men of that time and went to Central America to seek his fortune. Dunkley returned in the 1930s and set up his barber shop in a poor neighborhood of downtown Kingston. Although he had no training in art, he covered his shop and even the

Left, "Homage to Beethoven", a painting from the palette of National Gallery Director David Boxer. **Right**, the late artist Edna Manley relaxes at her home in Kingston.

barber's chair with colorful patterns, flowers and motifs. He also began painting on canvas, dark, almost morbid images: stunted tree trunks, embryonic rabbit holes and mesmerizing shapes and symbols that sometimes seem subtly Freudian.

Dunkley did not sell many of his paintings during his lifetime since they were so unusual, so non-European and so different. Today, his works are almost impossible to purchase and command the highest prices paid for Jamaican art.

Those who followed him captured untrained, untempered visions of Jamaican life at the grassroots with honesty and clarity. Gaston Tabois, the late Mallica Reynolds

artists developed a technique totally unique in style and theme. Kapo's paintings and woodcarvings include lush landscapes and "Garden of Eden" images. The Browns produce bright paintings that mesh with the colorful essence of their Rastafarian themes and motifs. McLaren brings the human side of Jamaican life to the canvas in detailed landscapes and cityscapes.

The early artists: Almost every weekend in Jamaica, an art exhibition opens. Art lovers and hangers-on, from a handful to a crowd, mill around holding glasses of pink rum punch, the traditional opening drink. They look at the latest offerings of the well-known and the up-and-coming. They chat. Usually

(who painted under the pseudonym "Kapo"), Everald and Sam Brown, Albert Artwell, Allan Zion and Sydney McLaren comprise the vanguard of the artists who are Jamaican originals. They draw their inspiration from the country's colorful and complex traditions and not from the dictates of outside influences.

Compared to the older and more internationally known works of the self-taught artists of neighboring Haiti, the works of the Jamaican school are less homogeneous and stylized and, consequently, often more interesting. Working in isolation from each other and from foreign influences, each of these

a Jamaican personality gives a speech which the artist's friends applaud politely. They laugh at the jokes. Then they resume their chatter. They buy the best of the works and spirit them away to private collections in their villas, apartments and more modest residences.

In this way, Jamaicans celebrate an artistic tradition that dates back even before the Europeans set foot in the Americas. The island's first inhabitants, the Arawaks, used cave walls instead of canvas. Arawak drawings have been compared to prehistoric African art and resemble ancient Hawaiian petroglyphs. Figures of birds and humans carrying spears and wearing headmasks have been discovered in Mountain River Cave in the parish of St Catherine.

The Arawaks, in turn, may have inspired the figures found in architectural friezes in Jamaica's first capital at Sevilla la Nueva which were created by equally anonymous Spanish artists who accompanied Christopher Columbus on his voyages. These pieces are on display at the Institute of Jamaica in Kingston.

The earliest published works of note were the so-called Spillsbury prints executed by an unknown English artist and printed by one "Mrs Spillsbury of London." They depicted the harbors of late 18th-century Jamaica.

into aquatints and bound in one volume. Isaac Mendes Belisario, an Italian Jew born in England, arrived in 1830 and set up a studio in downtown Kingston where he produced portraits. He is best known for 12 sketches of the slave custom of Junkanoo or John Canoe, a lively musical parade in grotesque costumes still celebrated during Christmas and New Year's holidays.

Joseph Bartholomew Kidd, a Scottish painter, produced a series of sensitive sketches of Jamaican estates and the city of Kingston. Another interesting artistic development was the commissioning and importation of some of history's finest works of religious neo-classic sculpture to trim the

William Beckford, a wealthy property owner, brought two artists to Jamaica in 1773: Philip Wickstead painted portraits of the island's plantocratic families and George Robertson painted landscapes.

More famous itinerant artists followed and succeeded in capturing for posterity the essence of 19th-century Jamaica. James Hakewill's watercolors were transformed

Left, the surrealistic flights of fancy of artist Colin Garland show through in his painting of "Mr and Mrs Goose". **Above**, one of the paintings that decorate the walls of Kingston's downtrodden Tivoli Gardens.

island's Anglican churches, tombs and monuments. Two famous pieces that still stand are the Rodney Memorial Statue in Spanish Town sculpted by John Bacon Sr., and the monument to Simon Clarke in the 18th-century Anglican Church in Lucea executed by John Flaxman.

But these early Jamaican works reflected a colonial society and virtually ignored the heritages of the African slaves and smaller pockets of indentured laborers from other countries. All that changed in the 20th century with the emergence of nationalism in Jamaica and other British colonies.

The 1930s spawned traumatic events which

prompted the island's black majority to join labor unions and political parties in a political awakening aimed at improving their lot in spite of continuing British control. The nationalistic feelings also surged through the veins of Jamaica's artists. A group of middle-class artists began to probe the Jamaican psyche, utilizing indigenous subjects and themes. European styles continued to influence their approach to brush and chisel, but their changing directions formed the nucleus of Jamaica's modern-art movement.

In the colonial social structure, some of these artists actually lived at the top. They were the privileged bourgeoisie among native Jamaicans. Among their leaders, in fact,

each other the work they had been doing, which generated extended critiques and heated arguments.

"The great thing was to be able to see ourselves as Jamaicans in Jamaica and try to free ourselves from the domination of English aesthetics," said Mrs Manley in an interview before her death. "It came out in the poetry. You had the poets in those days writing about the daffodils, snow and bitter winds they had never experienced. I told them, 'Why don't you describe the drought, when the sun gets up in the morning and is king of the world all day, and everything is parched? You can smell the seymour grass, and the sun goes down in a blaze of glory

was Edna Manley, the wife of one of the founding fathers of independent Jamaica, Norman Manley, and mother of former prime minister Michael. Mrs Manley mothered the infant art movement, helping to organize art classes at the Institute of Jamaica and inspiring others to meet and exchange ideas and opinions.

The personalities in Mrs Manley's circle included poet George Campbell, artist Albert Huie, interior decorator and furniture designer Burnett Webster, photographer Dennis Gick, sculptor Alvin Marriott and novelist Roger Mais. These dynamic talents held provocative meetings where they would show

only to come up again tomorrow. The drought is on.' That is a very Jamaican and artistic and poetic theme. And we had the most terrific arguments over this."

The Jamaican establishment at that time "thought we were bonkers," Mrs Manley added. Differences in attitudes toward the arts exploded in 1939 when a group of 40 liberals stormed the annual general meeting of the Institute of Jamaica. The Institute had been created "for the encouragement of arts, science and culture in Jamaica," but the board of directors was perpetuating a colonial interpretation of arts and culture.

"Our leader was a lawyer, Robert

Braithwaite," said Mrs Manley. "He pointed to the portraits of the English governors on the wall and said, 'Gentlemen! We have come to tell you to tear down these pictures and let the Jamaican paintings take their place.' There was pandemonium. But we knew they could not ignore us anymore."

The incident at the Institute meeting sparked prompt action. Mrs Manley and some volunteers began to give art classes. That mushroomed into larger, more formal training courses, until, in 1950, the Jamaica School of Art was finally established. The school has since trained most of the country's established artists.

During his directorship in the 1970s, Karl Craig expanded the school and opened its doors to a wider segment of Jamaican society. Its success, particularly in obtaining assistance from international funding agencies, led to the establishment of a Cultural Training Center in Kingston in 1976. The Center houses the Schools of Art, Music, Dance and Drama.

The National Gallery: The Institute also transformed a small collection of local art into a major establishment, the National Gallery. The paintings, sculptures, sketches and woodworks of most of the island's leading artists were initially housed in charming Devon House, itself a fine example of Jamaican architectural art. The elegant white wooden structure stands back from a wrought-iron gate on Hope Road in New Kingston. The National Gallery has since then moved to more secure premises in the Roy West building on Kingston's waterfront.

The Gallery's current curator, a noted artist in his own right, is Jamaican David Boxer, an art historian educated at Cornell University and Johns Hopkins University. Boxer has nurtured the young collection of works and has helped it to blossom into a major collection. The Gallery, in cooperation with the Smithsonian Institute, sent a representative group of Jamaican works on a North American tour in 1983.

By the 1960s and 70s, many young Jamaicans had been sent abroad to study. They returned home with new ideas and strong styles. They applied their nationalistic themes to their external experiences in Cubism, Modern Abstract, Nordic Expressionism, Surrealism and other contemporary techniques. Their work added another dimension to the island art in the Institute.

Leading names in the collection include Carl Abrahams, Karl Parboosingh, Ralph Campbell, David Pottinger, Cecil Baugh, Mrs Edna Manley, Barrington Watson, Colin Garland and Christopher Gonzalez.

Gonzalez trained at the Jamaica School of Art, where he later taught, and at the California College of Arts and Crafts in Oakland. His work as a sculptor earned him a commission from the Jamaican government to fashion a statue of the late reggae superstar Bob

Marley. This impressive work now stands in the National Gallery.

Noting that US artists look at his work as old-fashioned and romantic compared to their experiments in super realism and the abstract, Gonzalez said: "American art is less people-oriented than ours. In Jamaica, we still deal with people as human beings. Maybe they will say that Jamaica is a more primitive place, but the human element is much stronger. The artist reflects this in his work."

For the visitor to the island who has thrilled to the colorful spectrum of life in Jamaica, the focus on humanity makes Jamaican art that much more rewarding.

Left, David Pottinger adds the finishing touches. **Right**, former curator Vera Hyatt outside Jamaica's National Gallery.

To the uninformed, cricket comes across as an utterly preposterous game played by a faintly ludicrous group of men who should know better. It stirs fuzzy images of something played in slow motion by straight-faced men stuffed into starched white uniforms. Aficionados brandish pretentious words and phrases like "batting for a century," "googly," "popping crease" and "bowled for a duck." Matches drag on for days. It is the ultimate British cliché, an overwrought version of taking tea with crumpets, a bland mix of pomp and puffery.

To the knowledgeable, cricket is nothing of the sort. Not here in Jamaica. Not anywhere in the West Indies, for that matter. In Kingston's Sabina Park, the staging of a test match that pits the cricket stars of England against those of the Caribbean ignites as much excitement as a World Cup football match or a world heavyweight boxing championship. In Jamaica, test cricket is a celebration on the scale of Christmas, Thanksgiving and Independence Day.

Even more importantly, cricket has traditionally mirrored the essence of life in Jamaica, Trinidad, Barbados and other former bastions of British colonial power. "Cricket was a stage on which selected individuals played representative roles which were charged with social significance," wrote Trinidad's great essayist and cricket enthusiast, C.L.R. James, in his book *Beyond a Boundary*. James made a convincing case for the importance of cricket in assuring the British that their colonies in the Caribbean were prepared for self-rule in the first half of the 20th century.

Bails, stumps and wickets: The game of cricket has vague similarities to American baseball. A pitcher (called a "bowler") tries to hurl a ball (slightly smaller and heavier than a baseball) past a batsman. The batsman in turn attempts to hit the bowler's offering into the field, out of reach of the opposing team's defensive players.

Play revolves around a pair of inauspicious contraptions called "wickets," facing each other at a distance of 66 ft (20 meters) at opposite ends of a "pitch," or inner field. A wicket consists of three upright wooden sticks or "stumps." The stumps are driven into the ground a few inches apart (so that the ball cannot go through them) and topped with two round pieces of wood called "bails." The bails fall off when a bowled, batted or fielded ball hits or "breaks" the wicket.

It is the job of the batsman – armed with a

3-ft (1-meter) paddle, flat on one side and rounded on the other – to defend his wicket against the bowler. Standing in front of the wicket at the "popping crease," he swings at the bowled ball as it spins and rebounds off the pitch at speeds approaching 100 miles an hour (160 kph). He can hit the ball in any direction, behind as well as in front of him. A clean hit allows him to run to the second wicket opposite his own, while his batsman-teammate, who has been protecting that wicket, runs to his end. If both reach their opposite wicket safely, a run is scored.

The batsman and his teammate can continue to run back and forth between the

Left, legendary cricket star George Headley shows the form that made bowlers tremble in the 1930s, while **right**, youths dreaming to fill Headley's shoes play in the country.

wickets until a fielder returns the ball to the pitch and a wicket is threatened. If a batsman wallops a ball "beyond the boundary" of the playing field, it automatically scores six runs for his side. A boundary along the ground scores four runs.

A batsman can be dismissed in several ways. He can be bowled out (i.e., his wicket is broken by the bowler); run out (by a throw from a fielder); caught out (if a fielder catches a fly ball off the bat before it hits the ground); or stumped (if the opposition's wicketkeeper, akin to a baseball catcher, retrieves a ball and breaks the wicket with the batsman outside the popping crease). He can also be out if the ball hits his legs rather than the wicket. The

West Indies, Australia, New Zealand, India, Pakistan, Sri Lanka and South Africa), this can require 30 hours of competition spaced over five or six days, with breaks for lunch and tea. Time limitations or other restrictions are usually called upon to keep most games shorter. School matches are often kept to a pre-stated number of "overs" – series of six balls thrown by a bowler.

Given the timespan of typical cricket matches, it is not surprising to find scores ranging from 200 to 500 runs per team. On rare occasions, first-class cricket teams have tallied more than 1,000 runs in two innings.

Of course, this oversimplified description of the game overlooks innumerable strate-

ultimate achievement of a batsman in cricket is to achieve a "century" – 100 runs or more in a single innings. The antithesis is being "bowled for a duck" – going out without scoring.

11 men per side, 10 outs per innings: There are 11 men on a cricket side, and every one of them must bat before a side is retired and an innings has ended. Because there are two batsmen (at opposite wickets) in the game at one time, 10 outs constitute an innings. A match normally continues for two innings, until both sides have batted twice. In international test matches, which pit any two of the world's leading cricket nations (England,

gies, subtleties and idiosyncrasies.

The roots of Caribbean cricket: Cricket dates back to 16th-century England and has always been associated with that country and its larger associates, particularly India and Australia. By comparison, the small, indigenous populations of the British Commonwealth islands in the Caribbean have only begun making great strides in the sport during the past 50 years or so. Yet the list of Jamaican cricket greats continues to grow. And that of tiny Barbados, population about 280,000, is even longer.

One reason for the rapid rise of cricket in the West Indies was that the British Raj brandished the game as a byproduct of its colonial policy, often encouraging visiting teams to display the Union Jack and teach the locals some English "culture." West Indians from all levels of society learned quickly and players of European descent are still found in teams fielded by the West Indies. By the turn of the 20th century, most of the region's oldest clubs had come into existence and had begun inter-colony competitions (since succeeded by the annual Shell Shield matches). With limited other opportunities for education or advancement in society, young black men discovered that cricket could bring recognition and comparatively good incomes.

Some great names: In the eyes of the public,

to score two centuries in one test match at Lord's in London, the sport's world headquarters. If a comparison must be made, an American baseball player would have to hit a grand slam home run in every game of a World Series to equal the feat.

Headley's quiet personality and modesty bolstered his popularity. In one of the finest brief tributes ever paid to a sporting figure, a dean of England's elegant cricket writing fraternity, R.C. Robertson-Glasgow, wrote in *Cricket Prints*: "Great batting often has the beauty of the blast or the grandeur of the gale. In Headley's art, there is no noise. But it answers the test of greatness. As he walks down the pavilion steps, you can expect in

the name of one Jamaican still spells cricket – George Alphonso Headley. In cricket, Headley is on a par with his American baseball contemporary, Babe Ruth. Like another American contemporary, boxer Joe Louis, Headley was a black sporting hero with a constituency that stretched far beyond the field of play. Even the fans of Australia and, more significantly, England, flocked to watch George Headley bat. Among many other achievements, he remains the only man ever

Left, the team portrait of the Jamaican cricketers that faced their arch-rivals, Barbados, in 1925. Above, waiting to go on.

hope or fear. Only three or four can do this for you always."

In the 1930s, Trinidad produced the great all-rounder, Learie Constantine, equally skilled in batting and bowling. Cricket propelled Constantine through law school and the Trinidad government cabinet, into the post of High Commissioner to Great Britain, and finally into the history books as the first fully black member of the House of Lords.

In the same era, England's late Andy Sandham scored 325 runs at Kingston's Sabina Park, the first triple century in test history. During the same match, Headley scored the first of two test double centuries he was to make at Sabina. The next one occurred in 1935. Twenty-four years later, Garfield Sobers of Barbados put up a world record score of 365 runs for a test innings, again at Sabina Park. Sobers, whose statistics and abilities rank him as the sport's all-time leading all-rounder, was later knighted, and his batting record was only finally beaten by Brian Lara in 1994.

Other fine Jamaican players include batting stylists Lawrence Rowe; J.K. Holt Sr., the most famous Jamaican cricketer before Headley and father of the great J.K. Holt Jr.; O.G. "Collie" Smith, who rose from the ghetto to become one of the nation's finest all-rounders before his tragic death in an

automobile accident in the early prime of his career. Alfred Valentine, one of the game's best slow left-arm spin bowlers, made a major contribution to the West Indies' first overseas victory against England in 1950 – a feat which made him and his right-handed Trinidadian colleague, Sonny Ramadhin, heroes of a famous calypso.

More recently, the mid-1970s through the 1980s produced the No. 1 fast bowler in the world, and possibly the fastest bowler in history, Michael Holding. Considered one of the sport's legends, he is one of the main reasons for the West Indies' dominance of test cricket in that period. Now retired, Hold-

ing continues to be in demand as a commentator. His book on his life as a fast bowler is aptly titled *Whispering Death*.

Other sports: An abundance of evidence attests to Jamaicans' athletic prowess in several fields in the international arena. Their achievements in track and field have brought fame and glory not only to Jamaica, but also to the countries to which they have migrated and where they form the nucleus of Olympic teams.

The island has been producing Olympic medal winners since the 1950s, beginning with the unforgettable quartet of Herb McKenley, Arthur Wint, George Rhoden and Les Laing with a record-setting relay victory in Helsinki. More recent stars include Mel Spence, Donald Quarrie, Merlene Ottey and Grace Jackson Small.

Boxing has produced world champions such as Mike McCallum, Lloyd Honnegan, Trevor Berbick, and Simon Brown. Others have gone on to excel in sports not traditional in Jamaica: basketball (Patrick Ewing), baseball (Devon White) and, more recently, in the very un-Jamaican non-tropical sport of the bobsleigh competition. The Jamaican bobsleigh team comprised of ex-Jamaica Defence Force officers, evoked astonishment and mild amusement when they first entered the Winter Olympics held in Lake Placid in 1988. Initial reaction quickly turned to cheers and admiration when, despite an unfortunate spill which dashed their contending hopes, the four-man team turned in a daring performance in the final event.

The advent of satellite television in Jamaica has focused attention on traditional American sports such as basketball and NFL football. Spectator interest is keen and competitive with bets on the weekly NFL games and Superbowl parties celebrating the final event in true North American style. Basketball hoops have mushroomed in backyards and playing fields, particularly in the corporate area of Kingston, and youngsters are regularly seen practising "slam-dunks" in the style of Michael Jordan and Jamaica's own Patrick Ewing. Jamaicans at all levels of society have a keen appreciation of sports, whether as participants or spectators.

Left, Jamaican cricket fans, protected from the blazing sun by umbrellas, jam Sabina Park. **Right**, a class batsman is a national hero.

Nyam is a Jamaican word of African origin meaning "to eat." Once you discover the bounty of this fertile land, you may be tempted to *nyam* your way around the island.

Spicy and pungent, aromatic and enticing, greasy and filling, mouth-watering and hot; a blend of African, Chinese, Indian and European cuisines, yet individualistic in its appeal – this is Jamaican food. Unfortunately, the visitor who sticks to resort hotel restaurants will never be exposed to the incomparable taste of Jamaican cuisine nor to the great variety of seasonal fruit.

From jerk pork to ackee and salt fish, rundown to callaloo, curried goat to mannish water, Jamaican cooking is a little-known delight only now emerging on the international scene with new-found pride. Although some hotels have become more adventurous in recent years – adding ackee quiche and staple soups like pepperpot and red pea to their menus – these tend to be pale imitations of authentic Jamaican cuisine which is best experienced in home cooking. A close second are the wayside food stalls, many of which are located on visitor-driven routes, and are characterized by quaint shelters with equally quaint names.

The delicacy which arouses most curiosity in visitors is ackee, one of the main ingredients in the national dish. This red-skinned fruit with a taste all its own is treated like a vegetable and can only be eaten after the pod opens. Unripe and unopened ackee is poisonous. Inside are three yellow lobes with black seeds. The seeds are discarded and the lobes are carefully cleaned of a thin red membrane before being boiled. The cooked and drained lobes are then reheated gently (they disintegrate easily when cooked) with cooked onions, peppers and salted cod imported from Canada. As a Sunday breakfast special, ackee and salt fish is often served with a choice of roasted breadfruit, boiled green bananas, fried plantains, johnny cakes (fried flour dumplings from the English "journey cakes") or bammies (flat round breads made from cassava flour).

Left, the traditional way to carry a fruit basket.
Right, a street chef serves up crab claws.

Weekends are the times when Jamaicans can usually indulge themselves in cooking meals which require a certain amount of lengthy preparation.

The main course for Sunday lunch may be a roast of beef, pork or chicken. It is usually accompanied by steaming mounds of rice and peas, an assortment of white or yellow yams, sweet potatoes or pumpkin (collectively referred to in local parlance as "ground provisions" or "food"), carrots steamed with the squash-like cho-cho, fried or boiled ripe

plantains, and a simple salad of lettuce and sliced tomatoes. A feast fit for a king – or a gourmand.

Saturday's main meal is traditionally a hearty soup – red or gungo pea, pepperpot or beef soup, simmered with salt beef or pickled pig's tail, yams, dumplings, sweet potatoes, vegetables in season and accompanied by thick slabs of hard-dough bread.

Another popular dish is mackerel rundown ("run-dung" in the vernacular). Whole salted mackerel is soaked to rid it of excess salt, picked over carefully to get rid of the bones, and then cooked to a meltingly tasty stew in coconut milk, tomatoes, onions, scallion, thyme and hot country peppers. Traditional accompaniments for mackerel rundown are boiled green bananas, yams and boiled dumplings.

Seafood is exquisite, as is the bounty of the rivers and streams. A popular method of preparing freshly caught fish is called Escoveitch (es-ko-veech). The fish is cleaned and left whole, highly seasoned with salt and black pepper, then fried and left to marinate in vinegar, thinly sliced onions, cho-cho, carrots and hot peppers for hours, preferably overnight. It is eaten hot or cold. Peppered shrimps are a speciality of the Black River area. You can purchase a paper bag of these dried, exceedingly peppery tiny shrimps from wayside vendors. Elsewhere, you may be offered janga or jonga soup made from small river crayfish.

At times of celebration, there is the inescapable goat's head soup, or mannish water, which is an important part of any festive menu especially at country weddings. This is usually followed by curried goat and rice. Gourmet treats of other areas include turtle eggs in red wine, a delicacy of Clarendon; rare booby eggs from Goat Island (Port Esquivel), and fresh oysters with a blend of vinegar and pepper.

The variety of Jamaican foods and fruit is too numerous to list in detail, but some of the more unusual ones that you may encounter on your travels around the island include:

● Bammy, a round flat bread made from grated cassava (a tuberous root vegetable). It is fried, grilled or steamed.

● Breadfruit, a round, green starchy fruit that is a dietary staple. It can be baked, boiled, roasted, fried, made into chips, flour, or substituted for potatoes in salads.

● Callaloo, a leafy spinach-like vegetable.

● Cho-cho, also known as christophene or chayote. A pear-shaped, prickly skinned vegetable, light-green or white in color with a delicate flavor, similar to squash.

● Festival, a sausage-shaped, deep-fried cornmeal dumpling, usually served with fried fish, jerk pork or chicken at wayside stalls.

● Guinep, a small green fruit, borne in clusters like grapes. The leathery outer skin covers a soft orange-colored pulp, somewhat similar in taste to lychee. Large central seed.

● June plum, also called Jew plum. A tart fruit with a large spiky seed. Can be eaten fresh, stewed, or made into a delicious drink.

● Naseberry, also known as sapodilla. Small round brown fruit with a thin edible skin and sweet, delicately flavored pale brown pulp.

● Star apple, a round fruit about the size of an orange with shiny purple or green skin. So called because when it is cut in half, the pattern of the pale purple pulp forms an eight-pointed star. It is the basis of a dessert called Matrimony, which blends the pulp of the star apple with segments of orange sweetened with condensed milk.

Jerk cooking: Matthew Lewis, in his *Journal of a West India Proprietor*, was one of the first to describe the Jamaican eating experience. "We had at dinner a land tortoise and a barbecued pig, two of the richest dishes that

I ever tasted, the latter in particular, which was dressed in the true Maroon fashion.... I have eaten several other good Jamaica dishes, but none so excellent as this..."

Lewis didn't know it, but he was describing what is rather unflatteringly known as jerk cooking. No article on food and drink in Jamaica would be complete without a word about this latest food craze from Jamaica to hit the international market – jerk just as the Maroons used to do it.

The term refers to the special spices used to season the meat as well as the method by which it is cooked. The traditional method is on a barbecue of pimento wood over a pit dug in the ground in which a fire smoulders, a technique rather similar to Maori cooking in New Zealand.

The Maroons adopted the Arawak method of cooking meat over a *barbacoa* (from which comes the word "barbecue"), but it is their special seasoning of lime juice, crushed pimento berries, hot peppers and other spices that gives jerked meat its distinctive flavor. Four hundred years ago, they used this method to cook wild pigs in the mountain fastness of Portland. It is a method still used in Boston, Portland, where the best and most authentic jerk pork originates.

The two-hour drive to Portland for jerk pork along the winding, rugged coastline, or

the evenings, particularly at weekends, you will encounter several of these roadside jerk stands filling the air with the pungent smoke of jerk chicken, the cheapest and most easily available meat. More rarely it may be fish or pork. There are few, if any, wild pigs left in the hills around Portland and demand far outstrips the availability of farm-bred pigs. But so popular has this method of cooking become that some restaurants and bars offer it on their menus. Other establishments cook nothing but jerk pork or chicken. Jerk cooking is presently enjoying international acclaim in several cities in the United States, and a number of cook books based on jerk have been published.

over the equally winding mountain road, is too time-consuming for most busy Kingstonians. No problem! Ever-inventive Jamaican entrepreneurs have devised a portable barbecue made of oil drums sawn in half. The drums are cleaned and the halves fitted together with hinges and a funnel on top to allow smoke to escape. A fire is built in the bottom half, the seasoned meat rested on a grill and the whole contraption stood on a metal frame.

Driving through the streets of Kingston in

Left, fish and bammy. **Above**, Jerk pork stand at Boston Bay.

When your mouth waters for the taste of something spicy and your stomach longs for something filling, a paper-wrapped portion of jerk pork or chicken, with some slices of hard-dough bread, does the trick every time. Topped off with a cold Red Stripe beer, it is the Jamaican answer to the Englishman's fish-and-chips with a pint of best bitter.

Drinks all round: Drinking is an intrinsic part of the country's social pattern. When Jamaicans get together to relax, the question "what would you like to drink?" does not refer to coffee or tea, although you may have that if it's your preference. It is usually an offer of beer, rum, or any of the other locally available hard liquors mixed with a chaser or on the rocks, but always served ice-cold.

No matter where you go on the island, you are almost certain to find a bar. What's more, almost every corner grocery sells and serves beer and stout, as do many of the fast-food outlets. Most Jamaicans, from the rural villager to the city sophisticate, have their favorite local drinking spot. Indeed, the quickest way for a visitor to penetrate the local lifestyle is to drop into the neighborhood bar or rum shop.

Locally available drink runs the gamut from imported whiskies, wines and champagnes to white rum, beer and stout, accompanied by the continuous "bang" of domi-

noes in a back room. In the country parts, you may be confused by the patron's order: "Serve me a 'ot 'ops," (hot hops = beer which has not been chilled). It's quite popular. Jamaica produces an award-winning local beer, Red Stripe (also known as "The Policeman" because of the red stripe on the uniforms of the police force). Red Stripe's brewers, Desnoes & Geddes, also bottle Dragon Stout and Guinness.

There are a number of liqueurs native to Jamaica of which the most widely known is Tia Maria coffee liqueur, offered in better bars throughout the world. Other fine coffee and fruit liqueurs are produced by Sangster's

under the label "Old Jamaica" from their World's End factory in the Blue Mountains above Gordon Town. Unusual fruit flavors have been blended with selected aged Jamaican rums and have been winning international gold medals for several years. But as the world knows, it is rum that is synonymous with fine drinking in Jamaica.

Today, Jamaica produces a full range of rums, from light to dark, of which the best known brand is Appleton made by J. Wray & Nephew. Appleton rum is exported to 64 countries and there are two principal blends: Appleton White is light, smooth and mellow; Appleton Special is a blend of aged Jamaican dark rum with a distinctive taste of its own.

Something else to remember when ordering in a country bar: if you want, say, an Appleton Special with ginger ale, you have to be specific, otherwise you will be served white, 100 percent overproof rum chased with ginger beer – powerful stuff which could leave you gasping for breath.

If you visit Jamaica during the "winter" season, you may see bundles or plastic bags of spiky looking, dark red leaves on sale. This is sorrel and it is used to make a traditional drink at Christmas time. The leaves are covered with water to which a piece of ginger root, or a few pimento (allspice) berries, even a handful of cloves has been added. It is left to steep, then strained and sweetened with sugar. A dash of rum may be added to give it an extra "kick."

For those not inclined to alcoholic drink, the island's array of fruit produces some of the most refreshing, delicious and unusual juices. Not to be forgotten is the perennial favorite, coconut water and the succulent "jelly" or meat inside the nut. You may also want to try "Ting," a bottled grapefruit-based drink; a fizzy tamarind juice, or Irish Moss (made from seaweed). Alternatively, try a fresh fruit punch made from ripe bananas and a variety of fruit in season. Jamaican fruit juices have won several international contests, and are readily available at most resorts and even on roadsides.

Whatever your fancy, the salutation is "cheers!"

<u>Left</u>, rural children sell sticks of *ackee* near Flat Bridge. <u>Right</u>, old Jamaica liqueur at World's End in the Blue Mountains.

145

PARDON MY PATOIS

English-speaking visitors to Jamaica often wonder what language is spoken on the island, especially after they encounter their first Rastaman espousing the glories of "Jah" or a good-natured beachboy who inquires: "Everyt'ing kool, mon? Everyt'ing *irie?*" The newcomers soon think their tour guide lied in telling them everyone here speaks English. That is an understandable reaction – except to Jamaicans, who are under the impression that it is the Americans, British and Canadians who speak in their own unin-

"shoot the deer and kill them up." Jacques later uses the word "physic" to connote the act of purging. Jamaican country children all know that when their parents threaten to "physic" them, it means castor oil or Epsom salts ("salt physic") next morning.

Biblical influence: African slaves, brought to Jamaica centuries ago, adopted the speech mannerisms of their British masters. In their new Caribbean home, a rampant use of biblical phraseology crept into the distinctive patois. The Bible is a fixture in the homes of

telligible dialects. Indeed, Jamaicans do speak English, but some of it is so ancient that even the British have abandoned it. William Shakespeare and his contemporaries might understand, though.

For instance, Jamaicans use the word "up" as an intensifier. A car that is "smash up" is in much worse shape than one that has merely been in a smash. You "slip up" when you trip, you "soak up" when you make a mess of a job, and as even Americans know, you get "beat up" when you suffer a serious mugging.

Compare this to the character Jacques in Shakespeare's *As You Like It*. He tells of hunters who haunt the Forest of Arden and

Christians and Rastafarians alike. So when parting, a mere goodbye seems inadequate when one can say: "Peradventure I wi' see you tomorrow."

Some of the most colorful of Jamaican expressions can be traced back to the languages of West African countries like Ghana. Early arrivals from these lands found it difficult to pronounce barbaric language constructions like *th*. Thus, "the" became "de," "them" became "dem," and "that" became "dat" – a speech pattern that conformed with those of Africa and which persists here today. *Th* at the end of a word proved particularly tricky. If a Jamaican man says his girlfriend has beautiful "teet", rest assured he is complimenting her dental work, not her bustline.

To further simplify the Africans' transition to life in colonial Jamaica and its strange tongue, the peculiarities of English grammar were often simplified or totally abandoned. Both case and gender were ignored in favor of simply "him" – for men, for women, for you or I alike. A young girl or woman became "gal." But the plural became "de gal dem." In fact, the plural "dem" applies to almost everything – cars, people, dogs, even children.

Vowel games: Jamaicans play speech games with vowels, especially the letter *a*. A garden can become either a "gyarden" or a "gorden," depending on the gentility of the speaker.

The influence of Africa is also found in the way Jamaicans shift syllables and re-arrange the stress to suit their purposes. A mattress becomes a "mat-rass." A tomato becomes either "tomatis" or "salad" depending on its size. The ubiquitous surname Smith becomes unrecognizable to the Jamaican visitor as "Simmit." Words with African roots that linger in contemporary patois include *putta-putta* for mud, *duckanoo* for a particular kind of pudding, and "*Anansi* story" for fairy tale. (In the Akan language of Ghana, *Anansesem* means "words about the spider.")

More recent years have found yet another form of African influence creeping into patois – the language of the Rastafarians. Central to their speech is the emphasis on the singular "I" or the plural "I and I" to underline the importance of the individual. Thus, divine becomes "I-vine." Ethiopian is "I-thiopian" and fabulous has become *I-rie*.

Jamaicans regard time and distance as subservient to the individual. Thus the often misunderstood phase "soon come" should be interpreted to mean that the speaker will turn up sooner… or later.

Another source of confusion for the unwary is the use of measurements unknown elsewhere. In measuring land, the old English unit of chains is still employed. The original measuring chains used by surveyors were comprised of heavy wire links, each link exactly 7.9 inches (20 cm) long, so that the chain could be conveniently folded and carried in a bag. One hundred links equalled a chain of precisely 22 yards, the length of a cricket pitch. If a Jamaican tells you that your destination is "a few chains from here," it is not far away. If it is "a stone's throw," on the other hand, it may be anywhere. Traveling time is a flexible thing.

The ultimate key to Jamaican speech is the word *rass*. Originally, it meant backside, bum, derriere. It still retains that meaning in Jamaica, but as Humpty Dumpty told Alice it also "means what I intend it to mean." Thus, a man who is a *tiefin rass* is a dishonest thief. On the other hand, "Come here, you ole rass, mek I buy you a drink!" may be used when men greet their friends. Jamaicans may even say to each other with envy: "Dat is a rass house."

Or a man who spots an attractive woman walking past may lean over to his friend and smile, "Dat gal pretty to rass" – about which no further comment is necessary.

Left, "cuss-cuss never bore hole in skin" is the way Jamaicans on the telephone or **right,** chatting on the road would tell each other that "hard words break no bones."

PLACES

Get it together in Jamaica,
Soulful town, soulful people,
I see you're having fun.
Dancing to the reggae rhythm,
Oh, island in the sun! Come on and
Smile, you're in Jamaica!
— Bob Marley, from *Smile Jamaica*

The island of Jamaica provides a steady stream of surprises, fairly constant in mood and cadence, yet seductive and hypnotic in the way they brand themselves on your brain. Even the standard tour bus stops – Dunn's River Falls, Bamboo Avenue, Rose Hall Great House, the Blue Hole, the Rio Grande River rafting trip – provide experiences unique in the Caribbean. Greater rewards await the traveler who dares to turn down an unpaved country road and lose himself in the Cockpit Country, who puts on his or her hiking shoes and scales the Blue Mountains, or who saunters into a Darliston restaurant to order curry goat and breadfruit.

The travel section that follows gives a taste of both worlds: out-of-the way coves and crannies as well as the well-trodden trails. For the usual routes, you need only check with travel agencies or hotel tour desks for a list of guided tours. For the less-traveled byways, you will need to rent, beg or borrow a car, or join the Jamaican people on their buses and mini-vans.

This section has been subdivided into three main chapters. "The County of Surrey" offers a detailed look at Jamaica's business and governmental nerve center, the Kingston-lower St Andrew corporate area. Surrey also includes a tour of the Blue Mountains and a glance at historic Port Antonio.

"The County of Middlesex" starts with a visit to the tourist center of Ocho Rios, a good base from which to explore Jamaica's heartland. You will travel the north coast, then head south through the hills to South Middlesex, where the two main areas of interest are Spanish Town and Mandeville.

Finally, "The County of Cornwall" focuses on Jamaica's tourist capital – Montego Bay (or "MoBay") – and its coastal resort neighbors. There's also a brief dip into the mysterious Cockpit Country southeast of MoBay. The section ends at Negril, Jamaica's funkiest tourist development. As in any country, it's the human landscape that really counts. Meanwhile, most Jamaicans will enjoy meeting you as much as you will enjoy meeting them.

Preceding pages: the famed Bamboo Avenue, near Lacovia; climbing into the Blue Mountains; local country music club; resort pools at Ocho Rios. **Left**, waiting to go on at Carnival.

157

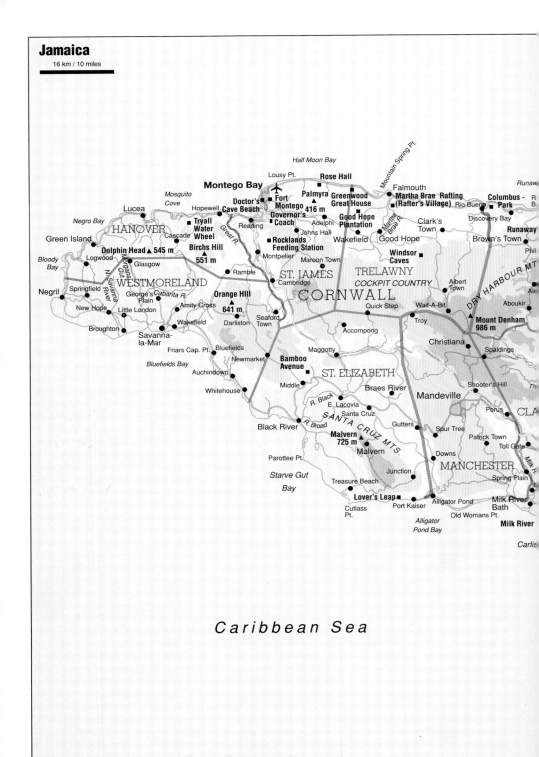

Jamaica

16 km / 10 miles

Half Moon Bay

Mountain Spring Pt.

Lousy Pt.

Rose Hall

Montego Bay

Falmouth

Runaw

Palmyra **Greenwood**
Great House

Martha Brae Rafting
(Rafter's Village)

Columbus -
Park

R
B

Mosquito
Cove

Doctor's
Cave Beach

Fort
Montego

Rio Bueno

Lucea

Hopewell

Governor's
Coach

416 m

Good Hope
Plantation

Clark's
Town

Discovery Bay

Negro Bay

Reading

Adelphi

Johns Hall

Good Hope

Runaway
Brown's Town

Green Island

HANOVER

Cascade

Tryall
Water
Wheel

Birchs Hill

Wakefield

Phil

Logwood

Dolphin Head ▲ 545 m

Montpelier

Windsor
Caves

Bloody
Bay

Glasgow

551 m

Maroon Town

ST. JAMES

TRELAWNY

Albert
Town

Ale

Ramble

Cambridge

COCKPIT COUNTRY

WESTMORELAND

Springfield

George's *Cabarita R.*
Plain

Orange Hill

CORNWALL

Quick Step

Wait-A-Bit

DRY HARBOUR MT

Aboukir

Negril

New Hope

Little London

Amity Cross

641 m

Seaford
Town

Troy

▲ **Mount Denham**
986 m

Broughton

Wakefield

Darliston

Accompong

Christiana

Spaldings

Savanna-
la-Mar

Friars Cap. Pt.

Bluefields

Maggotty

SANTA

CRUZ

Newmarket

Bamboo
Avenue

ST. ELIZABETH

Shooter's Hill

Th

Bluefields Bay

Auchindown

Middle

Braes River

Mandeville

CLA

Whitehouse

R. Black

E. Lacovia

Gutters

Porus

Santa Cruz

Spur Tree

Black River

R. Broad

Malvern
725 m

Patrick Town

Toll Gate

Parottee Pt.

Malvern

Downs

Junction

MANCHESTER

Starve Gut
Bay

Treasure Beach

Spring Plain

Lover's Leap ■

Alligator Pond

Milk River
Bath

Cutlass
Pt.

Port Kaiser

Old Womans Pt.

Milk River

Alligator
Pond Bay

Carlis

Caribbean Sea

158

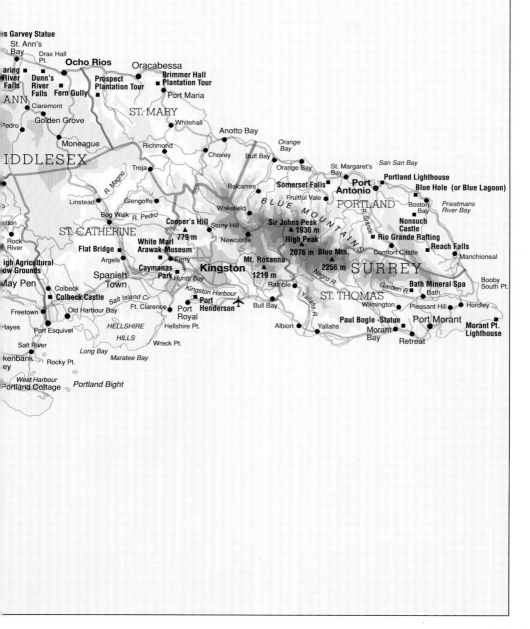

Caribbean Sea

s Garvey Statue
St. Ann's
Bay
Drax Hall
Pt.
Ocho Rios
Oracabessa
aring
River ■ ■ Dunn's ■ **Prospect** **Brimmer Hall**
Falls River **Plantation Tour** ■ **Plantation Tour**
Falls **Fern Gully** ■ Port Maria
ANN
Claremont
ST. MARY
Whitehall
Pedro
Golden Grove
Anotto Bay
Moneague
Richmond
Orange
Bay
IDDLESEX
Chovey
Buff Bay
Troja
Orange Bay
St. Margaret's San San Bay
Bay
Portland Lighthouse
Balcarres
Somerset Falls ■ **Port** ■ **Blue Hole (or Blue Lagoon)**
Linstead
Glengoffe ■ Fruitful Vale **Antonio**
Bog Walk R. Pedro Waketield **Nonsuch** Boston Priestmans
Castle Bay River Bay
elton
Cooper's Hill Stony Hill
Rock **ST. CATHERINE** ▲ Sir Johns Peak ■ **Rio Grande Rafting**
River **779 m** ▲ 1930 m
White Marl Newcastle **High Peak** ■ **Reach Falls**
igh Agricultural **Flat Bridge** ■ **Arawak-Museum** 2076 m **Blue Mtn.** Comfort Castle Manchioneal
ow Grounds Argels ■ ■ Ferry ▲
Caymanas Mt. Rosanna 2256 m **SURREY**
May Pen **Spanish** **Park** Hunts Bay ▲ Booby
Colbeck **Town** **Kingston** 1219 m Garden R. South Pt.
■ **Colbeck Castle** Salt Island Cr Ramble **Bath Mineral Spa**
Freetown Old Harbour Bay Kingston Harbour **ST. THOMAS** Bath
■ **Port** Bull Bay Wilmington Pleasant Hill Hordley
Hayes Ft. Clarence **Henderson** ✈ Yallais R.
Port Esquivel Port **Paul Bogle -Statue** **Port Morant**
Royal Albion Yallahs Morant **Morant Pt.**
Salt River **HELLSHIRE** Hellshire Pt. Bay **Lighthouse**
kenbank **HILLS** Wreck Pt. Retreat
ey Rocky Pt. Long Bay Maratee Bay
West Harbour
Portland Cottage Portland Bight

PORTLAND

BLUE MOUNTAINS

R. Magno

R. Grande

Negro R.

Jamaica's eastern protuberance packs into its 820 sq. miles (2,100 sq. km) more dramatic extremes than any other part of the island. Here in the County of Surrey, the cosmopolitan growth of modern Kingston stands shoulder to shoulder with the inaccessible reaches of the Blue Mountains. While daily mists descend to 3,000 ft (914 meters) on some parts of the mountains, coastal Kingston swelters under 60 percent sunshine annually.

Surrey embraces the parishes of St Thomas and Portland, and the corporate area of Kingston and St Andrew, comprising the capital city and surrounding areas.

Religious cults such as *kumina* flourish in St Thomas. Portland's mountains were the stronghold of freedom-fighting Maroons whose descendants still live in villages in the area. In Kingston itself, a fusion of the traditional and sophisticated modern takes place on the stages of theaters, in the museums and art galleries.

Surrey's principal highway, Route A4, clings to a coastline of beautiful beaches – white coral sands on the northern coast, occasionally black sands on the south. The foothills of the Blue Mountains offer spectacular and diversified scenery within easy driving distance of city and towns. The mountain roads themselves are narrow and twisting and should be tackled only by those with the right spirit of adventure.

The vegetation, from mountains to coast, is rich and varied. Untouched wilderness flanks slopes denuded by centuries of settlement. Hill savannas choked with guinea grass, but few trees, alternate with wet forests of overgrown foliage, tree ferns and mosses. Gnarled wind-blown trees of elfin woodlands are a contour line away from acres of Caribbean Pine in commercial forestry projects. Abundant rainfall feeds cascading streams which pour into coastal marshes.

Temperatures range from around 80°F (27°C) on the sea coast to 40°F (5°C) at Blue Mountain Peak, just 10 miles (16 km) inland. This climatic diversity has enabled Surrey residents to grow a bewildering array of vegetables, fruits and flowers from the four corners of the world. A farmer's garden might include yam vines as well as parsley, sage, rosemary and thyme, plus such decidedly tropical products as Search-Me-Heart and cho-cho. Peaches, strawberries, iceberg lettuce and asparagus grow on the mountain slopes.

Left, the County of Surrey is rich in tropical and mountainous vegetation.

163

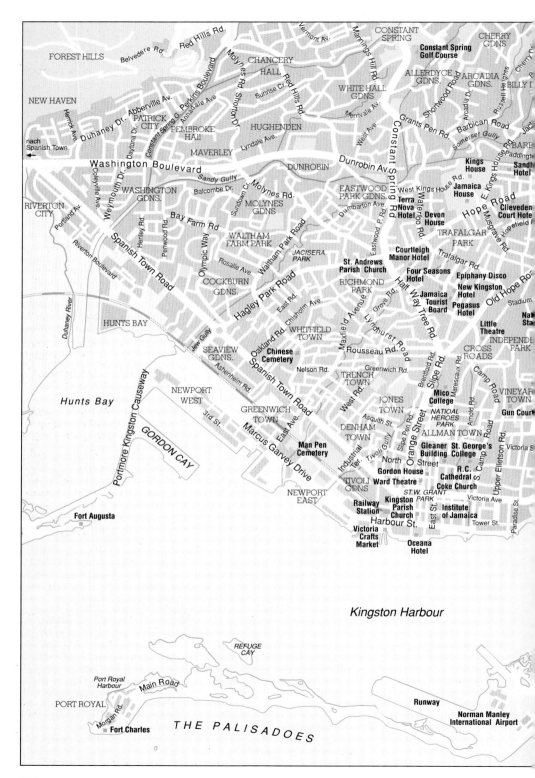

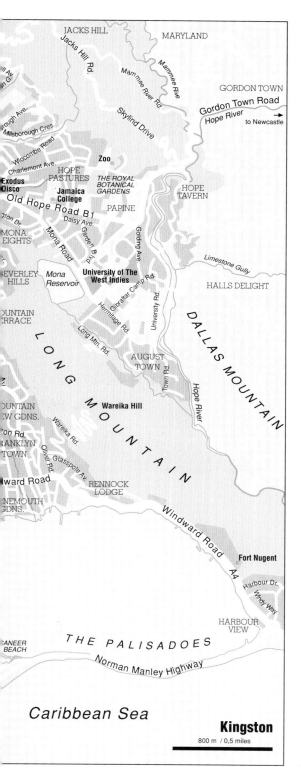

JACKS HILL

MARYLAND

Jacks Hill Rd.

Mammee River Rd.

Mammee River

GORDON TOWN

Gordon Town Road

Skyline Drive

Hope River

to Newcastle

Zoo

Wycombe Road

Charlemont Ave.

HOPE
PASTURES

THE ROYAL
BOTANICAL
GARDENS

HOPE
TAVERN

Exodus
Disco

Jamaica
College

Old Hope Road B1

PAPINE

Daisy Ave.

MONA
HEIGHTS

Mona Road

Golding Ave.

Garden B'lvd

Limestone Gully

EVERLEY
HILLS

Mona
Reservoir

University of The
West Indies

Camp Rd.

HALLS DELIGHT

Hermitage Rd.

Gibraltar Camp Rd.

University Rd.

OUNTAIN
ERRACE

Long Mtn. Rd.

D A L L A S   M O U N T A I N

L O N G

AUGUST
TOWN

Town Rd.

Hope River

OUNTAIN
W GDNS.

Wareika Hill

M O U N T A I N

on Rd.

RANKLYN
TOWN

Wareika Rd.

Oliver Rd.

Glasspole Av.

ward Road

RENNOCK
LODGE

NEMOUTH
GDNS.

Windward Road

Fort Nugent

A4

Harbour Dr.

Windy Way

HARBOUR
VIEW

CANEER
BEACH

T H E   P A L I S A D O E S

Norman Manley Highway

Caribbean Sea

Kingston

800 m / 0,5 miles

KINGSTON: THE LIVELY CAPITAL

If the expression urban sprawl had not existed, the city of Kingston would have invented it. Founded over 300 years ago, it has made up for its lack of elegance and graciousness with the exuberance and gusto of the perpetual adolescent. Kingston is a capital city which has defied all efforts of its city fathers, planners and various do-gooders to curb it, tame it, confine it, order it, or to discipline its citizens.

From every street corner, reggae music blares. Bars and betting shops jostle with churches as the most ubiquitous non-residential buildings in the city. Obsolescent narrow streets challenge drivers' nervous systems. Pound laws notwithstanding, animals wander at will. Street signs are usually absent. Amidst this endless chaos, Kingstonians have inbred a natural radar of direction and survival. They seem to find meaning or pattern in what outsiders consider so disordered.

Kingston is a city that has never caught up with itself, for it has never stopped growing. Its population is swelled daily by starry-eyed youths from the mountains who dream of hitting it big in the city. They inflate the numbers of "yard" or tenement dwellers, and their dreams and hopes burgeon into the city's headaches: outgrown water supplies, public transportation, sanitation services, schools, jobs and housing.

To make ends meet, many of these people have turned Kingston into a city of hustlers. Hawkers (known as higglers), their bargains purchased overseas, return to set up their wares on the sidewalks, competing with time-honored merchants who display goods indoors. The hustle on the sidewalk is known as "Ben Dung Plaza" – you have to bend down to buy. City fathers threaten and cajole, but Ben Dung Plaza, like the rest of Kingston, rolls on with a momentum of its own.

Kingston began as a well-designed

Preceding pages: overview of Kingston.

seaside town on the edge of a magnificent natural harbor. But it has voraciously gobbled up all of the Liguanea (pronounced *Li-ga-nee*) Plains and crept into the surrounding mountains. In the past decade, encouraged by a causeway across the western end of the harbor, Kingston has also embraced part of the promontory known as the Hellshire Hills, separating the harbor from the rest of the south coast.

A city of views: What redeems Kingston – and makes up for the noise, the squalor, the inconveniences and the heat – is the city's splendid setting. The readily accessible panoramic views make this evident. From Hellshire Beach at Naggo Head, the city unfolds, framed by the mountains. And from the hills – Beverly Drive (in Beverly Hills), Skyline Drive (on Jacks Hill), and the spectacular crest of Red Hills Road – are incomparable views of the city, plains, mountains and sea.

From its sweeping harbor, Kingston sprawls along the fan-shaped plain, rising imperceptibly for 8 miles (13 km)

into the foothills which surround it. Another 10 miles inland, the hills give way to the spectacular Blue Mountain Range and culminate in Blue Mountain Peak (7,402 ft/2,257 meters).

You can orient yourself by facing the mountains, your back to Kingston Harbor. On the east, to your right, is a rocky, low-lying hill near the coast. This is **Long Mountain**, whose northern flanks are covered with the **Beverly Hills** mansions of the nouveau riche. Halfway up the slope is the **Martello Tower**, built of stone in 1803 to guard against French invasion. Beyond is a higher limestone hill, **Wareika** (said to be an Arawak name), and behind that is **Dallas Mountain**, which takes its name from a family whose descendants emigrated to the United States and achieved great prominence. One of them, George Milfin Dallas, became America's vice-president (1845–48) and gave his name to the Texan city-cum-TV soap.

Looking westwards, the land drops slightly at the Hope River gorge and then rises sharply again in **Jacks Hill**. **The city as it once was.**

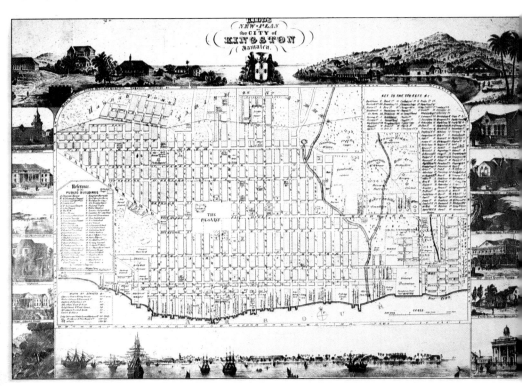

166

Skyline Drive is perched along its spine. Another dip in the landscape occurs where the residential suburb of **Stony Hill** and a major highway which leads to the north coast are located. Then the land rises again to the heights and residential areas of **Red Hills**.

"Under the Clock": Kingston is the Americas' largest English-speaking city south of Miami. Its population, estimated at 700,000, seems to grow daily.

Old timers will proudly claim that the only true Kingstonians are those "born under the clock" – that is, the clock of the **Kingston Parish Church**. This downtown landmark at the corner of King Street and South Parade dates from the late 17th or early 18th century: the oldest tombstone in its cemetery is dated 1699. Throughout Jamaica, during the time (before 1872) that the Church of England, or Anglican Church, prevailed as the sole official creed, the parish church was always one of the first public buildings erected in a settlement. The original Kingston Parish Church was destroyed in the 1907 earthquake;

the current structure was raised in 1911 based on the same design.

The interior of the church contains gifts from generations of worshippers. The high altar is flanked by statues of the Virgin Mary and St Thomas, gifts of the Chinese and Syrian communities respectively. Mystic Masonic emblems can be seen in the colored window in the northern chapel. A painting of the Pieta (by Susan Alexander) and stained glass windows (depicting Christ's resurrection and the Pentecost) look out on many interesting monuments within the church. Among these is the tomb of Admiral John Benbow, the English naval hero who died in Port Royal.

The square clock tower on the west side of the church was erected in memory of those who died in World War I. Its bell is much older, having been cast in 1715. But it is many centuries since all of Kingston fell within the shadow of the clock tower. The original section of the city (bounded roughly by today's North, East and West streets and the harbor) was laid out over 300 years ago

Kings House, *circa* **1890.**

to house survivors of the earthquake which destroyed Port Royal in 1692.

The dazed survivors were glad to escape the pall of devastation across the harbor and put some solid land under their feet – even if it was a *kraal* (enclosure) for Colonel Barry's hogs. Fevers, starvation and disease took their toll on 3,000 to 4,000 persons in the first weeks after the exodus. But by June, the governing council agreed to purchase 200 acres (81 hectare) of the *kraal* for £1,000 of public revenue.

The new city was laid out according to the rectangular grid pattern of European towns. In the north was an open square known as The Parade, the upper limit of which is marked by the **Ward Theater**. Today the theater, across the street from **Sir William Grant Park**, looks down on a monstrous confusion of ghetto shacks, traffic, vendors and buses.

The Ward occupies a site which has been used as a theater for centuries. The original stage on this site attracted many well-known English and American touring companies. But it was at a Kingston theater on another site (unknown today) that the famous American naval hero John Paul Jones made his debut as a professional actor. His theatrical career was brief: he took the job between ships and soon sailed off, later distinguishing himself in the US War of Independence.

The Ward was a gift to the city from Colonel Ward, nephew and partner in the famous rum firm of J. Wray and Nephew Limited. In 1825, John Wray, a wheelwright, started a business as a liquor dealer in the Shakespeare Tavern next door to the theater. (Another pub occupies the site today.) Eventually, Wray went into rum-making, perfecting a superior blend. The rest, as they say, is many billion glasses of Jamaica's favorite poison later.

Theatrical activity of every description is at home in the Ward. Most popular is the annual Pantomime which opens on Boxing Day (December 26) and runs for several months, usually until April or into May.

But back to The Parade. It was here in

Below, Ward Theater. **Right**, John Canoe dancer.

colonial times that the English Red-coats, shining with spit and polish, drilled for the edification and delight of the Jamaicans. They were often joined by the Militia, an island-wide force of callow clerks and bookkeepers, paunchy merchants or dyspeptic planters, led by doddering colonels and major generals. Militia duty was compulsory for all who qualified – usually freed men between 16 and 20 – and officer status, which gave social advantage, was eagerly sought and bought.

The Parade also served as a promenade for the local folk and a venue for public events such as the hanging of prisoners or putting them in the stocks. When the island worked itself into a state of hysteria over a threatened French invasion in 1694, a fort was temporarily erected on The Parade with guns pointing down King Street.

When the British troops and Militia took their parades to Up Park Camp, the Parade lost much of its splendor. In 1870 the garden was laid out and in 1914 it was officially named Victoria Park, in honor of the queen whose statue – once a prominent landmark – faced down King Street. The statue is said to have turned around on its pedestal to face the opposite direction during the 1907 earthquake. The north and south sections of the park are dominated by statues, executed by Jamaican Alvin Marriott, of two 20th-century Jamaican leaders, Sir Alexander Bustamante and Norman Washington Manley.

The park was officially renamed Sir William Grant Park in the mid-1970s, after a labor leader of the 1930s. Like most politicians and orators of the time, Grant's main platform was the steps of the Coke Church on the eastern side of the park.

The present **Coke Church** is on the site of the first Methodist chapel erected in Jamaica. It is named for the Reverend Dr. Coke, a Wesleyan missionary who came in 1789 to establish a mission. Coke Chapel was opened in 1790 but was soon closed when a grand jury found it "injurious to the general peace and quiet of the inhabitants." Mission-

The Parade, 18th century.

aries were frowned upon because of their activities among the slaves. Methodism flourished, however, and is today regarded as one of the largest organized religions in Jamaica.

On the waterfront: In recent decades, the focus of urban activity in Kingston has shifted. People have increasingly deserted downtown, and the heart of the old city has been left to decay – the old 18th-century town-houses turned into tenement yards for those too poor to move upwards.

However, a bold new development scheme has begun "to put new life in the old city," as the ads say. Only time will tell if the urban renewal project on the Kingston waterfront will set an example for the rest of the decaying city.

Until the 1960s, generations-old finger piers jutting into the sea were characteristic of Kingston's waterfront. But when the Kingston Waterfront Redevelopment Company was established to undertake renewal of the downtown area, a new commercial and shipping area – **Newport West** – was built from re-

claimed lands on the west side of the harbor. This modern port complex, known as **Port Bustamante**, has the capacity to handle more than one million tons of cargo annually. It includes a free zone and a trans-shipment port.

Where the old finger piers once stood, a new waterfront has been created. Modern Ocean Boulevard embraces a complex of high-rise buildings: hotels, apartments, offices and shops, collectively known as the **Kingston Waterfront**. This is only the first phase of an ambitious long-term program to transform a much more extensive area extending to the east.

One of the waterfront's highlights is the **Crafts Market**. Straw goods, carvings and embroidered goods are offered for sale along with more esoteric objects like dried calabashes. You may also find yo-yos made from cacoon, one of the largest seeds in the world. It grows on rampant vines found along river valleys and its pods can grow to 3 ft (1 meter) in length.

The original 19th-century Victoria

The Parade in the 1980s.

Crafts Market, at the foot of King Street in front of the Hotel Oceana, was one of the casualties of progress. In centuries past, this site was the location of a Sunday Market which attracted thousands of slaves, free people and white hucksters from surrounding parishes. When slavery ended, the market's character changed. It became known as the Christmas Grand-market, a special attraction for children who came to buy paper hats, balloons, *fee-fees* (whistles) and toys.

In front of the market was the famous Victoria Pier, landing place for nearly all famous visitors including kings, queens and other heads of state. Among the arrivals was Maximilian, Archduke of Austria, who with his wife Carlotta made a brief stop here in 1857 on their way to Veracruz to be crowned Emperor and Empress of Mexico.

The Roy West Building on the corner of Orange Street and Ocean Boulevard houses part of the Institute of Jamaica, including the **National Gallery**. The development of a national art move-

ment dates only to the 1930s, but since that time Jamaica has produced a number of exciting artists. Many of their works are on permanent show here.

Another waterfront attraction is the **Coin and Note Museum** in the Bank of Jamaica building. Although Jamaica switched to dollars and cents in 1967, older folks recall and sometimes still figure in pounds, shillings and pence, the old British coinage formerly in use. The folk names for these old coins live on in song and story: "*Carry me ackee go a Linstead Market, not a quattie wut sell*." Quatties might be seen in the museum, along with souvenir coin sets, tokens, tallies, pirate pieces of eight, and other fascinating fragments of the past. Tallies, incidentally, were substitutes for coins given to task workers such as banana loaders.

The decay of downtown was hastened by the spread of the city northwards. In the 1960s, a commercial revolution ·created North American-style shopping centers all over the city. Commerce became rapidly diffused and small

Kingston docks, about 1900.

shops or boutiques sprang up everywhere. The main shopping areas are now located along Constant Spring Road, Red Hills Road, and in Liguanea, Cross Roads and Manor Park.

King Street, the downtown area's main thoroughfare, is today a sorry spectacle. In 1909, when the public buildings flanking King Street were built, they were regarded as the last word in modernity and were featured in every photograph of Jamaican "progress." They were constructed of reinforced concrete, then a relatively new material, following the destruction of most of the old wood or mortar buildings in the earthquake and fire of 1907. The public buildings house the Treasury and Law Courts and offices.

Of the downtown areas, it is probably only lower **Duke Street** which retains some of its original flavor as a business and commercial center. Once the address of the best law firms, Duke Street is still full of attorneys' offices, but chambers there are no longer regarded as essential to success and prestige.

Duke Street contains some interesting buildings, among them the island's only **Jewish Synagogue** (at the corner of Charles Street). The United Congregation of Israelites represents an amalgamation in 1921 of two separate Jewish congregations – the Sephardic or Portuguese Jews and the Ashkenazi from England and Germany.

Another interesting religious structure on Duke Street is the **St Andrew Scots Kirk**. This octagonal church was built in 1814 when Scots were prominent in the island's commercial life. Jamaica's first Presbyterian church, it was damaged in the 1907 earthquake and thereafter reduced in size.

Further up Duke Street is **Gordon House**, where Parliament meets. Its name honors patriot and martyr George William Gordon, a noted legislator branded as one of the "villains" of the 1865 Morant Bay Rebellion, and now considered a national hero.

Directly across from Gordon House, facing Beeston Street, is one of Jamaica's most historic buildings. **Headquar-**

Modern container terminal at Kingston's Newport.

ters House, so called because it was once the seat of government and the military, was built in the 18th century by a prominent merchant and planter named Thomas Hibbert. He and three other rich merchants betted on who could build the most elegant townhouse, in order to secure the attentions of a certain beautiful lady. No one knows who won, and this is the only one of the four houses still standing.

On East Street are located the Main buildings housing the **Institute of Jamaica**. Founded in 1879 for the encouragement of literature, science and art, it has since functioned as a kind of mini-Smithsonian Institution. Divisions include the National Gallery, the Cultural Training Center (in which are located national schools of art, dance, drama, theatre), a Junior Center (located in the building opposite the East Street headquarters), a Muslims Division, an African Caribbean Institute (engaged in research on African traditions in Jamaica and the Caribbean), and a Publications Division.

Housed at East Street are the two major collections of the Institute – the **National Library of Jamaica** (formerly the West India Reference Library), containing the largest collection of West Indian material in the world, and the **National History Division**, which includes a small museum and a large herbarium. Before the University of the West Indies or the Scientific Research Council were established, the Natural History Division was the focus of Jamaica's scientific activity. It still plays a major role in the collection and classification of flora and fauna and the publication of research findings.

The **Gleaner Building** on North Street is the home of Jamaica's oldest newspaper, the *Daily Gleaner*. It was founded in 1834 by Joshua and Jacob De Cordova. Jacob, a civil engineer, later emigrated to Texas, where he laid out the town of Waco and served in the state legislature.

Further along North Street, the dome of **Holy Trinity Cathedral** marks the focal point of Roman Catholicism. The

Higgler stands at Kingston Parish Church.

174

island's largest Catholic church was once a landmark for those who arrived by sea. Established by the Spanish, Catholicism received a fresh impetus in the late 18th century with an influx of French Catholics from nearby Haiti. The church has pioneered educational institutions throughout the island, notably the Alpha Boys School.

Ghettos of the West: As Kingston expanded, polarities developed between "uptown" and "downtown" as economically and psychologically exclusive residential areas. The stereotyped "uptowners" were relatively wealthy folk who aspired to the middle-class norms of North America and Europe. They went downtown to work or shop, but left for their uptown suburbs in the evenings. The "downtowners" were ghetto dwellers who inhabited the decaying tenements and shacks. If they worked at all, it was for the uptowners whom they envied. Yet despite the downtowners' disadvantages, it was here that two of modern Jamaica's most vibrant cultural movements established

their roots: reggae and Rastafarianism.

The first songs of bondage and redemption came from an infamous settlement known as Back O'Wall. In the 1960s, this was converted into a model community, **Tivoli Gardens**. It became the centerpiece of the political constituency of then Prime Minister Edward Seaga, who first conceptualized Tivoli Gardens while serving as Minister of Finance in the 1960s. Tivoli Gardens, with its carefully planned pattern, modern buildings, community spirit and lovingly painted murals, was an oasis of hope in an area of decay.

Trench Town and other ghetto areas today are referred to in Kingston as the "West." Visitors who might feel the pull of the West are advised not to do so without a guide from the area; it can be rough. Post-independence political confrontation has left much of the former "downtown" divided into volatile territories which are, in the interest of self-preservation, rigorously defended against outsiders.

From horses to heroes: Horse racing

Mobile sound system in downtown Kingston.

was probably the most popular sport in Jamaica in colonial days. There were well-patronized race courses in each parish, and race days were occasions for social splendor. The first race on Kingston Race Track was run in 1816, and racing continued till the outbreak of World War II. In 1953, racing was moved to **Knutsford Park**, and soon thereafter to the modern **Caymanas Park** just across the county boundary in St Catherine.

Kingston Race Track later became George VI Memorial Park, and Kingston's war memorial or cenotaph was located there. In addition to racing, circuses and other amusements have traditionally found a home in the park. It has also been used as a tent city for refugees from natural disasters such as earthquakes. After independence in 1962, it was laid out as a shrine to the National Heroes, renamed **National Heroes Park**. Today their monuments can be viewed inside. There is also a bust of **General Antoneo Maceo**, a Cuban hero of the independence struggles who found

sanctuary in Jamaica on more than one occasion. The bust was presented by the people of Cuba in 1952.

Outside the park, in front of the Ministry of Education, is another monument to a Latin American revolutionary: **Simon Bolivar**, "The Liberator." Bolivar spent 7 months in Jamaica in 1817 while leading the struggles to free the Latin American colonies from Spanish rule. While here, he wrote the famous "Jamaica Letter" – regarded as one of the greatest documents of his career – and survived an assassination attempt at the boarding house where he lived at the northwest corner of Princess and Tower streets. The monument is a gift from Venezuela.

Streets of schools: Immediately north of National Heroes Circle, **Wolmer's School** marks the northern boundary of Kingston proper. It was founded over 300 years ago with proceeds from the estate of John Wolmer, a wealthy Kingston goldsmith. It started out strictly as a boys' school; the girls' school was founded later.

Dance Theater Co. rehearsal.

Mico College, next door to Wolmer's is one of the oldest teacher-training institutions in the world. It indirectly owes its establishment to a London gentleman who refused to wed any of his aunt's six nieces, in spite of a £1,000 dowry involved! The strings-attached inheritance which the wealthy Lady Mico had left him in her will was instead invested, and the income was later used to rescue Christians captured by Barbary pirates.

When piracy was stamped out, the Lady Mico Trust lay dormant for 200 years, growing to an enormous sum. It was used by English philanthropists to start Mico Schools throughout the West Indies to educate the soon-to-be freed slave population. The Kingston college, established in 1834, is the only Mico institution still existing. Now co-educational, it was originally a boy's school. It has produced many of Jamaica's outstanding citizens, including the first native governor-general, Sir Clifford Campbell. At one time, Mico also trained missionaries for service in West Africa.

The college was moved to its present location in 1896; the main building dates from 1909.

The street on which these schools are located – **Marescaux Road** – sometimes offers an excellent opportunity to see Jamaica's national flower. The *lignum vitae* is a small tree whose branches might go unnoticed until they begin flowering around mid-July. At first, there is a light dusting of purple on the leaves; eventually, the tiny purple blossoms with their bright yellow stamens entirely cover the boughs. The plant fascinates a certain white butterfly (*Kricogonia lyside*) and, in some seasons, the blossoms can hardly be seen for the thousands of these creatures which set each tree shimmering.

Lignum vitae's name is Latin for "wood of life," and this gives an indication of how highly valued the plant has been in the past. As a medicine, its gum is reputed to be a cure for venereal disease and many other ailments. Its wood is so heavy it will sink in water, which makes it ideal for specialized purposes such as ship's propeller-shaft bearings, mortars, mallets, pulleys and policemen's batons. The attractive wood is also used to make furniture and curios.

Refuge in the "Pens": By the 18th century, Kingston's rich merchants were discovering that it was much cooler and healthier to live in the foothills. They moved to more expansive new homes surrounded by a great deal of land. These were known as "pens", for there was now space for their horses and other livestock, and enough acreage to grow their own grass. At about 10 o'clock every morning, these merchants would leave their pens and bustle importantly into town, usually in small open carriages called "kitareens." Many place and street names in Kingston today still retain the word "pen" – as in Delacree Pen, Slipe Pen Road and Rest Pen.

One of the oldest and most splendid of these pen residences was built in 1694 and has been in continuous use since. Known as **Vale Royal**, it is now the Prime Minister's official home. Located on Montrose Road off Lady Musgrave Road, it has undergone a sensitive resto-

Kingston bar decor.

ration in recent years. The most notable feature of its striking facade is a rooftop lookout tower, typical of early Kingston houses. This would have been equipped with a spyglass for keeping an eye on doings in the harbor. Vale Royal was built by Simon Taylor, one of the richest men of his time.

Beyond the area of pen residences, sugar estates once covered the Liguanea Plains. The estates gave their names to many Kingston locations, including Hope, Liguanea, Constant Spring, Mona and Barbican.

Urban expansion northwards led to the creation of several important crossroads, one of which still retains that prosaic name. **Cross Roads** is a busy junction poised between uptown and downtown, though it gained significance only early in this century when the name Cross Roads became official. It had been known as Montgomery's Corner after a lieutenant who was thrown from his horse here. The white **Carib Theater** for generations has been the setting for glamor and thrills born in the world of Hollywood. The clock tower here was erected in memory of the Jamaican servicemen who died in World War II.

Not far to the east of Cross Roads is **Up Park Camp** on South Camp Road. Best known simply as "Camp," it was established in 1784 as the home of British regiments stationed in Jamaica and is now headquarters of the Jamaica Defence Force. Duppy Gate, the southern entrance, recalls the legend of an officer of the old West India Regiment whose ghost regularly called out the guard there for inspection.

Kingston's cultural core: South Camp Road leads to **Tom Redcam Drive**, Jamaica's "cultural" street, named for a former poet laureate of Jamaica. Here are located the public library service, the Little Theater, and the headquarters of the Anglican Church.

The library system, established in the 1950s, is highly regarded. An islandwide system of main parish libraries, branch libraries, a schools library service, and a book-mobile service is administered from here.

The **Little Theater** was built in 1961

through the untiring efforts of Henry and Greta Fowler, who founded the Little Theater Movement in 1942. The movement, which established the Jamaica School of Drama (now incorporated into the Cultural Training Center), also sponsors the annual Pantomime. The Little Theater is used by theatrical groups throughout the year, two of which have won national and international acclaim and hold annual seasons here: the National Dance Theater Company and the Jamaican Folk Singers.

The architecturally exciting **Cultural Training Center** on Arthur Wint Drive just around the corner from Tom Redcam Drive houses the national schools of Dance, Drama, Art and Music. The Center not only instructs performers; it trains teachers for the island's schools and takes in a few students from other Caribbean islands. Placing all the schools in close proximity is expected to develop cross-fertilization in the arts. Students are encouraged to explore other forms outside their own disciplines.

Arthur Wint Drive continues around

Caymanas Park races.

the northern end of Camp to the **National Stadium**. The stadium was built for independence celebrations in 1962 and has been the venue of major sporting events since that time. The **National Arena** next door hosts other sports and more diverse activities, including a two-day National Flower Show in July and a biennial trade exposition. At the entrance to the stadium is a statue by sculptor Alvin Marriott, symbolic of Jamaican athletic prowess. **Arthur Wint Drive** is named after a famed Jamaican athlete who won a gold medal in the 400-meter run at the 1948 London Olympics, bringing international fame to his tiny island home. Wint was also a member of Jamaica's gold medal-winning 1,600-meter relay team at the 1952 Olympics in Helsinki.

Half Way Tree: From Cross Roads, busy Half Way Tree Road leads north to Constant Spring. Aqueducts flanking the road were built in the 1770s to carry sugar to this former estate.

As early as 1696 the name **Half Way Tree** was in use, a reference to the giant *kapok* (silk cotton) tree which once threw its huge buttresses in all directions here. Before the tree died of old age in the 1870s, it was a resting place for market women traveling from the hills to town with their wares. Roads west to Spanish Town, north to the coast via Stony Hill, and east to the mountains via Papine all join here.

A few yards south of Half Way Tree's main intersection is the **St Andrew Parish Church**, the island's oldest church. Registers date to 1666; the first building was raised here in 1692. The foundation of the present structure was laid in 1700, though it has undergone many renovations since then.

The community of Half Way Tree is the center of government of the parish of St Andrew. Parish law courts sit here.

East of Half Way Tree, via Hope and Trafalgar roads, **New Kingston**, built on what was once the Knutsford Park Race Tracks, accommodates many leading hotels including the Jamaica Pegasus and the Wyndham New Kingston.

Hope Road itself leads to scenic drives

Vale Royal.

in the mountains to the northeast. It contains several places of interest en route, including the stately Devon House at the junction of Trafalgar Road. **Devon House** was built in 1881 by a black Jamaican who made his fortune in South America, some say as a gold miner. George Stiebel was also a builder, so his house was harmoniously constructed. It is regarded today as the best preserved example of classical architecture in Jamaica. Each room is a period piece of exclusive style.

The government bought and restored the house in the 1960s and opened it to the public. Former stables surrounding the building were converted to craft shops and a popular bar and restaurant known as the Grog Shop was opened. For a time, Devon House was the home of the National Gallery; but with the removal of the gallery to downtown Kingston, Devon House has reverted to its original concept.

The modern **Jamaica House**, further north, was built in the 1960s as the residence of the Prime Minister. It served that purpose only for a short time, and was soon converted into the Prime Minister's office instead.

At the traffic lights by East Kings House Road and Hope Road is **Kings House**, official residence of the Governor-General. Originally the residence of the Bishop of Jamaica, the building was wrecked in the earthquake of 1907 and rebuilt to a design by Sir Charles Nicholson. Visitors may view the attractive 200-acre (80-hectare) grounds.

The **Bob Marley Museum** is unmistakable just beyond the Lady Musgrave intersection. It flies the Ethiopian flag and has renderings of hit Marley records painted on the wall in front.

The busy intersection further north is known as **Matilda's Corner**, probably after a French Haitian refugee who settled here. The official name for the wider area is Liguanea, a name which may derive from the iguana, the large lizard which was much esteemed by the native Arawaks.

Hope Road leads to **Hope Gardens** and the campus of the **University of the**

Half Way Tree, about 1890.

West Indies. Major Richard Hope, who came here with the conquering British Army in 1655, gave his name to this area. Hope's land grant, which extended from the hills at Newcastle to the harbor, was one of the most progressive estates on the island. By 1758, his descendants built stone aqueducts to carry water from the Hope River to turn the estate mills. The city's first public water supply came from this source and sections of the aqueduct are still in use in the vicinity of Hope Gardens and Mona Heights.

Hope Gardens have been a favorite sanctuary for sweethearts and amateur photographers since it was built over a century ago. The gardens were laid out in 1881 on 200 acres acquired by the government from Hope Estate. They were officially designated the Royal Botanical Gardens in 1953, on the occasion of a visit by Queen Elizabeth II. The gardens have been somewhat neglected in recent years, but efforts are being made to revitalize the complex, which includes a small zoo. Children

are also attracted on weekends to **Coconut Park**, a small funland.

University of the West Indies: The lovely campus of the University of the West Indies (UWI), called "You-wee" by initiates, is wedged in the hills between Long Mountain and Dallas Mountain. From small beginnings in 1948 with 33 medical students, the university has grown to embrace three campuses – in Jamaica, Barbados and Trinidad – and university centers in the other Caribbean territories which support it. This is a regional institution and the crests of all its member states can be seen inside the the Chapel.

Located near the main entrance, the Chapel is the foremost visitor attraction on campus. The old cutstone building of classically simple lines was formerly the sugar warehouse of Gales Valley estate in Trelawny. It was pulled down and reassembled here stone by stone as directed by its last owner. The original owner and the date of construction – "Edward Morant Gale: 1799" – are written at the top of the pediment just under

Devon House in oils.

the roof. This is by no means the university's only connection with sugar. The campus embraces parts of the old Mona and Papine estates, and ruined aqueducts and sugar works are throughout the grounds.

The Gordon Town Road beyond Papine travels along the gorge of the Hope River for some miles, climbing to the **Blue Mountain Inn** – regarded as Jamaica's most romantic dining place if not its most expensive. Established in 1754 as a plantation coffee house, it is set at the foot of waterfalls where the Mammee River joins the Hope.

A left turn above the inn leads eventually to **Newcastle**; a right turn goes to **Gordon Town**, Mavis Bank and other hill villages, and ultimately to the **Blue Mountain Peak** walking trail.

The Hope gained fame at the turn of the 20th century as the "Healing Stream" of the self-proclaimed Prophet Bedward, who attracted thousands of followers to his church at **August Town**, below the university. Bedward's much-publicized announcement that he would fly to heaven on a certain day was not fulfilled, but that did not dampen his followers' ardor.

Support did fall off, however, when the authorities decided to confine him to an insane asylum. Nonetheless, there are faithful Bedwardites to this day, and some scholars see a political element in their activities.

The Hellshire Hills: Southwest of Kingston, off Marcus Garvey Drive and across the causeway on the west side of the harbor, are the city's bedroom communities and some of its favorite beaches.

In a few short years, the Hellshire area has gone from uninhabited headland to urban extension of Kingston. **Portmore**, at the entrance to the region, is now home to 80,000 Jamaicans, with an additional 70,000 to be accommodated by expansion into the Hellshire Hills. Long-range plans for the 45-sq. mile (117-sq. km) promontory include provisions for natural areas and forest parks; but much of its original character is disappearing beneath the demands of a burgeoning population. It is also the new home of the annual **Reggae Sunsplash** festival, staged at Jamworld.

As you drive across the causeway, look to the west toward Caymanas Park and an area called **Passage Fort**. Formerly on the mouth of the Rio Cobre river (which has since shifted course), Passage Fort was the island's principal shipping port in Spanish Town's early years as capital, before the development of Kingston Harbour. It was here that a British fleet landed in 1655, later marching 6 miles (10 km) inland to capture Spanish Town and end Spanish rule in Jamaica. The imposing structure on the left is **Fort Augusta** prison; it was originally constructed in the mid-18th century as the major fortification on the western side of the harbor.

Where the road forks, proceed left through Portmore. At the end of this community are remains of the charming old 18th-century village of **Port Henderson**. Six of the original buildings have been restored by the Jamaica National Trust Commission. Among them is **Rodney's Arms**, a bar and restaurant.

Below, Twin Sisters' Cave near Hellshire Beach. Right, a sister's salute at the beach.

PORT ROYAL: LAIR OF THE BUCCANEERS

The quiet fishing village of **Port Royal**, resting at the tip of the 7-mile-long (11-km) Palisadoes spit, sleeps on a turbulent past. Famed as the principal port of the pirates of the Caribbean in the late 17th century, it also was once the regional headquarters for the British Royal Navy – at a time when seapower controlled the world.

Today, little remains of Port Royal's glorious past. But a large scale restoration is planned to make the town one of the truly significant historic attractions of the Americas.

The name Port Royal evokes tales and legends of fabulous wealth beneath the ocean waves. The sea floor, in fact, is where most of the town ended up when it was destroyed by a devastating earthquake and tidal wave in 1692. Underwater searches so far have revealed little actual treasure, but many fascinating and historically valuable artifacts. Some of these can be seen at the **Archaeological Museum**, located in the former naval hospital (built in 1819).

Port Royal's booty was the gift of the buccaneers, who carried it here from every city they sacked and every ship they robbed on the high seas. These "Brethren of the Coast" had the long-standing approval of British authorities since they were acting against England's deadly enemies: the Spaniards.

The buccaneers themselves hardly ever got rich. There were too many temptations in Port Royal, including very friendly women, and up to 40 taverns. Port Royal soon gained a reputation as "the wickedest city in the world." Christian moralists said it could not go unpunished, and pointed to the ruinous 1692 quake as retribution.

But the town refused to die. Some of the survivors returned to rebuild their houses, and though Port Royal could never be the same again, it achieved a different character as a naval port.

The great British admiral Horatio Nelson once trod the streets of Port

Giddy House near Fort Charles, Port Royal.

Royal, and visitors can still follow in his footsteps at **Fort Charles**. As a 20-year-old officer in the Royal Navy, Nelson was left in charge of the fort's batteries in 1779 when a French invasion was feared. The attack never came, probably because the fort's 104-gun complement was the strongest in the British Caribbean, but Nelson spent many anxious hours pacing the deck. Today the platform is known as **Nelson's Quarterdeck**.

Fort Charles was Port Royal's original structure, its foundations having been laid by the British shortly after their capture of Jamaica in 1655. Today it houses a small **Maritime Museum**.

Another attraction in Port Royal is the **Giddy House**, so-called because it leans at an apparently impossible angle. An old artillery store, it was tilted by the 1907 quake.

A fascinating reminder of the 1692 quake is found in the epitaph on **Galdy's Tomb** in St Peter's churchyard. Mr Galdy was swallowed up by the earth during the tremor, but there must have been something unappetizing about him – for he was spewed out again, living to a ripe old age to tell and retell the tale.

The highway from Kingston to Port Royal skims across the **The Palisadoes**, an alluvial strip created by centuries of sand, gravel and debris deposits from mountain streams. The alluvium joined a string of small islets of which Port Royal was one. The spit encloses Kingston Harbor and acts as a breakwater.

The road was built in 1936. Previously, a ferry – still operating from the foot of King Street – was the only form of transportation between Kingston and Port Royal. The highway cuts through what was once a flourishing coconut plantation, but has now reverted to its indigenous vegetation, including many native species of cacti and mangrove.

The broadest part of the Palisadoes is today occupied by the **Norman Manley International Airport** which began as a supplementary landing strip during World War II for seaplanes which set down in Kingston Harbor.

Modern buccaneers in Kingston Harbor.

HIGH IN THE BLUE MOUNTAINS

The majestic **Blue Mountains** range from Kingston's northern suburbs to the north coast. They encompass the tallest mountain on the island, a high-altitude botanical garden, a national park and bird sanctuary, old plantations, great houses, and magnificent hill walks.

At least three days should be devoted to exploring the Blue Mountains. A sturdy, preferably compact vehicle is recommended for covering the rugged roads. Those from Kingston to Mavis Bank via Guava Ridge and Kingston to Hardwar Gap are paved and passable in all weather. But unpaved roads connecting Content Gap and Section and the Yallahs Crossing can be difficult during or immediately after heavy rains. Route B1 follows Hope Road from Half Way Tree to Papine. Your last chance to fill up is at the Papine Service Station. At Papine, B1 passes left round the little park and becomes Gordon Town Road.

It follows the Hope River Valley past **Blue Mountain Inn**, a restaurant that was formerly the "Great House" of a coffee plantation. The coffee produced was shipped in wooden casks, made up the road at **The Cooperage** by imported Irish coopers, who were quartered farther up the Mammee River Road at the village still called **Irish Town**.

At Cooperage, the road forks. Continue straight ahead to a village called **Industry**, a slightly incongruous name in view of the normal level of activity there. Three miles (5 km) from Papine, 1,200 ft (366 meters) up the valley, stands **Gordon Town**, a metropolis by Blue Mountain standards. It has a police station, a courthouse, a post office, two schools, a clinic and its share of bars.

Gordon Town was the site of Jamaica's first botanical garden, established by Hinton East in 1770 at **Spring Garden**. East introduced hundreds of foreign plant species from places as diverse as China and Sweden. Many of his imports – including hibiscus, azalea, cassia, magnolia, oleander, croton and

jasmine – permanently altered the Jamaican scene. Nothing survives of the original garden except the profusion of attractive plants around Gordon Town.

Higglers and hairpins: The road to **Guava Ridge** leaves the town square from the police station, crosses a narrow bridge over the Hope River, and climbs above the town along the side of the river valley. As the road twists and turns in and out of a succession of valleys, the red roofs of the Newcastle army camp constantly appear, then recede from view, 4,000 ft (1,220 meters) up across the valley, straggling down the mountain-side. From here, Newcastle looks like some lost Inca city in the Andes, especially in low-hanging clouds.

A succession of tiny houses dot this route. Some cling precariously to the hillside, a small patch of banana, coffee and vegetables around them. Down below the road, many more can be seen scattered over the valley floor. Such small holdings supply most of Kingston's vegetable and fruit needs. As the weekend approaches, the road fills up with brightly painted market trucks carrying unbelievable loads of higglers with their baskets of produce to sell to city markets. This was the free land settled by the newly emancipated slaves in 1834. The pattern of their agricultural life has not changed significantly since then.

Two hairpin bends straddle the 11-mile (18-km) post as the road climbs steadily around the sides of the mountains. Shortly before the 13-mile (21-km) post on the left hand side is **World's End.** Here, some of Jamaica's most famous liqueurs and rums are produced under the **Sangster's "Old Jamaica"** label. Dr Ian Sangster, originally from Scotland, began production in 1973.

This attractive little factory straddles several levels as it descends the side of the valley to a visitor's terrace commanding a fine view of Newcastle. Tours (including product sampling and purchasing) are available.

A hotel in the pines: A junction beside the bus shelter beyond World's End at an elevation of 3,000 ft (914 meters) forks right through the scattered township of Guava Ridge and descends via

Mavis Bank to the Yallahs River at 1,700 ft (519 meters). The left fork ascends after a mile to the gates of **Pine Grove Hotel**. Besides panoramic views over Kingston and around the mountains, the hotel offers chalet accommodation and typical Jamaican food.

Pine Grove is the best central point from which to explore the Blue Mountains. Sit here in the evening with the mountains all around, while the sky changes from blue through turquoise to pink and the lights of the capital gradually come to life far below.

After Pine Grove, the road passes **Valda** at 3,758 ft (1,145 meters), then drops steadily to **Content Gap**, a village connected by footpath to Gordon Town, 4 miles (6 km) and 1,800 ft (550 meters) below. At the round water tank the left-hand track offers an easy one-mile walk up to **Charlottenburg House**, a well-preserved Great House furnished with antique Jamaican furniture. Former slave quarters, dating from coffee plantation days, still stand adjacent to the house. The durable and attractive hard-

Blue Mountain coffee beans on the bush.

wood used in the construction is local cedar, cut from the plantation when it was cleared for coffee.

Past **St Peters**, there is a junction with the road to **Clydesdale**, a picturesque forestry station on the River Clyde, 1½ miles (2½ km) up a bumpy little road. Also once a coffee plantation, it still has coffee-drying barbecues and an old water wheel. The Forestry Department rents the two-bedroomed main house at Clydesdale. Linen, towels and essentials are not provided. The house looks down on Clydesdale town above thousands of tiny conifer seedlings, standing in serried ranks. The entrance road is to the left of the seedling beds.

A flowery high: A worthwhile side-trip from Clydesdale takes you to the **Cinchona Botanical Gardens**. Follow the descending road on the right which passes below the old wooden coffee-mill house. About 100 yards later the dirt road divides. The branch on the right leads 2 miles (3 km) up to **Top Mountain**, where a rough Jeep road on the left side (if you come to some houses of the Yallahs Valley Land Authority, you've gone too far) leads slowly, if scenically, up to **Cinchona**. If you don't have a jeep, park at Top Mountain for a breathtaking if strenuous walk of more than 1,000 ft (300 meters).

The "main" road at Top Mountain junction leads on to **Westphalia**; from here, a bridle road beside the water tanks leads one mile up to the lower end of Cinchona. The left-hand fork from Clydesdale passes a picnic rondel on the left en route to Cinchona. It is quite steep, but is by far the easiest route.

The Cinchona Botanical Gardens cling to a magnificent stretch of ridge which is 4,500–5,500 ft (1,371–1,677 meters) above the valleys of the Yallahs, Clyde and Green rivers. Cinchona may have the most inspiring site of any botanical garden in the world. It was founded in 1868 as a center for the cultivation of Assam tea and cinchona trees, whose bark was in great demand as a source of quinine for the treatment of malaria.

The cinchona is a native of the high

Sorting beans at Mavis Bank Coffee Factory.

Andes. Its medicinal properties were passed to the Spaniards by the Quechua, descendants of the Incas. An experimental few hundred acres were planted around Cinchona and proved initially profitable. Later, however, large-scale production in India proved to be cheaper, and the Jamaican plantations of both cinchona and tea failed. The plantation shrank to an expatriate's dream, a "European Garden," established by an English gardener to supply Kingston with flowers and vegetables. As a result of its success, the trade remains an important source of income for local people.

Cinchona affords views in all directions, with John Crow Peak and St John's Peak to the north, the main ridge of the Blue Mountains stretching east (and viewed spectacularly from the **Panorama Walk** on the east side of the gardens), and Kingston and the sea shimmering away to the hot south.

The uninhabited Great House was formerly the home of Jamaica's Superintendent of Gardens. Well-tended lawns bordered by a profusion of flowers front the house. Around the lawns is a veritable labyrinth of paths and walks that lead through the loosely arranged trees. These include many imported types: some huge specimens of eucalyptus, easily recognizable by their spear-shaped leaves and peeling whitish barks; juniper; cork oak, whose bark is in fact cork; Chinese cypress; ferns and tree ferns; rubber trees, whose leaves when plucked emit a white latex; and some fine examples of Blue Mountain yacca, a tall tree with tiny dagger-shaped leaves and reddish marks on its smooth trunk.

Follow the main route half a mile after the Clydesdale detour to a small road on the right leading to **Silver Hill Coffee Factory**. Between September and February, you can see workers picking the red coffee berries. They remove the outer pulp from the two inner green beans to prepare them for drying, husking and roasting.

In the Blue Mountains, optimum soil and climatic condition combine to produce coffee of exceptionally fine flavor, believed to be the most expensive and **Newcastle.**

sought-after in the world. After the introduction of coffee in 1728, its cultivation spread through the Blue Mountains. Most of the Great Houses here were plantation homes built during the halcyon years 1800 to 1840, when coffee exports rose to 17,000 tons per year. After emancipation, the large plantations declined and were split up among small farmers. That system has never produced more than a fraction of the earlier tonnages. Silver Hill is one of the four coffee factories that operate in the Blue Mountains.

Misty roads and militiamen: At **Section** the road joins route B1, which connects Kingston to the north coast at **Buff Bay**. The partially paved road on the right drops north through the mountains via villages with engaging names like **Birnamwood** and **Tranquility**, to Buff Bay. But bear left to **Hardwar Gap**. The hills around the Gap constitute the **Blue Mountain** and **John Crow Mountain National Parks** and **Conservation Area**, a fine example of montane mist forest. The area has an annual rainfall of over 100 inches (250 cm), with wet clinging mists occurring daily.

In the almost constant moisture, the flora is quite distinct even from that of Newcastle, only 2 miles (3 km) away. Pine trees predominate among the many tree types, while a striking feature is the profusion of a wide selection of Jamaica's 550 types of fern, including the high tree ferns, *Cyathea arborea.* Some of the trees grow to over 30 ft (9 m) and many support climbing plants and even orchids. The bird songs that fill the forest include the harsh cry of the red-headed Jamaican woodpecker and the hauntingly plaintive call of the solitaire thrush. Picnic areas with views of Kingston speckle the hillside in Hollywell Park. The Forestry Department rents log cabins at reasonable rates.

From **Hardwar Gap**, follow B1 to **Newcastle** along the contours of **Mount Horeb**, with views over the Mammee River valley. Newcastle is a military camp built between 3,500 ft (1,067 meters) and 4,500 ft (1,372 meters). The road passes right through the parade

Military graveyard in Newcastle.

ground and you may find yourself in the middle of a military drill.

General Sir William Gomm established the camp in 1841 in an attempt to reduce the high death rate from yellow fever that occurred at lower altitudes.

The Jamaican Defence Forces now command Newcastle. Visitors may use the bar and facilities of the Sergeants' Mess, located in the building above the parade ground. The army also rents out a series of comfortable cottages a mile above the camp.

The Japanese connection: From Newcastle, the road drops steadily to the few houses of **Irish Town**, passing the signposted entrance drive up to **Craighton Great House**. This old property was purchased in 1981 by the UCC Coffee Company of Japan to expand production of Blue Mountain coffee for the Japanese market, which virtually absorbs all Jamaica's production.

At the 13-mile (21-km) marker, a signposted road leads to **Bamboo Lodge**, a small attractive hotel which was formerly a British Naval Hospital claiming association with Admiral Nelson, commander of Port Royal in 1799.

Below Bamboo Lodge is **Belancita**, home of the late Sir Alexander Bustamante. The road continues down the mountainside to the Mammee River, whose course it then follows to the Blue Mountain Inn at Cooperage Junction where you turn south for Kingston.

The most popular approach to **Blue Mountain Peak** itself begins from Guava Ridge. The road descends through pine woods along the broad valley of the Falls River to Mavis Bank. After one of the bends, a panoramic view of the Grand Ridge including the Blue Mountain Peak suddenly unfolds. The Peak is a rather rounded hump amid a series of others almost equally high.

Shortly before Mavis Bank, where the main road bears left over a bridge, a dirt road leads into the local **Mavis Bank Coffee Factory** where the preparation and roasting of Blue Mountain coffee beans may be seen. The factory is owned and operated by former government minister Keble Munn, and processes about 12,000 bushels annually.

The raw coffee is purchased from 4,000 Blue Mountain farms. The most prized coffee is a form called "rat-cut." Rats eat the ripe berries and expel the beans. The resultant seedlings are extremely sturdy and produce superior berry-bearing plants.

The main road passes above the coffee factory before reaching Mavis Bank, a small township that nevertheless boasts both a police station and a post office. A broad dirt track continues straight through the Yallahs River at **Mahogany Vale**, then climbs steeply to **Hagley Gap**, the nearest village to the Peak. Here at the tiny square in front of the village store, take the dirt road to the left. Climb for one mile to **Farm Hill**, bear right and continue for half a mile to **Whitfield Hall**, 5 miles (8 km) and 3,200 ft (975 meters) below the Peak. The house is clean and homey, if somewhat ascetic, and resembles a European youth hostel. Start your hike from here.

Scaling Blue Mountain: Only the hardy will succeed in reaching the summit of Blue Mountain Peak, a three-hour scramble up a rough track. The climb begins in a montane mist forest, a rare remnant of Jamaica's original forests. Its name derives from the characteristic mist which often lies on the peaks between 10 am and 4 pm. This reduces the incidental sunlight greatly, thus affecting the flora.

The **Elfin Woodland** starts about 5,500 ft (1,677 meters), petering out in windswept scrub on the summit. It is an open and eerie woodland of mainly short, twisted, gnarled trees, often laden with lichens, mosses and ferns. A dwarf species of orchid grows here in the swirling mist. Other flowers which grow well are honeysuckle, rhododendron, ginger lilies and the lesser known *merianias* (called "Jamaica Rose"), whose hanging rose-like blossoms appear to be lit from within when bathed in sunlight.

Once on the Peak, there is an incredible view over most of Jamaica. In clear weather, you can see as far north as Cuba. It can be cold, so take a sweater and a swig of rum. There is a small house with toilet and cooking facilities but this must be booked in advance.

Soldier at attention, Newcastle.

PORT ANTONIO AND COUNTRY COMFORTS

North of the Blue Mountains, Jamaica slopes gently back to the Caribbean. Surrey's coastline, carved out by volcanic activity, boasts the most ruggedly beautiful scenery on the island. This is Country, as Jamaicans call any region that lies outside Kingston.

Route A4 winds through local fishing villages and hidden coves of jagged rock and secret sandpits. The seas swell in on northern fronts and currents crash against cliff and sand in some of the island's biggest breakers. From Surrey's western boundary below Annotto Bay east around the coast through Port Antonio, Morant Bay and Yallahs back to Kingston, the discriminating visitor will discover some of the Caribbean's most breathtaking vistas.

The heart of this region is **Port Antonio**, once the cradle of Jamaica's tourist trade. In the 1890s, visitors arriving by ship marveled at the little town perched above the twin harbors. Poet Ella Wheeler Wilcox called it "the most exquisite harbor on earth."

Most first-time visitors who don't arrive by cruise ship come by car from the north-coast resorts or from Kingston. The popular sight-saturated approach from Kingston is via Route A3, usually just called the Junction.

To follow this route you should take Constant Spring Road north out of Kingston. Bear right onto Long Lane after negotiating the Manor Park roundabout. The road will swing north again to become Stony Hill Road, Route A3. A detour on Gibson Road past the red slate-roofed **Stony Hill Hotel** provides majestic views of Kingston and an insight into the lives of Jamaica's elite, who live behind barred entrance gates guarded by security dogs in the mansions on the hillcrest.

The main route takes you through the bustling center of **Stony Hill** and through smaller towns like **Golden Spring**. Drivers should take care around the increasingly hairpin corners and narrowing roads. Buses and trucks rarely slow down when slipping through them.

Castleton Gardens on the boundary of Surrey and Middlesex counties demands a visit. Established in 1862, it has blossomed into a showcase of exotic Jamaican flora. The highway bisects its 15 acres (6 hectares). Huge trees provide shade and cool rest spots in the upper half. The lower part runs along the bank of the **Wag Water River** with which the road plays tag from this point on. For a tip, guides willingly introduce you to fascinating plants like the *strychnos* – from which strychnine poisons and medicine are derived. Further on, inviting bamboo lines the river, usually a mere trickle that exposes enormous, water-worn boulders.

The views become more spectacular beyond the gardens. Look out for a graceful suspension bridge at boulder-crested **Mahoe Hill**. The road eventually winds down out of the Wag Water ravine into broad plains of sugar cane reminiscent of those found on the Big Island of Hawaii.

Turn east when the road dead-ends at

Left, the Junction Road to Portland. Below, plant with exotic characteristics at Castleton.

the Caribbean. **Annotto Bay** takes its name from an orange dye made from a Central American tree that once grew in the area. The town, like most in north-coast Surrey, has a weather-beaten **train station** that hasn't been used since Hurricane Allen shredded Portland's railway tracks in 1980. There's also an imaginatively-structured **Baptist chapel** built in 1894, just beyond the market square.

You cross back into Surrey and the parish of Portland at **Windsor Castle**. Further east at **Buff Bay** is the junction with the sensational but tortuous back route from Kingston. This road climbs up through Newcastle, then plummets 4,500 ft (1,372 meters) from Hardware Gap to the Buff Bay River gorge.

Of rats and rafts: The road winds east, turning inland into thick, wet foliage, beyond **Spring Garden**. William Bancroft Espeut lived on an estate here, where he introduced the mongoose in 1872. Plagued by rats that annually damaged some £45,000 worth of his sugar crop, Espeut imported nine mongooses from India. Though they ate the rats, they also preyed on birds, crabs, lizards, domestic stock and fruit and became as much of a pest as the rats. Wildlife experts blame the mongoose for nearly decimating the populations of coney and Jamaican iguana.

The only evidence of recent volcanic activity on the island is a low ridge about 600-ft (183-meter) high just beyond **Orange Bay**. It was formed by lava believed to have poured from a fissure in the earth.

Take a dip in the cool clear waters of Somerset Falls near **Hope Bay**. There's a small admission charge here, as well as a restaurant and changing facilities. Swim or take a boat beyond the small trickles at the top of the stair for a look at bigger, more secluded waterfalls in a blue-green grotto.

Another road swings inland at Hope Bay. It provides spectacular views of the Blue Mountains before rejoining the coast road at **St Margaret's Bay**. Here, on the old **Burlington Estate** grounds, a tree exemplifies the region's fertility

Cruising the Rio Grande.

by growing out of the factory chimney.

A bridge crosses the **Rio Grande**, the island's largest river. Maroons and other residents once floated bananas down the stream on long rafts; now they do the same journeys with tourists. In the 1940s, Port Antonio's most notorious resident, movie idol Errol Flynn, arrived and began organizing raft races. The Earl of Mansfield later built the landing site, shops and restaurant at **Rafters Rest**.

A swift ride on a 30-ft-long (9-meter) raft is still one of Jamaica's major tourist attractions. Licensed raftsmen, some of whom have spent up to 10 years as apprentices, guide your craft through gentle rapids with long poles. The 2½-hour trip begins at **Berrydale**, (or 3 hours from Grant's Level) north of Port Antonio off Red Hassel Road. About 150 rafts work the river, but it rarely appears crowded. The sight of mothers washing children or clothes, or kids swinging from vines along the banks, makes the trip an exotic adventure for most visitors.

The Rio Grande rises nearly 3,000 ft (900 meters) up into the mountainous interior of Portland. Torrential rainfalls often swell it beyond its banks. Portland's wet reputation results from the meeting of the moist northeast trade winds with the Blue Mountains. The winds, forced to rise, mix with ever-cooler air and form pregnant clouds. They drop most of their load here, leaving leeward areas such as Kingston parched. As much as 300 inches (762 cm) of rain falls annually in parts of inland Portland.

Twin harbors: Portland's rugged terrain long deterred settlement of this part of the island. Here, nature was so unbridled that early settlers probably felt threatened by its very presence. Even the Arawak Indians seem to have shunned Portland. No signs of their presence have been found here.

The first Europeans here were the Spaniards. They named the Rio Grande and the twin harbors just east of it – Puerto San Francisco and Puerto Anton, from which Portland's principal city got its name. They are now known rather

Port Antonio gateway.

prosaically as **West Harbor** and **East Harbor**.

The Spaniards carved a few *hatos*, cattle ranches, out of the jungle, but made no serious strides toward settlement. Portland remained virtually unknown territory long after the British settled the rest of the island.

The British created the parish of Portland in 1723. Fifty years later, Port Antonio had no more than 20 houses. The government offered free land and slaves to prospective settlers, as well as seven years' freedom from land taxes, arrests or prosecutions. Two barrels of beef and one of flour would be given to everyone until they reaped their first crop. But only the most desperate of settlers took up the challenge, discouraged as they were by heavy tropical downpours, the dense jungles, and the swampy, mosquito-infested coastline. Raids by the feared mountain Maroons also deterred pioneers.

To combat the invasions from Maroons or Spaniards, the British began to build **Fort George** in 1729 on the peninsular bluff that juts into the harbors. Its 10-ft-thick (3-meter) masoned walls had spaces for 22 guns. The old barracks have been turned into classrooms, and the parade grounds from a playfield for the **Titchfield School** compound. The existing cannons date from a later period but are mounted on the original gun emplacements.

The island to the north, originally intended for the town's site, was also acquired by the British military. The navy established a formidable installation there, but only the name, **Navy Island**, lingers. The island became more famous when it was purchased in the 1940s by lusty Errol Flynn, whom Jamaicans fondly recall as having staged wild Hollywood parties there. The likes of Clara Bow, Bette Davis and Ginger Rogers became part of the swinging Port Antonio scene.

Flynn is long gone and Port Antonio has settled back into its serene role as a resort for visitors wanting to get away from the commercial tourist scenes at Ocho Rios and Montego Bay. Just south

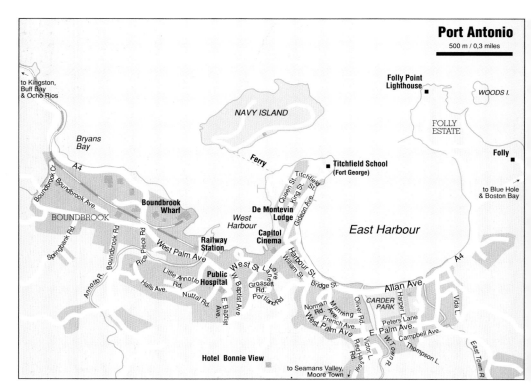

of Titchfield School on the peninsula is one of adventurous visitors' favorite haunts, **DeMontevin Lodge**, built circa 1898 at the corner of Fort George Street and Musgrave. If you don't intend to stay, at least sample an authentic Jamaican meal of suckling pig, codfish and ackee, or lobster. This is by arrangement only: you must phone in your order before you are ready to eat.

DeMontevin Lodge sits on "**The Hill**," once an exclusive residential area restricted by race, class and wealth. The British named the town Titchfield after the English estate of the Duke of Portland. The Hill became Upper Titchfield. The common people lived in Lower Titchfield along the seashore.

After the signing of a treaty with the Maroons in 1739, Titchfield grew more rapidly with the steadily increasing influx of sugar-cane money. By the end of the 18th century, Portland had 38 large estates and more than 100 smaller ones. But while sugar readily grew in most of Jamaica's soil and climate, heavy rain took its toll. By 1854, only four estates remained; all had vanished by the turn of the century.

But another green crop saved Port Antonio from economic ruin. As the large estates dwindled, Jamaicans carved them into smaller plots where peasants began to grow yams and other "ground provisions" as root crops are called. They also began to grow bananas.

The banana business: The empty wharves and vacant warehouses of modern Port Antonio provide little evidence that this town was once the world's banana capital, the very stereotype of Harry Belafonte's "Banana Boat" song, where men and women carried heavy banana bunches on their heads as they swayed and sang, "Day-O."

If you time your trip right, you may still see bananas being loaded at **Boundbrook Wharf** near the railroad crossing when you drive into town from the west. Packaged elsewhere, they will be loaded into the ships mechanically.

The Spanish brought the banana to the West Indies from the Canary Islands in 1516. The trade was later founded on

Early view of Port Antonio.

a large, sweet, creamy fruit called the *Gros Michel* (and pronounced "Gross Mitchell" by Jamaicans) which was initially wiped out by Panama disease. The *Gros Michel* can sometimes be bought in the markets or on the roadside, but no longer exists in large enough quantities to be exported.

For the first 350 years after it arrived, the banana was disparaged as animal food. But canny Yankee sea captains loaded them green, watched them ripen on board ship, and found they could sell them for a profit on the eastern seaboard of the United States.

Captain George Busch carried the first bunch of bananas from Port Maria, west of Port Antonio, in 1869. Captain Lorenzo Dow Baker turned bananas into an industry in 1871 when he sold 1,450 stems at a US$2,000 profit in Boston. Baker organized planting, collection and marketing systems among the peasants in Portland's interior. His efforts grew into the Boston Fruit Company, later acquired by the giant United Fruit conglomerate.

With fleets of empty banana boats traveling to Jamaica to pick up their cargos, the enterprising Baker filled them with tourists seeking refuge from harsh winters, simultaneously touching off Port Antonio's tourist trade. He built the first Titchfield Hotel on "The Hill" in 1905.

Bananas became big business in Port Antonio. In the town's heyday, weekly sailings of banana boats were said to exceed weekly departures from the big British port of Liverpool. The arrival of a ship in those days was signalled by the blowing of a conch shell. All hands rushed to the fields to cut down mature fruit with machetes. Then they wrapped it in banana "trash," or dried leaves, for its short journey to the docks.

The banana plant is a tree with a succulent stem (sometimes used as animal fodder) formed by overlapping leaf bases. The mature plant sends out a purple bud revealing rows of tiny flowers when it opens. The flowers develop into small "fingers." Each grows into a banana. A cluster of fingers forms a

Below, view toward Titchfield from DeMontevin's Lodge. **Right, banana man.**

"hand." Several hands make up a bunch.

When bananas were unloaded from trucks, two checkers would take a "stem count" of each bunch. Nine hands or more were considered a "bunch;" eight hands were a three-quarter bunch. Anything less was rejected. "Six hand, seven hand, eight hand, bunch!" as the song says. When a carrier walked the line, he received a metal disc showing the bunch count, to be redeemed later. Another long human chain, this one mainly female, carried the bunches aboard the truck. Here the famed "tallyman" of Belafonte's song gave each carrier a "tally" to be redeemed.

The plaintive songs of banana workers were very real reflections of their lives. "Mi back dis a bruck with the bare exhaustion," they sang as they carried heavy loads from dawn to dusk, earning only 25 to 70 cents per day. Portland-born Evan Jones, screenwriter of *Funeral in Berlin* and other movies, wrote in his poem "Song of the Banana Man":

Thank God and this big right hand.
I will live and die a banana man.

Devastating hurricanes and Panama disease eventually crippled the banana industry. The trade passed temporarily into the hands of large operators who had the means and the resources to control the disease; today, it is back in the hands of small-to medium-sized growers. The government controls marketing and shipping. Bananas continue to be a major crop, but the days of the tallyman have ended.

Many varieties of the banana and its fat cousin, the plantain, can be sampled at the **Town Market.** All you have to do to locate it is follow your nose and the crowds of clutter and color opposite the cenotaph on West Street. Port Antonio's best food market days are Thursday and Saturday.

The bonnie view from Bonnie View: From ground level, particularly around the market, Port Antonio displays a dingy, dusty, lived-in look. But a drive up Richmond Hill changes all that. Follow the signs to the **Bonnie View Hotel.** Built in 1943 as a honeymoon retreat, the hotel's chief attraction has always

Maroons in Moore Town, about 1920.

204

been its view. Here, the noise of the city vanishes in the hill air, and gives way to sweeping panoramas of Port Antonio, its twin harbors, Navy Island and Portland.

Some consider it charming, others annoying, that Port Antonio lacks a cohesive infrastructure to stimulate its tourist trade. For many visitors, however, the town represents seclusion. Port Antonio has thrived as a hideaway for the "rich and famous," including in the early days, Bette Davis, Ginger Rogers, J. P. Morgan and Errol Flynn.

Mrs Patrice Flynn, Errol Flynn's widow, has balked at allowing her husband's remains to be buried in Port Antonio as he had wished, to the dismay of Jamaicans who still delight in relating tales about the star. He was buried instead in Forest Lawn cemetery in Hollywood.

But Mrs Flynn later returned to the area and has lived ever since at the Flynn ranch. Situated on Priestman's River near Boston Bay, the ranch is surrounded by fields of coconuts, pine-

Anglican Churchyard, Moore Town.

apples, pimentos, bananas and about 2,000 head of cattle.

The Maroons of Moore Town: One worthwhile side trip from Port Antonio takes you to **Moore Town**, the capital of the Windward Maroons' community. Before you go, try to contact the leader of this proud, secretive people through the local office of the Tourist Board, or the trip could prove pointless. If he agrees to meet you and introduce you to Moore Town and his people's fabled history, prepare for a rocky, 10-mile (16-km) ride up a steep, winding dirt road into the John Crow Mountains.

Take Sommers Town Road behind Port Antonio. Turn left at the town of **Fellowship**. Through **Newington** and **Windsor**, you will be struck by the wild blends of river, vegetation and mountains. Turn left again at **Seaman's Valley**. The last small dirt road leads to Moore Town. As you enter on your left, there's an **Anglican Church** fronted by a serene graveyard. The church, one of seven in Moore Town, is the community's oldest building.

A bridge crosses the **Wildcane (Negro) River**. Moore Town's school is the low rambling set of buildings on your left. More than a century old, it has an enrolment of about 300 children aged 6 to 15 years. **Bump Grave** is across from the school, a simple stone monument wherein lies the body of national hero Nanny, the founder of the town and legendary chieftainess of the Windward Maroons. Here, the flagpole flies the Maroon flag next to the Jamaican flag. **Cornwall Barracks**, another Maroon settlement, lies just across the river.

Maroons from throughout the region – from Comfort Castle, Ginger House and Seaman's Valley – travel to Moore Town annually to celebrate Nanny's canonization as a national hero in 1975. The *abeng* horns and Coromantee drums call them here. *Kumina* African-origin ancestral dances last deep into the night and stories of old are told. High up on the Blue Mountain Ridge to the northwest is a trapezoid-shaped bump, believed to be the site of the legendary **Nanny Town**.

A rich man's Folly: Brooding **Christ**

Church on Port Antonio's Harbor Street is a neo-Romanesque style Anglican Church built in 1840 by English architect Annesley Voysey. The Boston Fruit Company donated its lectern in 1900.

East of East Harbor rises another fascinating bit of Parthenon-type architecture now simply called **Folly**. It is the subject of a favorite romantic legend. As the story goes, a rich man built the mansion for his bride. He stocked its gardens with flowers, birds and animals – all of them white – then brought his lady to Jamaica for the honeymoon. Just as he carried her over the threshold, the concrete that had been foolishly mixed with sea water began to crumble. So did the rich man's dreams. His bride burst into tears at the omen and fled, never to return to him or his mansion.

In reality, a Connecticut jeweler named Alfred Mitchell built the mansion in 1905 and lived there occasionally with his family until his death in 1912. His wife, one of the Tiffanys of New York, was already a grandmother when they moved in. The building began to fall apart in the 1930s. Salt air rusted the steel reinforcement rods and the roof caved in.

Just east of Port Antonio is a castle-like mansion begun several years ago by a European baroness who reportedly encountered some financial problems. It is now the private residence of Earl Levy, owner of the Trident hotel.

The price of paradise: East of Port Antonio, several high-priced hotels have been cloaked in some of Jamaica's most splendid scenery. You will first pass the **Trident**, an elaborate reincarnation of a regional favorite that succumbed first to Hurricane Allen and then to Hurricane Gilbert. Set on 17 acres (7 hectares) of coastline, this hotel sprawls along the rocky, volcanic coast offering luxurious suites and villas and a four-room chateau. Patrice Wymore Flynn owns a boutique here.

In 1956, Canadian biscuit heir Garfield Weston opened a resort that further enhanced this area's elite aura. **Frenchman's Cove**, tucked back from the road in a magnificent setting on the lava rock

Below, Folly. **Right**, Cannon at Frenchman's Cove.

cliff, is a cottage-style colony. In its glory days, the luxury cottages rented for £1,000 a week, a fortune in the 1950s. For that price, everything a vacationer could possibly want – and then some – was included: personal servants, all food and drink, sports equipment and activities, a golf cart for zipping around the expansive grounds, caviar flown in from Russia, French champagne, and free airplane rides up and down the coast.

The author V. S. Naipaul spent several days here in 1962 and wrote in *The Middle Passage*: "Within 24 hours my interest in food and drink disappeared. Everything was at the end of the telephone, and it was my duty to have exactly what I wanted. But how could I be sure what I wanted best?"

The glory didn't last. Frenchman's Cove eventually went bankrupt. The beach and grounds are occasionally used for fund-raising functions and parties.

As you round a bend along the water beyond Frenchman's Cove, you will see the kind of picturesque island you thought existed only in the movies. **Monkey Island**, also called Pellew Island, no longer has any monkeys. But you can swim or boat to it across the unimaginably blue waters of **San San Bay**. But beware of sea urchins, which can leave a nasty sting in an unsuspecting swimmers' foot.

Just a half-mile further, bear left past palatial private villas to the **Blue Hole** otherwise known as Blue Lagoon. Its intense natural color is a result of the depth of the lagoon, estimated by realists at 210 ft (64 meters) and by romanticists as bottomless. The area is good for swimming, snorkeling or picnicking. Fine hotels here include **Dragon Bay**, with its lily ponds, almond trees, dragon fountain and private beach, and **Goblin Hill villas**, back from the beach but with a glorious clifftop view.

Spelunkers (cavers) can wander up into the hills beyond **Sherwood Forest** to the **Nonsuch Caves**. They are dry and can easily be negotiated with the aid of local guides.

Boston Bay beyond the Blue Hole is

Monkey Island, San San Bay.

a necessary stop for gourmands of uniquely Jamaican cuisine. Here the local people make what is reputed to be the island's best jerk pork. This delicacy was the creation of Maroons who seasoned wild pigs with herbs, pimento (or allspice) and pit-barbecued it on pimento wood. Jerking takes several hours, so you probably won't be able to buy any before mid-morning. And most will have been eaten by mid-afternoon.

Mrs Flynn's **Priestman's River Plantation** lies a few miles east of Boston Bay. From here, the road winds around rocky cliffs slapped by waves, through small villages, and past outcroppings of dense rainforest, all reminiscent of Maui's Hana Coast. Enjoy the scenery until you reach **Manchioneal.**

From here, you can also reach **Reach Falls**. Take the turnoff just before the Driver's River bridge, then continue a mile or two inland until you come to a fork in the rocky road. A hand-scrawled sign directs you to the spot. It's a tricky walk down stone stairs carved into a cliff to the bottom. Few tourists venture to this out-of-the-way spot, so except for the local guides or a freelance mento drummer, you should have the lovely cool water and falls all to yourself. Climb up into the caves under the falls themselves for a look.

When the United Nations drew up a "national physical plan" for Jamaica in 1970, the committee members found the Manchioneal area so magnificent that the establishment of a coastal wilderness area was recommended.

Quakers and Africans: On top of the hill east of Manchioneal is the **Happy Grove School**, founded by Quakers for East Indian sugar workers in 1898. Soon after, you leave the parish of Portland and cross into St Thomas. The scenery begins to change. The plains at the island's eastern tip are laden with palm and sugar cane, an impressive view of which is available as the road winds down **Quaw Hill**.

Turn off at **Golden Grove** onto a long road that leads to **Morant Point Lighthouse**. Built in 1841, the 100-ft (30-meter) high cast-iron structure is listed

Villas on the Blue Hole.

by the Jamaica National Trust as a historic monument. Engineer George Grove is better known to musicians as the author of *Grove's Dictionary of Music and Musicians.*

Jamaicans today regard St Thomas as one of the parishes where the African heritage is strongest. Here, the ancestor worship cult of *kumina* flourishes.

Among St Thomas' many historical relics are the overgrown ruins of the oldest house in Jamaica – **Stokes Hall**, slightly off the highway near Golden Grove. In 1656, Governor Luke Stokes, seeking colonists, attracted 1,000 settlers from the Leeward islands of Nevis and St Kitts. Less than three months later, Stokes and his wife died, along with two-thirds of the other pioneers. The disease-ridden Morant swamps had taken their toll.

But Stokes' three sons survived, and although all were under 15 years of age at the time, they apparently prospered. One is believed to have erected Stokes Hall. Like many plantation houses, it was built with loopholes in the walls through which guns could be fired in case of attack, a grim reminder of those hard times.

Continue on the A4 to **Bowden** and **Port Morant**, both of which were busy harbors in the days of sugar and bananas. Port Morant was guarded by **Fort Lindsay** (now in ruins) on Morant Point and **Fort William** on the other side. Bowden, on the eastern end of the harbor, gave its name to the **Bowden Formation**, which has yielded extensive fossil remains from the late Miocene geological period. Several hundred species of marine shells have been discovered in this formation.

The legacy of Morant Bay: At Port Morant beaches like **Lyssons** and **Roselle**, you can mingle with the people of St Thomas. The shores swing toward Kingston in soft undulating curves quite different from the jagged beauty of the Portland coast.

The parish capital at **Morant Bay** was the site of the famous rebellion of 1865. The bloody reprisals in which national heroes Paul Bogle and George

Rugged Portland coast near Manchioneal.

William Gordon were executed, along with hundreds of other residents, live on in a dramatic **Statue of Bogle** that dominates the town square. Created by Edna Manley, the sculpture depicts a defiant Bogle clutching a machete in a crucifix pose.

The statue stands in front of the **Courthouse**, a reconstruction of the one burned out during that rebellion. Gordon and 18 others were hanged from a boom in front of the courthouse, while Bogle and his brother were hanged from the center arch of the gutted building.

Seventy-nine skeletons were found behind the wall of the old **Morant Bay Fort**, behind the courthouse, during excavations in 1965. A mass grave and monument have been installed under the fort cannons. The fort dates to 1773, but the three cannons were installed early in the 19th century. The **Parish Church** nearby was built in 1881.

Today, Morant Bay has forgotten its melodramatic past and turned into a quiet town with unusual street names like Soul Street and Debtor's Lane.

Water of life: For a pleasant side trip into inland St Thomas, take the road from Morant Bay through **Airy Castle** to the Bath Spa and Botanic Gardens. The mineral bath opened in 1699 after a runaway slave discovered its waters and claimed it had cured chronic ulcers on his legs. The government bought the spring and 1,300 acres (526 hectares) of surrounding land, and immediately it began to record cases of cures. A certain Mr Watson had a "dry bellyache eased by the first draught of the water," and a Mr Gordon was cured of "lowness of spirit and a depraved appetite."

The mineral baths do have therapeutic value for treating rheumatic ailments and skin diseases. Hot water reaching 128°F (53°C) and "cold" water at 115°F (46°C) miraculously pour from the same igneous rocks above the Sulphur River, and are mixed in the baths to proper bathing temperature. They contain high percentages of lime and sulphur.

Once known as the Bath of St Thomas the Apostle, little of the spa's early splendor remains today. But the spring

Former Holland estate in St Thomas near Morant Point, 19th century.

continues to attract health addicts from around the world.

Nearby is the Western Hemisphere's second oldest botanical garden, established in 1779. The breadfruit trees in one corner are offsprings of those brought from Tahiti in 1793 by Captain William Bligh of *Bounty* fame.

From Morant Bay, the highway traverses Jamaica's longest span, **Busta-mante Bridge** across the Morant River. The arid district of **Yallahs** provides a dusty change of scenery. The huge **Yallahs Ponds**, south of the highway, are separated from the sea by an arm of land. With twice the salinity of sea water, they provided salty supplies for early settlers.

The **Yallahs River** is usually a dry riverbed filled with enormous boulders. But it can become a raging torrent during the rainy season, since its source lies 4,500 ft (1,372 meters) up in the Blue Mountains. A huge landslip upriver occurred when a mountain fell into the valley during the 1692 earthquake. A 1,000-ft (300-meter) escarpment left be-hind is called **Judgement Cliff** because the rubble buried a plantation belonging to a wicked Dutchman – or so say the locals. The best view of the cliff is from **Easington**.

The road soon bends back into beautiful valleys, the foothills of the Blue Mountains. At the hamlet of **Eleven Miles**, keep a watch for the roadside marker commemorating Three-Fingered Jack. This Jamaican equivalent of Robin Hood was an escaped slave who was courtly to ladies and the poor, but cruel to male travelers and British soldiers. He pillaged until his death at the hands of the Maroons in 1781.

Evening light falls upon these mountain roads like a sprinkle of dew. The road bottoms out at **Bull Bay**, home of a community of fervent Rastafarians. A road from the settlement leads up to the small but lovely **Cane River Falls**.

Wickle Wackie and **Copacabana Beach** are disappointing dirt slivers, despite their alluring names. Harbor View's popular drive-in cinema and Kingston lie just beyond.

Middlesex, as its name implies, spans the heartland of the island. Its attractions run the gamut of the Jamaican experience: from the commercial tourism center of Ocho Rios to history-rich Spanish Town, from industrial hubs like May Pen and Mandeville to sparsely inhabited strips of wild terrain around Alligator Pond and Gut River.

There are also the "Northern Reaches, Sandy Beaches" of the parishes of St Mary and St Ann. Coastal towns here rely heavily on the influx of foreign visitors. But a few miles inland, the hotels and their trappings vanish. Cows and rolling pastures take over a landscape studded with intriguingly-named places like Walker's Wood, Golden Grove and Cave Valley.

Spanish Town and South Middlesex are another matter. The only hotels here are small local establishments. Otherwise, it's a wide-open land of unexplored enchantments where you can spy on the gentle giant of the sea, the manatee, and bathe in a spa more radioactive than any in Europe. Children peddle pouches of delicious raw cashew nuts along the railway tracks near Old Harbor. Fishermen will sell you enormous lobsters just caught off the dusty beach at Rocky Point.

Three parishes comprise the southern part of Middlesex: St Catherine, where Spanish Town looks much as it did in the days when the British still ruled; Clarendon, rich in the traditions of Pocomania around its capital of May Pen; and Manchester, spread out across a rolling mountain plateau pock-marked by bauxite mines. Acres of sugar cane and citrus bind these parishes together and sustain them.

Preceding pages: falling flowers on the edge of Walker's Wood. **Left,** landscaped tourism in Ocho Rios.

OCHO RIOS AND SURROUNDINGS

The northern region of the county of Middlesex reflects two sides of Jamaica. There is the beach-fringed coast where fishing villages huddle between the major tourist resorts and modern hotels. Then, there is the interior, tourist-free small towns and hamlets where Jamaicans earn a simple, but seemingly adequate, living from the soil.

Both sides of this intriguing heartland can be explored on solid roads. Routes A1 and A3 skirt the coast and Route B11 winds inland almost parallel to this coast. A tangle of crossroads connect the routes, so you can drive by any portion without having to double back. Along the coast, you will find tourist meccas and Columbus country, as well as the town where James Bond, Agent 007, was born. The inland roads offer glimpses into typical Jamaican lifestyles and scenic hills.

At the core of this part of the county lies one of Jamaica's premier travel destinations, **Ocho Rios**. You may wish to make your "base camp" in one of its plush hotels or villas, or perhaps in more modest accommodations, as you wander into other parts of northern Middlesex on jaunts of a day or two.

The most popular route to Ocho Rios from Kingston follows A1 through Spanish Town, along the lovely Rio Cobre river, through Linstead and Ewarton with its massive Alcan bauxite complex, then up **Mount Diablo** and down into the parish of St Ann. At the crest of the mountain, you will look into an enormous red earthern sea, one of the unfortunate legacies of a bauxite-mining industry that has otherwise brought a measure of prosperity to many Jamaican communities. Just before, you will come to a wide-open tract that is a popular spot to stop, stretch your legs, and fill your belly with saltfish, yams, corn and fresh fruit from roadside chefs and vendors.

Past **Moneague**, where Route A1 forks west to an inland route covered **Fern Gully**.

later in this chapter, you follow A3 into **Walker's Wood**. This area lives up to its name with a dense, pastoral Tolkien-esque setting of rounded hills, pastures and valleys criss-crossed by stone walls. The British countryside couldn't look more British. Take the road to **Friendship Farm**. It offers a farm tour, and also incomparable views of the storybook scenery from its handsome Great House and swimming pool.

Two miles past the farm on A3, you suddenly plunge from daylight into semi-darkness down the roller-coaster ride of **Fern Gully**. Once a river bed, dense growths of ferns and trees blanket the road and block the sun. But don't allow the surreal surroundings to distract you from the tricky drive. The road is often slippery and its corners are sharp, so low gear is recommended. Its fern population has diminished some, probably because of vandals and car exhaust fumes, but Fern Gully still pleases the senses.

Ocho Rios, cruise capital: Billboards announcing the American chain hotels and Kentucky Fried Chicken fast-food franchises bring you out of Fern Gully and back to 20th-century reality. You have entered *Ocho Rios*, the navel of island tourism. Ocho Rios is hardly a town: it is more like a village mugged by tourist development. Its hotels, houses and shops are haphazardly strung out along the coastal strip.

Ocho Rios' name is not what is purports to be. There are not eight rivers in the town, although its Spanish translation might suggest that. Its original name in *español* was *Las Chorreras*, "the waterfalls," obviously a reference to the magnificent Dunn's River cascades just west of town. Apparently, English settlers heard wrong. It's been called Ocho Rios ever since.

Ocho Rios' only historical claim to fame is as the lair of pirate John Davis. Rich local planters were said to have subsidized Davis' enterprising rape-and-plunder expeditions, which included sacking the city of St Augustine in Florida. The only reminders of those days are the walls and cannon of an old

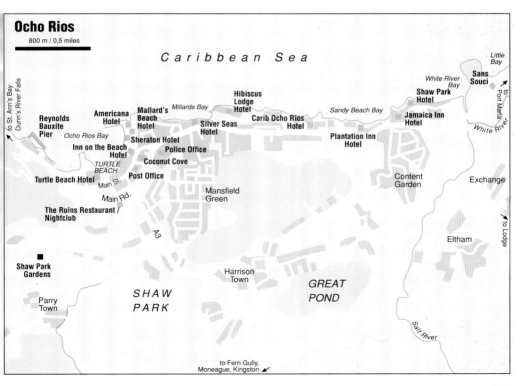

Ocho Rios

800 m / 0,5 miles

C a r i b b e a n   S e a

Little Bay

White River Bay

Sans Souci

to Port Maria

to St. Ann's Bay
Dunn's River Falls

Shaw Park Hotel

Hibiscus Lodge Hotel

Millards Bay

Sandy Beach Bay

White River

Reynolds Bauxite Pier

Americana Hotel

Mallard's Beach Hotel

Silver Seas Hotel

Carib Ocho Rios Hotel

Jamaica Inn Hotel

Ocho Rios Bay

Sheraton Hotel

Plantation Inn Hotel

Inn on the Beach Hotel

TURTLE BEACH

Coconut Cove

Police Office

Turtle Beach Hotel

Post Office

Main St.

Main Rd.

Mansfield Green

Content Garden

Exchange

The Ruins Restaurant / Nightclub

A3

Eltham

to Lodge

Shaw Park Gardens

Harrison Town

GREAT POND

Parry Town

SHAW PARK

Salt River

to Fern Gully, Moneague, Kingston

fort, buried in dust from the Reynolds bauxite terminal next to it.

The town's growth as a magnet for tourists began in the 1950s. That reputation has accelerated in recent years, Ocho Rios has surpassed Montego Bay and Port Antonio to become Jamaica's top cruise ship destination. It's an attraction in itself to rise early in the morning to watch the enormous luxury liners inching into a berth at the wharf near the bauxite terminal.

Passengers are usually greeted in "Love Boat" style by an old mento or calypso band and dancers. Two of the monstrous ships often moor in Ocho Rios Bay at the same time. Their arrival turns sleepy Ocho Rios into an anthill of activity. Higglers, craftsmen, taxi drivers and mini-van operators all jockey for good positions from which to be the first to offer their wares or services to free-spending cruise passengers.

Scaling the falls: For a John Crow's view of Ocho Rios, try **Shaw Park Gardens** up the hill to the west of A3 as you enter the town from Fern Gully.

These landscaped grounds were once the setting for the old Shaw Park Hotel, since closed but latterly resurrected as the Shaw Park Beach far below these heights. There are also a variety of flowers and trees, a rushing stream and waterfalls in the gardens.

But the main attraction of Ocho Rios – and probably of the entire island – drops 600 ft (180 meters) to the sea coast in a series of cascades two miles west of the town center. **Dunn's River Falls** have been delighting visitors since Spanish times. They are the most spectacular of a series of waterfalls that gush from lush, wooded limestone cliffs along this ridge. A large park, full of snack bars, souvenir stands and woodcarvers' shops, has grown up around these falls. But the tradition at Dunn's River Falls is to climb them.

Stairs lead downhill through a tunnel under Route A1 to a beach where you can check your clothes and valuables in a locker. You must purchase a ticket: this entitles you to climb with (or without) an official guide. It's a common

Ocho Rios is Jamaica's top cruise ship destination.

sight to see a guide, his dreadlocks dangling among the dozens of cameras strung around his neck, leading a daisy chain of tourists up the rocks, through the falls to the top.

Take the climb slowly and check your footing. The rocks are slick in spots and the torrents powerful enough to knock you over. There are several spots along the way to exit back to dry land if the climb becomes too nerve-wracking.

A smaller, less crowded spot for showering in a waterfall is located less than a mile west of Dunn's River by the hydroelectric station. The best section of **Roaring River** falls on a private property called **Laughing Waters**. Scenes for the first of the James Bond epics, *Dr. No*, were shot here.

Rum and resorts: The other prime draws in Ocho Rios are its strands of white sands, **Turtle Beach** and **Mallards Beach**. At night, you can reggae with Jamaicans in the Jamaican Grande hotel's disco or try the romantic setting of The Ruins night club, where music plays against the background of a waterfall.

Route A3 twists and turns east through Ocho Rios' most pleasant area. Here, hotels like the Plantation Inn, Carib Ocho Rios and the Sans Souci Lido nestle amid the trees and nudge the rocky coast. One of the grandest old lodgings is the Jamaica Inn perched on a cliff above a secluded slice of beach. Here, time has stopped. Waiters in white coats serve you rum punch: trade winds trickle through the trees; and the scent of jasmine fills the air.

Continue east to the **White River**. Once lined with handsome Jamaica tall palms, the mysterious Lethal Yellowing disease has taken its toll. Only the trunks of the trees remain; they are being replaced with the sturdier, but less attractive, Malayan Dwarf. Dead stumps are processed into parquet flooring.

Tuesday and Saturday nights, exotic torches burn along the bank for "A Night on the White River." Guests get a romantic cruise down the stream to a forest clearing for dinner, drinks, a show and dancing.

A signposted road near the river leads

Dunn's River Falls.

inland one mile to the grounds of **Prospect Estate**. It opens daily for tours of the plantation, the White River gorge, **Sir Harold's Viewpoint** over the coast, and a lane of memorial trees planted by such eminent and varied notables as Winston Churchill, Noel Coward, Charlie Chaplin and former Canadian Prime Minister Pierre Trudeau. Prospect Estate takes young men from poor backgrounds and trains them as "cadets" who live and work on the estate while learning useful skills.

East of White River, Annabella Proudlock has handsomely restored **Harmony Hall** Great House. Inside, you will find a bar, a restaurant and a gallery where you can buy work by some of Jamaica's leading artists and craftsmen.

Couples, for couples: Further east and across the road, commanding another nice beach on the turquoise waters of the Caribbean, rises **Couples**, formerly the Tower Isle Hotel.

Unlike its Negril affiliate, Hedonism II, only couples are permitted here. A marriage certificate is not necessary, and wedding services can be arranged as part of its package for those who impulsively decide to tie the knot. Ceremonies are performed on the tiny offshore island with the tower – after suntanning hours. During the day, the island is strictly reserved for those who prefer to swim and sunbathe in the nude. Couples earned a flurry of publicity when it opened with its advertising poster of two lions, one a well-endowed female, mating.

From Couples, Route A3 continues down the increasingly scenic coast. **Rio Nuevo** is the spot where Great Britain finalized its claim on Jamaica in June 1658 by routing the displaced Spanish governor Ysassi and his men from a stockade above the river mouth. A small monument marks the site of the last battle.

A side road that leads south from here, Route B13, provides a picturesque tour past banana plantations up the Rio Nuevo valley to **Retreat**, where a suspension footbridge straddles the river. The beautiful old **Holy Trinity Church**

The view from Noel Coward's room at Firefly.

and an abandoned sugar mill lie further on. The road climbs to Gayle and Guy's Hill, where there's a junction with a road to **Highgate**.

James Bond, bird-watcher: East of Rio Nueva, Route A3 enters Jamaica's most lovely coastal country. The gorgeous seascapes extend all the way to Manchioneal at the eastern end of the island. The first point of interest is in **Oracabessa**, "Golden Head" – from the Spanish word *oro* for gold and *cabeza* for head.

Opposite an Esso gas station north of the main road is a small lane leading to a beach lined with traditional dugout canoes. Imposing gateposts, surmounted by black wood-carved pineapples, mark the entrance to an old home that gave birth to the world's most famous, albeit fictional secret agent: "007," otherwise known as James Bond.

The home is called **Goldeneye**. It was owned by Ian Fleming, author of the 13 James Bond novels that have sold more than 18 million copies in 23 languages. Fleming wintered here from 1946 until his death in 1964. Ironically, he borrowed the name for his secret agent from a most unlikely source.

In *Ian Fleming Introduces Jamaica*, he explained: "I was looking for a name for my hero – nothing like Peregrine Carruthers or Standfast Maltravers – and I found it, on the cover of one of my Jamaican bibles. *Birds of the West Indies* by James Bond, an ornithological classic." Fleming goes on to add: "Would these books have been born if I had not been living in the gorgeous vacuum of a Jamaican holiday? I doubt it."

The literary juices of yet another famous author and playwright flowed just down the coast from Oracabessa near the town of Port Maria. Watch for the sign that directs you off the A3 and up a rutted dirt road to **Firefly**. Here, the actor, playwright and master of waspish British wit, Sir Noël Coward, spent many of the last 23 years of his life. He died here on March 26, 1973, and is buried in a simple grave in an idyllic spot on the lawns in front of the house. The house is now a protected property of the National Heritage Foundation Trust (NHFT).

During his years at Firefly, Coward entertained the likes of the Queen Mother of England and her daughter, Princess Margaret. The property has been leased from the NHFT by Chris Blackwell, himself a native of St Mary. He has painstakingly restored the buildings and grounds to reflect, as accurately as possible, the way it was when Coward was alive. There is a guided tour of the property and a regular program of musical and theatrical entertainment throughout the year.

East of Firefly, **Port Maria** springs up after you round a rocky cliff. It has the standard town trappings – a courthouse built in 1820 and a church that dates from 1861. A bridge joins a noisy shopping section to a quiet residential area. A sign at the church gates points you to the **Tacky Monument** that commemorates the leader of the Easter slave rebellion of 1760.

One worthwhile side trip from Port Maria leads up Route B13 to **Brimmer Hall** and its plantation tour. Here, you

Relaxing on Port Maria monument.

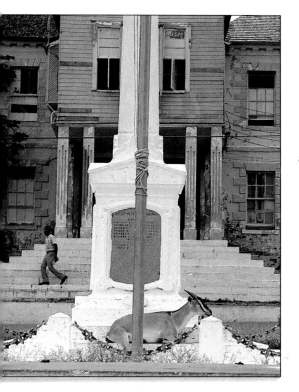

can ride a tour wagon through acres of banana, coconut, pimento and other crops. You can also tour the Great House, have a Jamaican lunch of curry goat or ackee and salt fish, and take a swim in the pool.

Beyond Port Maria, A3 curves back inland through thick rainforests. Look for the shop near **Whitehall** where a Rastaman sells solid cast-iron pots. Whitehall also marks the junction with Route B2, an off-the-beaten track drive through the country to Bog Walk and then back to Kingston or Ocho Rios. Alternatively, you can take the Junction Road that breaks off to Kingston just before reaching Annotto Bay; or you can continue east on to Portland and Port Antonio. The road west from Ocho Rios passes Dunn's River Falls and Roaring River.

Take Route A3 west past Sandals Dunns River Hotel, then swing by **Drax Hall**, a polo playing field. Polo was, of course, imported by the British colonial elite. Now the game is open to any sport-minded Jamaican who has a horse.

Prior to reaching **St Ann's Bay**, the road transits plantations of elegant coconut palms that have thus far managed to resist the blight of Lethal Yellowing. These palms mark the approaches to **Sevilla Nueva**, the first Spanish settlement in Jamaica.

We are now entering Columbus Country. In fact, foreign research scientists are working with the Jamaican government to find the hulks of the last two caravels abandoned here by Columbus in 1504. The government also plans to reconstruct Spanish townsite ruins with an archaeological park at the **Seville Estate**.

The modern history of Jamaica began near present-day St Ann's Bay, just north of the junction of routes A1 and A3. The town has been bypassed by the new trunk road (the A.G.R. Byfield Highways), but leaving the bypass makes for a worthwhile detour to this pleasant parish capital.

The courthouse on the main street, next to the parish church, was built in 1866. Beyond the town on the landward **Port Maria as it looked about 1830.**

side of the road is a **Statue of Columbus**, cast in his native town of Genoa, Italy. Behind the statue is a **Catholic Church**. It was built in 1939 of stones from a variety of local sources, including those from the ruins of the original Spanish Church of Peter Martyr, which stood slightly west of the present church. Peter Martyr of Anghiera was a 16th-century soldier-turned-priest who authored a book about the New World – but never set foot in Jamaica.

A more fitting island tribute is the **Marcus Garvey Monument** fronting the town library. Garvey was born in St Ann's Bay in 1887 and has been elevated to national hero status because of his work in developing among black people a sense of pride and identity in their African heritage.

Route A1 swings south into the mountains from St Ann's Bay to **Claremont**, a bauxite center once called Finger Post. It proceeds to Moneague, where roads connect to Kingston or Ocho Rios.

A detour from Claremont leads some 5 miles (8 km) to the village of **Pedro**, where Jamaica's most macabre ruin stands. In the hill tower of **Edinburgh Castle** lived Lewis Hutchinson, a sadistic red-haired Scotsman. In the 1760s, this ex-medical student murdered more than 40 travelers by shooting them from the slit windows of his tower. The bodies were robbed and decapitated; they are thought to have been thrown down a nearby sinkhole.

Hutchinson was captured while trying to board a ship offshore. He was unrepentant. Before being hanged, he left £100 for the erection of a monument to himself with the requested inscription to read: "Their sentence, pride and malice I defy. Despise their power, and like a Roman I die." The monument was not erected.

The ruins of the first Spanish settlement in Jamaica at Sevilla Nueva lie just west of St Ann's Bay. After crossing the river, take the dirt road behind the gate that crosses the seaward side of the main road. Castle ruins have been discovered to the right of the road, while the remains of a Spanish sugar mill, surely the

Brimmer Hall Plantation.

island's first, are strewn to the left of the road. These buildings are believed to have been some of the few structures constructed in the settlement before the Spanish decided to pack up and relocate their capital at Villa de la Vega, the modern-day Spanish Town.

Beyond this cradle of modern Jamaican history, Route A1 continues through the sugar cane country of Priory and the Llandovery Central Factory to the charmingly-named Laughlands. Just before Laughlands are the Chukka Cove polo playing fields, the north coast's polo center.

Runaway Bay, so-called because the last Spaniards allegedly left Jamaica from here after their final defeat by the British, is a booming tourist area. On entering, you'll find a settlement of small conical habitations, like a Hottentot housing scheme. This is Club Caribbean, tourist accommodations with individual cottages arranged around a central clubhouse that contains a restaurant and bar.

Next is the Jamaica, Jamaica! Hotel, one of the most expensive in the area. It has an 18-hole golf course, on the opposite side of the road. The Franklin D Resort, or FDR, is next. It is one of only two all-inclusive hotels that caters for families. Accommodation is condominium style. A string of smaller hotels and guest houses follow. **Eaton Hall** is notable for being built on the foundations of an old English fort, complete with an underground passage that leads to the cliffs.

Beaches and hotels are Runaway Bay's claim to fame. As a town, it is non-existent. Much of it consists of **Cardiff Hall**, a vast estate of privately owned houses. A short detour up the road by the Shell Service Station leads to the Runaway Bay HEART Academy; the main training center for the hospitality trade.

Well-signposted beyond are the **Runaway Caves** and **Green Grotto**, the most accessible of Jamaica's large limestone caves. Guided tours take in about 1½ miles (2 km) of the caverns, and include a sail across an eerie grotto

Left, Marcus Garvey, St Ann's son. **Right**, Polo at Drax Hall about 1920.

120 ft (37 meters) below the earth's surface. Discreet lighting brings out the grotesque beauty of the stalactites and stalagmites. A fascinating property of some formations is that they are hollow. The guide, by cunningly striking them with a stick, coaxes primitive music from them. Outside the caves is a 160-ft-deep (49 meters) lagoon.

Discovery Bay, 5 miles (8 km) further on, is slowly developing under the stimulus of the Kaiser bauxite operation. But many tourists are put off by the presence of the great, dusty Port Rhodes bauxite shipping terminal in the middle of the bay. Guided tours of the mine and plant are combined with a stop at **Armadale Approved School**, where you can listen to performances of traditional songs.

Beyond the bauxite terminal, with its huge green storage dome, is **Columbus Park**, which despite its name is a pleasant open-air museum on the cliff with a panoramic view over the bay. Cannons and sugar-mill fragments (including a water wheel and the old cast-iron pans used for boiling juice down to sugar) are on display. You will also find a stone crest of the Clan Campbell of Argyll dated 1774, taken from Knapdale in St Ann parish.

Discovery Bay's name originates from the claim that Columbus first landed here in 1494. He called it *Puerto Seco*, "dry harbor," because of its lack of water. Today **Puerto Seco** beach is open to the public. Opposite is **Columbus Plaza**, containing a bank, bar, supermarket, and other modern amenities that would have impressed the navigator.

The road crosses the Rio Bueno river by the **Bengal Bridge** – a stylish stone structure of 1798 which serves as a boundary marker between St Ann and Trelawny parishes. It is an interesting combination of both bridge and hill: its eastern end is much higher than its western end.

Rio Bueno, in a bay at the mouth of the river of the same name, also has claims to being Columbus' landing site. It is an unspoiled fishing village, the main street of which has some old stone

Carreras tobacco farm.

houses. **Gallery Jo James**, with its little jetty behind, serves light though expensive meals.

St Mark's Church at the water's edge, fronted by its walled churchyard, is photogenic. Inside, a J. B. Kidd print shows how Rio Bueno looked in the 1830s. At the far end of town was **Fort Dundas**, built in 1778 to command both sea and bay.

From Brown's Town to Marley's tomb: Route B3 from Runaway Bay, and a smaller road from Puerto Seco, both lead south into the main structures on the enormous **Orange Valley Estate** property. If you can arrange a tour of this private estate, you will see a sugarworks factory that looks very much as it did some two centuries ago.

Another lovely estate that looks like a slice of the British courtryside is **Minard**, behind imposing gateposts south of Orange Valley.

Minard's first owner was a man named Brown. It is for him that the next community on this route, **Brown's Town**, is named. A quaint and picturesque country town, it is built up and down the sides of hills and valleys.

Facing the central market, an arresting example of 19th-century Gothic architecture, is **St Mark's Church**. It was completed in 1895. The main street also features a twin post office and police station, each with stone arches, and balconies and tile roofs that give them a distinctly Spanish look. Above these two structures is a Georgian courthouse, well-built in cut stone with a pillared portico. The many-tiered layout gives Brown's Town a Mediterranean flavor that is good for camera buffs but hard on the legs.

At the fork in the middle of town, you can proceed south on B3 through splendid hills and dales to **Alexandria**.

Reggae fans will want to ask directions here to the **tomb** of Jamaica's international superstar, Bob Marley, who was born near the village of Nine Miles. Fans and reggae stars make a pilgrimage to this site on Marley's birthday in February, when they play his music long into the night.

Below, Brown's Town market. Right, typical rural scene.

228

SPANISH TOWN AND SOUTH MIDDLESEX

The southern half of Middlesex County is a land of enormous variety. Sites of great historical importance – including Spanish Town, Jamaica's original capital, and caves once inhabited by the Arawaks – are part of a landscape that encompasses bauxite-filled plateau country, green rolling "English" hills, and undeveloped coastal grasslands.

Most visitors are introduced to the region at **Spanish Town**, 14 miles (23 km) west of Kingston on Route A1. The approach leads across the **Ferry River**, which until the early 20th century was still important as the last staging post for horses and carriages traveling from Kingston to the west of the island. Planned by a son of Christopher Columbus, Spanish Town was a colonial capital from the early 1500s to 1872.

Three miles (5 km) outside of Spanish Town is the **White Marl Arawak Museum**. Located on the site of a large

Left, Rodney Memorial, Spanish Town.

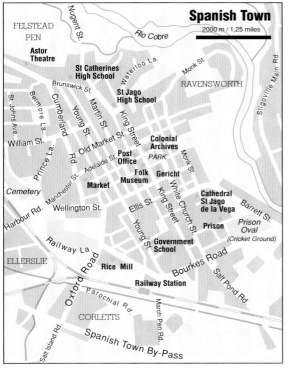

Arawak village of centuries past, the building is said to be a replica of an Arawak hut. Important archaeological finds were made here.

A short distance further on, the main highway passes an **Iron Bridge** regarded as a national monument. Indeed, this span over the Rio Cobre, while no longer in use, is the oldest surviving cast-iron bridge in this part of the world.

From the time of its founding by the Spanish in 1523, until the British moved the capital to Kingston in 1872, Spanish Town was the seat of Jamaican government. The Spaniards called it *Villa de la Vega*, "the town on the plain," while the English (after their 1655 conquest) preferred St Jago, in honor of St James of Compostella, the patron saint of Spain. But gradually people simply began to call it Spanish Town, even though all of its Spanish buildings had disappeared by the 18th century.

In the center of Spanish Town is the **Square**, surrounded on all sides by Georgian-style buildings constructed during the heyday of sugar. On the east side is the **Parish Council Office**, formerly the House of Assembly. Built in 1762, it is notable for the superb brickwork of its long, shady colonnade and the pillared wooden balcony above. Opposite, on the west side of the square, are the remains of **King's House**, also dating from 1762. It was gutted by fire in 1925, leaving only the grand portico and facade. An interesting archaeological museum, displaying artifacts found here, has been erected on the site.

Demanding a closer look is the **Jamaican People's Museum of Craft and Technology**, located in the adjacent former stables. Its collection features relics from years past – everything from home furnishings to a village store.

On the south side of the square is the **Court House**, built in 1819. Still in active use by parish magistrates, it attracts a vociferous throng of defendants, witnesses and onlookers outside its doors when court is in session. The building's upstairs-floor contains the **Town Hall**, where concerts, plays and other public entertainments are held.

The **Rodney Memorial** at the north

end of the square was sculpted in Italian marble by the noted English artist John Bacon. It was erected in the late 18th century as a token of gratitude to Admiral George Rodney for saving the West Indies from French domination with his famous victory at sea over the Count de Grasse in 1782. Rodney is depicted in the dress of a Roman emperor; apparently, this was the artistic convention of the day. The statue is missing a hand and a few additional chips, the result of a feud between the residents of Spanish Town and Kingston. When it was removed to Kingston with the island administration, Spanish Town citizens were outraged and went to reclaim the statue. It has remained in Spanish Town ever since.

Behind Rodney's statue is the **Archives Office**, where many historical documents are kept, and the **Records Office**, where legal records for the entire nation are stored, from birth certificates and wills to title-deeds. Among the old records still on hand is the last will and testament of Sir Henry Morgan, the 17th-century buccaneer-turned-governor.

A short five-block walk back in the direction of Kingston on Barrett Street will take you to the **Cathedral Church of St James**, also known as the Cathedral of St Jago de la Vega. Constructed in 1523, this small house of worship was the first cathedral to be built in the New World. The British replaced it in 1666, and the current structure was raised in 1714 after a hurricane destroyed the original.

The cathedral church is built of brick in the form of a cross. The wooden steeple was added in 1831. In and around it are tombs and memorials to 17th-century settlers and notables of later centuries. Since 1843, it has been the cathedral of the Jamaica diocese of the Church of England.

From Spanish Town to Bog Walk the road follows the Rio Cobre river to **Flat Bridge**, a Spanish relic set just a few feet above water level between towering vertical walls of limestone. Heavy rains frequently make this bridge im-

Rio Cobre river *circa* 1800.

passable. A high-water mark of 1933 is indicated on the rock face, 25 ft (8 meters) above the bridge.

At the roundabout, the left fork leads to **Bog Walk**, on the main A1 highway between Spanish Town and St Ann's Bay. Bog Walk is one of the oldest settlements in Jamaica, a rest-stop for cattle wagons carrying hogsheads of sugar from nearby estates to ships waiting at Passage Fort. Today, Bog Walk is a railway junction and the site of a milk condensery, sugar factory and citrus packing plant.

North of Bog Walk, A1 continues through the town of **Linstead**, whose market (beneath the little square clock tower) is the subject of a famous folk song. Seven miles (11 km) further is **Ewarton**. Alcan has a major alumina factory here; bauxite is supplied by ropeway from a mining area 6 miles north, processed, then shipped to Port Esquivel.

Route A2 begins in Spanish Town and continues west through Mandeville to Savanna-la-Mar. Twelve miles (19 km) down this route is **Old Harbour**, best known for its iron Victorian clock tower. Such towers can be found all over the island, having been constructed mainly between 1890 and 1930. This one is unusual, it has been maintained in excellent condition, and usually keeps accurate time.

Colbeck Castle is located 2 miles (3 km) north of Old Harbour on a side road. Once perhaps the largest building in the Caribbean, it is generally thought to have been built in the late 17th century by an English settler named Colonel John Colbeck, as protection against Maroon attacks and possible invasion by the French. The main walls of this huge brick mansion are still erect, although the roof and floors are gone. Beam slots in the higher walls give an idea of the size of timbers which were used in construction. Four underground slave quarters can be seen at each corner of the castle. The building is in the midst of what is now a large tobacco farm.

A short distance west of Old Harbour on A2 is the **Bodles Agricultural Sta-**

The river in recent years.

tion, where some of Jamaica's finest dairy cattle are bred. The Jamaica Hope, the world's first tropically adapted dairy cow, was developed here by Dr T. P. Lecky as a cross between the Jersey and Brahmin breeds. It is particularly hardy and heat-tolerant. Crosses of Holstein and Frisian breeds have also been quite successful.

Opposite Bodles, beside a railway crossing, is the entrance road to **Port Esquivel**, a deepwater port of the Alcan Jamaican Company. From here, alumina is shipped to smelters in British Columbia and Scandinavia. You can visit the port by calling the firm's Kingston office in advance; they will arrange to have a pass waiting for you at the gate.

In Old Harbour Bay, beyond Port Esquivel, lie the two **Goat Islands**. Great Goat Island was an American naval base during World War II. Some of the old fortifications, barracks and ammunitions stores can still be seen, although the island now is used only by occasional fishermen. Further down the coast in Vere is the site of another former US base, Fort Symonds, now known as **Vernam Field**.

Crocodiles and sugar: At **Freetown**, Route B12 branches south toward Lionel Town and Milk River. It first passes through mangrove swamps, a large refuge for Jamaica's declining crocodile population, then enters **Salt River**. This was once a major port for shipping sugar, despite its lack of deep-water facilities. The estates on the surrounding plains of Vere can still be seen, although many have amalgamated under the influence of Tate and Lyle and its Jamaican subsidiary, the West Indies Sugar Company (Wisco).

A small road leads south to **Rocky Point**, a scattered fishing village where the local delicacy is turtle eggs in red wine. North of this hamlet is the town of **Alley**, with its sugar factory windmill-turned-library and its 18th-century St Peter's Church, surrounded by old tombstones and huge *kapok* (silk cotton) trees.

May Pen, the halfway point between Spanish Town and Mandeville, is the market center for Clarendon, Jamaica's largest parish. Fridays and Saturdays are market days; May Pen's downtown area becomes colorful, crowded and chaotic. The Clarendon capital, along with the parish church and hospital is actually at Chapelton, north of here, but May Pen is far more active commercially. Here, the famous Trout Hall citrus products are canned, under direction of the Sharpe family, developers of the *ugli* fruit.

A visit to **Trout Hall** and its surrounding citrus orchards is very rewarding. Let the Sharpes know of your planned visit by telephoning the May Pen or Kingston office of the Citrus Company of Jamaica, then head north on B3 out of May Pen.

After passing through the old sugar capital of **Chapelton**, now notable chiefly for its war memorial clock tower, parish church and hospital, you'll travel up the Rio Minho valley. The citrus plantation is located at the junction of routes B3 and B4.

From Trout Hall, you can continue north to Runaway Bay, passing en route through **Cave Valley**, site of a Saturday

Old Harbour clock tower.

morning donkey, mule and horse market. Or you can proceed west through Frankfield and Guinea Corn to the town of **Spaldings**.

On the boundary of Clarendon and Manchester parishes, Spaldings is famous for its co-educational **Knox College**, founded in 1947 by the Church of Scotland and the Presbyterian Church of Jamaica. Based on the progressive concept that education must extend beyond the classroom, this boarding school offers a wide curriculum of academic subjects; a printing works, farm and meat-processing plant make it almost self-sufficient.

Spaldings sits at about 3,000 ft (900 meters) elevation, giving it a cool year-round climate. The ginger grown in this region is said to be the best in the world.

Returning to Route A2, a few miles west of May Pen are the **Denbigh Agricultural Show Grounds**. The island's biggest show is held here annually over the long Independence Day weekend in early August. Just south of May Pen is the **Halse Hall** alumina plant, owned by Alcoa Minerals of Jamaica. It takes its name from the Halse Hall Great House, the focal point of the company's operations. Halse House has been beautifully restored. Contact Alcoa's Kingston office ahead of time if you wish to visit.

At Toll Gate, 8 miles west of May Pen, Route B12 branches south toward Milk River. **Milk River Bath**, not far from the river's mouth, is the island's leading spa. The spring waters here, known since the 17th century, are the most radioactive on earth: three times more than Karlsbad in Czechoslovakia, and 50 times more than Vichy in France! The minerals in the water are said to have curative powers for those suffering from gout, sciatica, lumbago, rheumatism, neuralgia, eczema, and liver and kidney complaints. The baths have recently been refurbished, and the Milk River Bath Hotel is ideal for weekends of bathing, swimming and fishing.

Beyond Toll Gate, Route A2 crosses the Manchester parish line and enters **Porus**, a thriving market town for citrus, coffee and other cash crops of the

region. Leave this mini-metropolis via **Melrose Hill**, which climbs about 2,000 ft (610 meters) in 5 miles (8 km); you should stop to admire the view from roadside shops which sell delicious roast corn and yams to weary travelers.

Jamaica's "Last Resort": A new highway winds into clean, cool **Mandeville** town, cradled in a hollow at about 2,000 ft (610 meters) elevation. Often called "the most English town in Jamaica," it now boasts a resident population heavy in North Americans employed in the bauxite industry.

Mandeville is the capital of the parish of Manchester, created in 1814 from pieces of other parishes. The parish was named after the Jamaican governor, the Duke of Manchester, and the town after the duke's heir, the Earl of Mandeville. Mandeville's pleasant climate (in the 70s Fahrenheit in the summer, 60s in the winter) appealed to many English colonialists, who came to think of it as their "last resort." But while some retired here, many more stayed only long enough to make their fortunes in coffee and pimento before heading home to the British Isles.

There are few points of particular interest in Mandeville itself. The Georgian courthouse and stone parish church were built around the central green soon after the town was founded. The oldest golf course on the island, the nine-hole **Manchester Club**, is located a half-mile from the town center. The major hotels include the Mandeville, built on the site of the 18th-century British garrison's hill station barracks and the Hotel Astra. The latter can arrange overnight visits to **Marshall's Pen**, an 18th-century great house set on a 300-acre (120-hectare) cattle farm.

The countryside around Mandeville is rich in citrus fruits, particularly oranges and tangerines, grown on small farms by independent cultivators. An odd but tasty fruit called the "ortanique," a unique natural cross of the orange and tangerine, was discovered here and propagated by Charles Jackson.

The mining of bauxite: Jamaica is the world's largest producer of bauxite, and a visit to a mining operation and alumina factory should be included on any itinerary. Most hotels can arrange tours, or permission can be obtained from head offices in major towns.

Perhaps the most easily reached operation is Alcan's **Kirkvine Works**, just off the new highway on the northeast approach to Mandeville. You can't miss its red bauxite "lake" at the foot of Shooter's Hill. This was Jamaica's first alumina plant (completed in 1957, although mining began in 1952) and is still the country's largest.

Alcan (more properly, the Canadian Aluminum Corporation) is the largest of four multinational firms in Jamaica. The other three are American: Alcoa, Kaiser and Reynolds. Between them, they annually claim well over 10 million tons of bauxite from Jamaican soil.

Bauxite is an iron-rich mineral containing approximately 50 percent aluminum oxide. Commercially exploitable bauxite lies close to the earth's surface: thus it is mined in open pits. The ore is then transported to a processing plant, where it is crushed, washed,

Dangerous territory for goats.

kiln-dried, powdered, and shipped to another factory for refining into alumina. This product is ultimately smelted into aluminum. Four to 6 tons of bauxite ore will yield a single ton of aluminum.

Most of the valley northeast of Mandeville belongs to Alcan. This includes **Shooter's Hill**; at its peak is the tomb of Alexander Woodburn Heron, the original owner of the property. Heron's tomb and an adjacent lookout are preserved by Alcan. The view across the island is fantastic: on clear days, Blue Mountain Peak, 60 miles (100 km) to the east, is easily seen.

Another attraction at the base of Shooter's Hill is of more interest to gourmets. At the crossroads where Route B4, B5 and B6 converge is the famous **Pickapepper factory**. This sauce, which is sold throughout the world, is similar to Worcestershire Sauce. Jamaicans insist it is much tastier.

Proceeding north on B5, the road passes through **Walderston**, founded by a Moravian missionary who bought the land and sold it in parcels to free slaves. His descendants still live in the village. The road continues through lovely mountain vegetation to the **Villa Bella** hotel, and on to **Christiana**, a trading center for ginger, bananas, Irish potatoes, and other hill-country crops. You can return to Mandeville via **Mile Gully**, notable for its lovely early 19th-century church, and **Grove Place**, site of the island's largest livestock breeding research station.

South to the coast: From Mandeville, there is easy access to Jamaica's south coast. Start west, via Route A2. At the top of a steep descent down **Spur Tree Hill**, turn into the Alpart (Aluminum Partners of Jamaica) Farm's parking lot and gaze across a 2,000-ft (610-meter) dropoff into eastern St Elizabeth parish. Directly in front of you are the Malvern Hills. To your right or north, lie the peat-rich swamps of the Black River, the ganja-rich plains of Elim, and the rum-rich Appleton Estate. To your left, or south, is the world's largest open-field bauxite mine at Nain. While it is an eyesore in the daytime, it turns into a

Country bus at Alligator Pond.

veritable fairyland of lights at night.

The steep descent to appropriately named **Gutters** has seemingly endless hairpin bends. But tiny cookshops selling "curry goat" line the route, providing energy to continue. Turn south at Gutters and proceed through Downs to Alligator Pond on the south coast. (Another route from Mandeville winds through Newport, Rudds Corner and Plowden Hill to Alligator Pond).

Alligator Pond is a quiet fishing village, outside the influence of the tourist industry. The early-morning fish market attracts mainly local people, and the proliferation of bars caters primarily to fishermen. Accommodation is limited to a few small cottages.

An 18-mile (29-km) dirt road follows the Long Bay coastline through Gut River to Milk River. The latter portion of the route is almost impassable without a four-wheel-drive vehicle. Vegetation along the rutted road changes from tall grass and palms to treeless rocks and cacti. It seems more like Africa than the Caribbean. But the ancient Arawaks must have found the terrain hospitable, for numerous artifacts and rock carvings have been found here.

The road passes close to **God's Well**, a 160-ft (49-meter) deep limestone sinkhole with clear turquoise water. It was named by a man who claimed to have been cured of a terminal illness by bathing in its waters.

The chief attraction of this coastline is the colony of manatees which make it their home. At **Canoe Valley**, local conservationists will meet your car and guide you to a lookout. The manatee, sometimes called "sea cow," is a sluggish marine vegetarian that frequents shallow coastal waters and estuaries. Adults range from 8–15 ft (3–5 meters) in length, and attain weights up to 1,500 pounds (680 kg). Once common throughout the Caribbean, man has hunted this seal-like mammal for its meat, hide and fat until it has become rare. You may be lucky enough to see a family of manatees. They neither see nor hear well, so they communicate primarily by nuzzling one another.

Below, bulldozing for bauxite. Right, bauxite-rich earth near Mandeville.

238

THE COUNTY OF CORNWALL

Cornwall and its English namesake have at least one thing in common: a beautiful seacoast setting. But while Cornwall in the United Kingdom is a land of rocky terrain, frequent rain and sea mists, Cornwall in Jamaica is one of the Caribbean's foremost centers for tourism, sugar and rum production.

Montego Bay and its immediate surroundings attract a seemingly endless invasion of sun seekers to their sandy beaches. Direct flights connect major cities on North America's east coast with Montego Bay and its famed hotel strip. Exclusive restaurants and night clubs, and endless daytime recreational opportunities, keep visitors returning year after year. Off the beaches, old legends like that of the White Witch of Rose Hall blend with newer sensations like the Reggae Sunfest festival to give the north coast of Cornwall a flavor all of its own (Sunsplash has been relocated to Kingston, and Sunfest has taken its place in MoBay).

At the western point of Cornwall county, and indeed of the entire island of Jamaica, is Negril Beach, the most popular destination for young ganja-smoking, nude-bathing foreigners. A journey through south Cornwall leads from here through the sugar estates of the Westmoreland Plain around Savanna-la-Mar and Frome, into the hill country with its old German settlement of Seaford Town, past the lovely beaches of Bluefields Bay to the fishing town of Black River, into rum-making and ganja-growing country north of Santa Cruz, and finally to the tranquility of Lover's Leap and Treasure Beach, far from the beaten tourist track.

Five parishes comprise Cornwall county: St Elizabeth and Westmoreland in the south; Hanover, St James and Trelawny in the north. The isolated reaches of the fabled Cockpit Country, parts of which remain unexplored even today, comprise a large percentage of Trelawny and parts of both St James and St Elizabeth. This strong-hold of the Maroon culture maintains an autonomy from the rest of Jamaica. It is the most traditional and to many the most fascinating part of an amazing country.

Preceding pages: Rose Hall Great House. **Left**, the popular Doctor's Cave Beach, Montego Bay.

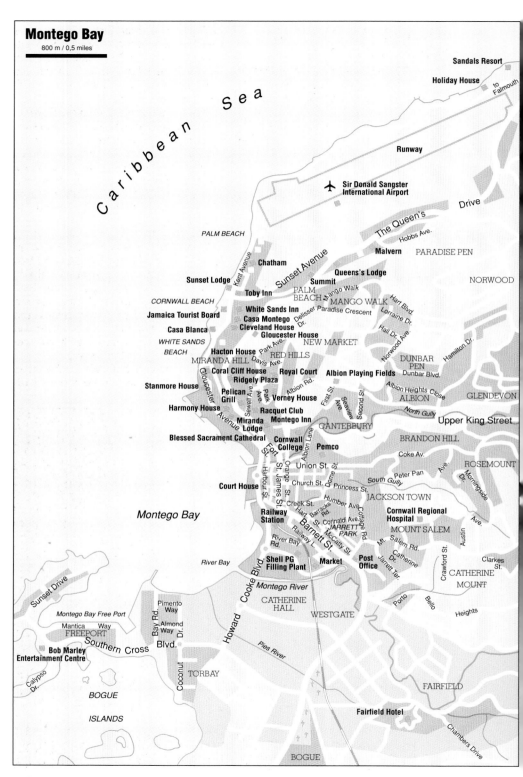

Montego Bay

800 m / 0,5 miles

Caribbean Sea

Sandals Resort

Holiday House

to Falmouth

Runway

✈ Sir Donald Sangster
International Airport

The Queen's Drive

Hobbs Ave.

PALM BEACH

Malvern

PARADISE PEN

Chatham

Queens's Lodge

Sunset Avenue

NORWOOD

Sunset Lodge

Kent Avenue

Summit

Mango Walk

CORNWALL BEACH

Toby Inn

PALM
BEACH

MANGO WALK

Hart Blvd

Jamaica Tourist Board

White Sands Inn

Delisser Paradise Crescent

Lorraine Dr.

Casa Montego

Dr.

Casa Blanca

Cleveland House

Hall Dr.

WHITE SANDS
BEACH

Gloucester House

NEW MARKET

Hacton House

Park Ave.

Norwood Ave.

Hamilton Dr.

MIRANDA HILL

Davis Ave.

RED HILLS

DUNBAR
PEN

Coral Cliff House

Royal Court

Albion Playing Fields

Dunbar Blvd.

Stanmore House

Ridgely Plaza

Albion Rd.

Albion Heights Close

GLENDEVON

Gloucester Avenue

Pelican
Grill

Park Ave.

Sewell Ave.

Verney House

First St.

Seaview Ave.

Second St.

ALBION

Harmony House

Racquet Club

North Gully

Upper King Street

Miranda
Lodge

Montego Inn

CANTERBURY

BRANDON HILL

Blessed Sacrament Cathedral

Fort St.

Cornwall
College

Albion Lane

Pemco

Coke Av.

ROSEMOUNT

Orange St.

Union St.

Dome St.

Peter Pan

Ave.

Morningside Dr.

Montego Bay

Court House

Harbour St.

St. James St.

Church St.

Princess St.

South Gully

JACKSON TOWN

Cornwall Regional
Hospital

Ave.

Railway
Station

Creek St.

Humber Ave.

Cottage Rd.

MOUNT SALEM

Austin

Barnett St.

Hart

Barracks Rd.

Corinaldi Ave.

JARRETT
PARK

McCatty St.

Mt. Salem Rd.

Catherine
Dr.

Crawford St.

Clarkes
St.

River Bay
Rd.

Railway L.

River Bay

Shell PG
Filling Plant

Market

Post
Office

Jarrett Ter.

CATHERINE
MOUNT

Sunset Drive

Montego River

Howard Cooke Blvd

CATHERINE
HALL

WESTGATE

Porto

Bello

Heights

Montego Bay Free Port

Pimento
Way

Bay Rd.

Almond
Way

Coconut Dr.

Pies River

FAIRFIELD

Mantica Way

FREEPORT

Southern Cross Blvd.

Bob Marley
Entertainment Centre

Calypso
Dr.

TORBAY

BOGUE

ISLANDS

Fairfield Hotel

Chambers Drive

BOGUE

DOWN THE WAY AT MONTEGO BAY

In many ways, **Montego Bay** and its north coast suburbs are the least Jamaican part of Jamaica – an "Independent Republic of Montego Bay" built almost exclusively around the annual invasion of hundreds of thousands of international sun worshippers.

The phenomenon has resulted in a riotous clash of cultures where young men with their hair in dreadlocks walk arm-in-arm with visiting co-eds; where Chicago businessmen chat up bikini-clad Jamaican girls; where retired couples chase goats off the golf greens before putting; where waistcoated waiters serve champagne and caviar in plush hilltop restaurants overlooking valleys of wooden shacks and poverty. It's all relatively new, but it is nevertheless somehow suitably off-beat to make it typically Jamaican.

Other than Kingston, Montego Bay is Jamaica's only city, a helter-skelter de-velopment without distinct boundaries that has slowly swallowed up the coast-line as far east as Rose Hall, as far west as the Tryall Club, and as far north into the Caribbean as sailboats, windsurfers and jet-skis will take you.

This is all tourist territory. Beyond, Jamaica itself slowly resurfaces in such historic places as Falmouth and Lucea and in typical small towns like Green Island, Anchovy and Duncans. Thus, visitors can spend daytime hours exploring Jamaica – and return home to the "independent republic" of Montego Bay at night.

Bay of butter: To modern visitors, **Montego Bay** means soft beaches, transparent waters, exotic living. To the first European visitors, it meant lard. Historians believe the word "montego" evolved from *manteca,* Spanish for lard or butter. Early Spanish occupants used the bay for shipping fat from wild and domesticated pigs and cattle. Now most people simply call it MoBay.

Christopher Columbus anchored in the bay, a crescent of beach that rolls

Riding the wind over Montego Bay.

into gentle hills, during his first visit to Jamaica in 1494. He found Arawak villages onshore; there are stories that claim Columbus recruited one of the Indians as a crew member. But the Spanish did not establish a settlement here until about 1655.

Ten years after that, the British established the parish of St James, named for King James II, but settlers trickled in slowly during the latter part of the 17th and early 18th centuries. Potential residents feared the bay's vulnerability to attacks from pirates and from Maroons living in the nearby Cockpit Country. But by 1773, Montego Bay boasted the island's only newspaper outside Kingston, the *Cornwall Chronicle*, and it even had a regular theatrical season, making it a respectable center for the north coast's aristocracy.

Fires destroyed chunks of the town in 1795 and 1811. And "Daddy" Sam Sharpe led area slaves in revolt during the winter of 1831–32. British authorities reacted by hanging him in The Parade on May 23, 1832, and by murdering an estimated 500 of his followers. Then, MoBay lapsed into a period of decline until the seeds of its tourist industry were planted around the turn of the 20th century.

The feature that made Montego Bay's future, **Doctor's Cave Beach**, still draws the tourists of today. The beach took its name from Dr Alexander McCatty, who owned it and turned it into a semi-public bathing club in 1906. A small nearby cave no longer exists. Another doctor, British osteopath Sir Herbert Baker, further heightened the allure of the beach in the 1920s by claiming its waters could cure a variety of ailments. You pay a small fee for use of the beach and its facilities.

The subsequent development of a series of hotels along Kent and Gloucester avenues have created MoBay's **Strip**, a scaled-down version of Waikiki or Miami Beach.

Arriving in MoBay: Most travelers get their first look at Montego Bay from the window of an airplane and many never see much more of the island than this. **19th-century Montego Bay.**

Sir Donald Sangster International Airport serves destinations in the United States, Europe and the rest of the Caribbean, and has connections to Kingston's Norman Manley International Airport. The loveliest drive into MoBay is west up **Queen's Drive**, which skirts the cliff above the beach strip.

Queen's Drive bends back down **Miranda Hill** past the remnants of **Fort Montego**. Three of its 17 original cannons remain pointed seaward. Its massive powder magazine lies landward. No one is sure when the fort was built, but historians first described it in 1752.

Fort Montego's contribution to the struggle for power in the Caribbean was negligible. It only fired its guns twice: once to celebrate the surrender of Havana (a defective cannon exploded and killed a gunner); and the second time in 1795 when local soldiers fired at what they believed to be a French privateer entering the harbor. They missed, fortunately. The privateer turned out to be a British ship.

At the roundabout you can swing back north along Gloucester Avenue to the Strip beaches. To the south, the roads converge into **St James Street**, the main thoroughfare through town. It leads to the inevitable town square. Formerly known as Charles Square and The Parade, it is now called **Sam Sharpe Square**.

The square is a miniature version of The Parade in Kingston, a jumble of tacky new buildings and crumbling old structures, dusted by fumes from automobiles and buses. In its northwest corner is an attractive little building called **The Cage**. As its name implies, it was once used for imprisoning runaway slaves, and (in those bad old days) any blacks found on the streets after 3pm on Sunday were considered runaways. The Cage dates to 1806.

At the corner of Union and East streets is another reminder of that grim era, **The Slave Ring**, a decaying stone amphitheater once believed to have been used as a slave market and later the scene of cockfights.

Church Street, which crosses St

The Richmond Hill Hotel.

James Street west of the square, has a fine old plantation house now the Town House Restaurant at No. 16. **St James Parish Church** rises opposite it on Church and St Claver streets. Built from limestone, the church is a fine example of modified Georgian architecture. Its foundation stone was laid in 1775. Artist James Hakewill described it as "the handsomest church in the island" at that period.

The elegant monuments inside include a tribute to Rosa Palmer sculpted by Britain's John Bacon, who also executed the Rodney Memorial in Spanish Town. The lady draped over the urn has faint purple markings in the marble around her neck and nostrils which have contributed to the theory that Rosa Palmer may have actually been the legendary, but probably fictional "White Witch of Rose Hall" who murdered many husbands and lovers until she was strangled by a slave.

Poverty and elegance: For a good view of Montego Bay and a startling look at the gap between its affluent visitors and poor residents, take Church Street back to Union then head east up the steep hill to the rather sophisticated **Richmond Hill Hotel**.

To see a rather different style of life, peek into the valley called **Canterbury** which is not very well hidden by the stone wall in the parking lot. Thousands of small wooden dwellings cling precariously to a hillside devoid of paved streets and other modern amenities. Here live many of the poorly-paid personnel who wait on you in hotels and restaurants and try to sell you souvenirs along the streets of MoBay.

Their ramshackle homes are made from plywood, cardboard, corrugated tin, concrete and any other building materials that the residents can lay their hands on. The steady din of life hovers above the whole surrealistic scene. Yet you're only steps away from the comfort and Old World elegance of Richmond Hill Hotel, formerly the 18th-century Spanish-style residence of a local plantation owner.

Back down Union Street, take Dome

MoBay crafts market.

Street to its junction with Creek Street. The small, unimportant-looking structure in the intersection is called **The Dome**. In the 18th century it controlled distribution of the small river called **The Creek**, once the main source of water for MoBay. Its architectural style might be called "Creek Orthodox," reminiscent of the white domes that litter the far off isles of Greece.

Reggae Sunsplash: Continue east on Humber Avenue around the corner to Cottage Park Road. Behind the wall west of the road lies **Jarrett Park**, once the home of the world's biggest reggae music festival, Reggae Sunsplash, now relocated to Kingston. Sunsplash is a marvelous concept that brings mainly young people of all creeds and colors together for a week-long celebration of Jamaican life and rhythms, which usually takes place around the first week in August.

MoBay offers a variety of day and nightlife. When you finish para-sailing above coral waters, dance to the latest reggae and funk at **Disco Inferno** (in the shopping center across from the Holiday Inn) or at the aptly-named **Cave** at the Seawind Resort in Freeport. Here you bend down to enter a dark catacomb of a dance hall, where you pay for your drinks with tiny plastic bananas that you can snap together and string around your neck.

Haggling with higglers: Harbour Street's wharves still hum with activity when fishermen come ashore with their daily catch, and MoBay still ships its share of fruit, produce and other goods from the port area.

The local **Crafts Market** is located along Harbor Street, where you can haggle over prices for souvenirs, Bob Marley T-shirts, or fruit from a higgler's head basket and even have your hair turned into a mass of African-style braids and beads.

To look at a genuine Jamaican market, however, head for the **Fustic Street Market** off Barnett Street, where women higglers reign supreme. The practice dates back to early colonial times when slaves brought their sales

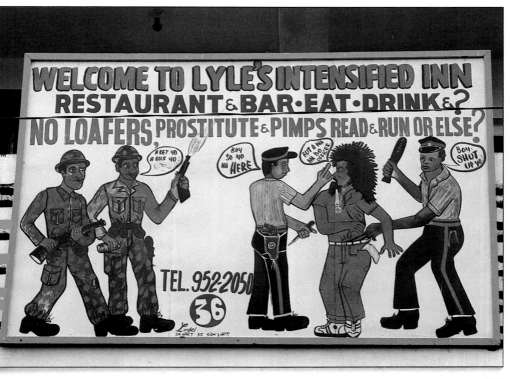

Targeting the market in MoBay.

practices from West Africa. Here, as in Africa, the "Market Mammy" is an important person.

Markets first bloomed on the sugar estates or at busy crossroads where slaves and free persons alike met to trade and barter. Each slave received a plot of land for cultivation. What he didn't eat, he traded. Some also crafted baskets or *bankras,* clay bowls called *yabbas,* and "jackass rope," tobacco twisted and rolled into long ropes to make it easier to carry while traveling.

The men usually did the cultivating and manufacturing. The women became salespeople. They controlled the money. Often, the peasant women walked as many as 20 miles (32 km) loaded with goods to sell at the market. Today, higglers remain the queens of the trade. The young ones dress in contemporary fashions, but the older women cling to the age-old uniform of a large apron with huge pockets worn over a dress. They wear head ties and keep their money buried in their bosoms in cloth "threadbags."

It's a tough life. Higglers have developed a reputation for being loud and quarrelsome. But approach them with a smile and a query, and you will find that most warm up to you quickly. They are certainly not shy.

Route A1 east of Montego follows Queen's Drive past another shanty village and an airport runway. The junction turns left to **Sandals Montego Bay**, another of the popular all-inclusive complexes where one price buys all accommodations, entertainment, food and beverage. Only couples are allowed into Sandals, so don't try to get in with your children.

Further east lie more hotels, from the inevitable **Holiday Inn** to the plush **Half-Moon Club**. Considered to be one of the island's top three hotels, the Half-Moon takes its name from the shape of its perfect beach. It has 360 acres (146 hectares) of gardens and manicured lawns, its own championship golf course which was designed by Robert Trent Jones, tennis courts, saunas and prices to match.

Rose Hall Great House.

250

The White Witch of Rose Hall: Looming mightily on a ridge just east of the Half-Moon is one of Jamaica's premier attractions, **Rose Hall Great House**. Drive up the road and pay the stiff admission charge for a look at this plantation house built about 1770 by John Palmer, when he served as the *custos* (queen's representative) of the parish of St James. It was restored by American millionaire John Rollins, who was a former governor of Delaware.

In Rose Hall Rollins and his wife have attempted to recreate the typical grandeur of an 18th-century plantation house. Its antiques and art treasures are museum-quality pieces dating to the 17th century.

Still, Rose Hall's trappings and restoration remain overshadowed by its famous legend. One of the many versions says Annie was an English woman tutored in the black arts of voodoo by a Haitian priestess. She came to Jamaica and supposedly, at age 18, married John Palmer. Three years later, Palmer died, reportedly poisoned by the petite and pretty but sadistic Annie. She later stabbed a second husband to death and strangled a third. The legend also says that she took slaves as lovers and murdered them when she got bored. Finally, the slaves rebelled and murdered Annie in her bed in 1833.

Naturally, Rose Hall is now said to be haunted by the ghost of the "White Witch," Annie Palmer.

The legend makes a great story, but probably is more fictional than factual. There *was* an Annie Palmer at Rose Hall. But she wasn't English, she had only one husband, and she died a respected citizen in 1846. Rosa Palmer of Rose Hall did have Irish connections and four husbands. But she kept the last one for 23 years. In fact it was he who buried her at the age of 72 in the Montego Bay churchyard.

A side road leads from the main road past the right corner of Rose Hall to the walled burial ground of the Moulton Barrett family, 200 yards (183 meters) below the 19th-century Great House. The Barrett family, which produced

Modest dwelling near Rose Hall.

poetess Elizabeth Barrett Browning, lived in the **Cinnamon Hill Great House** further up the road. The latter has since been modernized and restored, and purchased by American country-and-western star Johnny Cash. Cash and his family make yearly visits to his Jamaican hideaway, although it is a hard place to go unnoticed. Cash has become a valued patron of the Montego Bay SOS Children's Village, which provides family-type homes for destitute and abandoned children.

Route A1 continues east past souvenir stands which are chockablock with conch shells to reach yet another mansion. **Greenwood Great House** was also built by the Barrett family between 1780 and 1800. It's now owned and operated by Bob and Ann Betton. Its antiques include the largest collection of rare musical instruments in the western hemisphere.

The next major town, **Falmouth**, virtually dates *in toto* from the time the famous Barrett family of Cinnamon Hill roamed Jamaica. It was developed as a sugar port during a period of wealth and good taste – the end of the 18th century. The good taste is reflected in its broad streets and well-built stone and wooden houses.

The Georgian heritage here is better preserved than elsewhere on the island. The greatest concentration of Georgian buildings is on **Market Street**, west of the central **Water Square** with its small ornamental fountain.

The **Post Office** has a well-balanced upper window pattern that sits boldly on a support of semicircular arches. At the bottom of the street is the **Methodist Manse**, built in 1799 by the Barretts, a stone-and-wood house with elegant wrought-iron balconies and fine Adam-style doorways and friezes.

Adjacent to Water Square is the 1815-era **Courthouse**, one of the finest Georgian buildings in Jamaica despite a poor restoration attempt after a fire in 1926. A double exterior staircase leads up to a portico with a pediment supported by four doric columns. The building now houses the offices of the town council.

Left, north coast artist. **Below**, Falmouth Square.

On leaving town via Upper Harbor Street, you pass by the 1801 **Phoenix Foundary**, one of Jamaica's earliest iron works.

Like Port Antonio in the east, Falmouth has its rafting river, the **Martha Brae**. There's a **Rafter's Village** a mile upriver at the neck of an oxbow in the stream. It has a restaurant, bar, and boutiques. The trip downriver takes 1½ hours; you will be driven back to the village afterwards.

East of Falmouth on Route A1, there is a phosphorescent lagoon at **Rock**. At night, microscopic organisms glisten when the water is agitated with a stick or a stone. **Glistening Waters** seafood restaurant in front of the lagoon serves good fresh food at reasonable prices. **Fisherman's Law**, the small hotel next door, caters to divers and deep sea fishermen. You can charter deep-sea fishing boats here to try your luck at catching a marlin, kingfish, wahoo or barracuda. Or take the dive boat and explore the off-shore reefs.

An impressive ruin, **Stewart Castle**, can be reached a mile up a dirt road from the main highway past Rock. The structure appears to be a large home that was fortified with thick stone walls perforated with musket and cannonade firing slits. It appears to date from the early 18th century when large landowners constructed such dwellings to protect themselves from attacks by Maroons, slaves or pirates. Designated as a national monument, Stewart Castle is slated for renovation.

At **Silver Sands**, an excellent beach cottage colony, you can head south up Route B10 for a look at the **Long Pond Sugar Factory and Distillery**, where Jamaica's famous Gold Label Rum is manufactured.

Then head back west at **Clark's Town** on Route B11, or continue south to Duanvale and Sherwood Content on the fringes of the almost inaccessible **Cockpit Country**. The latter is discussed in more detail in the following chapter.

West of MoBay: West of MoBay, a spur road off A1 leads to a shopping complex designed to cater for passengers who spill out of passing cruise ships. Its products are in-bond (duty-free) as well as out-of-bond. Beyond are the twin towers of the **Sea-wind Hotel** complex and a yacht marina.

West of **Reading** is a junction with a road that jogs across the island to Savanna-la-Mar on the south coast. The road climbs up **Long Hill**, providing views over town and coast. Two miles up, a signpost indicates the route to Rock Pleasant. A bird sanctuary owned by Lisa Salmon is half a mile along this route.

Bird-watchers carrying their bird society cards are welcome all day, but for the general public **Rocklands** bird feeding starts daily at 3pm. Miss Salmon, who insists that Rocklands is a "bird-feeding station" as opposed to a sanctuary, calls many of the feathered visitors by name. Even the skittish doctor birds are so tame they feed from your hand here. Miss Salmon established the station in 1958.

The road continues to **Anchovy**, then to the town of **Montpelier**, center of the local dairy and beef cattle industry. The

Country dominoes match.

road's right-hand fork proceeds to Savanna-la-Mar via Ramble.

West on A1 beyond Reading, the scene is graced by some large and elegant homes, many owned by wealthy winter visitors. Shortly after crossing the parish boundary into Hanover at **Great River**, round, beehive-like gate-posts on the right seaward side indicate the location of the **Round Hill Hotel**, one of the most exclusive and expensive in Jamaica. It is also one of the most beautiful, enjoying an incomparable setting on its own private beach. A list of guest names over the years resembles *Who's Who* and includes rock star Paul McCartney and US Senator Edward Kennedy. Fashion designer Ralph Lauren of "Polo" fame owns the estate west of Round Hill.

Sugar and golf at Tryall: Four miles (7 km) later on the left is the magnificent **Tryall Water Wheel** and ruins. The wheel is still turned by water carried via aqueduct from the **Flint River**. Its brick chimney was rebuilt in 1834 after the old sugar works were destroyed during

Tryall Water Wheel.

the rebellion of 1831. The water wheel turned the single three-roll crushing mill. In the old days, the mill could also be turned by means of wind power (the island is dotted with old sugar towers which carried sails), animal power or even human power. On the right is the picturesque Tryall championship golf course. Above on the hill is the small but exclusive Tryall Hotel.

Beyond **Sandy Bay** are perhaps the finest sugar-estate ruins in Jamaica, **Kenilworth Estate**. The sugar factory buildings, which are located a mile south of the main road, were built on a far grander scale and more durably than the adjacent Great House. The first block is the sugar mill, with long, deep, rectangular housing for the water wheel (which probably looked like the one at Tryall). The two-story building is beautifully constructed of limestone in two different shades, with oval Palladian windows trimmed in light stone and an arched front doorway reached by a semicircular flight of steps.

The second block, the sugar-boiling

house and distillery, is in the form of a long central room with two wings. The sloped hillside accommodates the furnaces on a lower level.

About 25 miles (40 km) beyond Montego Bay is the quiet little town of **Lucea**, administrative center of Hanover parish. Once a busy port for the shipment of sugar, its economy now is based around bananas and molasses. Pimento, ginger and yams grown in the surrounding districts are also important products. The new town center was dedicated by Queen Elizabeth II during her 1966 visit to Jamaica. Lucea's 19th-century **Courthouse** is an attractive stone and wood structure with a clock tower supported by columns in Corinthian style.

Fort Charlotte, behind the school and the Public Works Department, is another Jamaican fort which never actually fired a cannonball in anger. Named after George III's queen, this octagonal structure had ports for 20 guns; three remain. It commands a lovely little turquoise harbor.

Backtrack to the main road which continues west in and out of little nooks like **Cousins Cove**, **Davis Cove** and **Negro Bay**. A paved road from Davis Cove leads 2 miles (3 km) inland to **Blenheim**, birthplace of national hero and Jamaica's first prime minister, Alexander Bustamante, who came from relatively humble origins. Bustamante's father, Robert Clarke, was an overseer on the Blenheim Estate. His famous son was born in the overseer's home at Blenheim. The house has latterly been reconstructed on its original site as a national monument.

The next town on the main road is misleadingly-named **Green Island**, with a fishing-village flavor and an old Presbyterian chapel. There are several important transport junctions in Green Island with roads that spiderweb up into the hills toward Savanna-la-Mar. Beyond it, Route A1 cuts a steady course down the coast to Jamaica's center of hedonism, **Negril**, which is dealt with in detail in the chapter *Negril and South Cornwall*.

Damp Scamper (below,) and passing the time in Green Island (right).

CONQUERING THE COCKPIT COUNTRY

One of the most mysterious and intriguing blemishes in the Jamaican landscape is the Cockpit Country, a potholed limestone plateau that cuts into its mountainous surroundings like a missing piece from a giant jigsaw puzzle. It's a land that looks much like it did when mighty Maroon warriors first staked their claim some four centuries ago.

A four-wheel-drive vehicle will take you only along its outer fringes. The best view of the eerie landscape is from an airplane or helicopter. Otherwise, you must mount a small expedition and hike into the Cockpit Country.

Maroon Town, on the northwestern edge of the Cockpit Country, is as good as any to begin a brief automobile tour of the surroundings. Maroons settled here a long time ago, but no longer live in the village.

A side road off the main track slices through banana plantations to **Flagstaff**, formerly a Maroon settlement called Trelawny Town.

You must backtrack to the main road from here, then head south past Elderslie where a sign will point to the Maroon capital of the Cockpit Country, **Accompong**. The village is scattered over several miles, but has a square flanked by shops, a church and a school. Cudjoe Day is celebrated here on January 6.

Backtrack again to the main road. It dead-ends in the town of **Quick Step**, in the **District of Look Behind**. You can swing back west again on Route B11 to **Sherwood Content**. A side road here darts back into the Cockpits from here to **Windsor Cave**.

The cave's first two chambers can be easily negotiated. Step carefully through the layers of "rat bat" manure. More advanced spelunkers will find the cave plunges to uncharted depths.

Beyond Sherwood Content and Windsor Cave, much of the Cockpit Country is said to remain unexplored. Ask around, and you might find someone to take you there.

NEGRIL AND SOUTH CORNWALL

Beaches and sugar: these are the main calling cards of southern Cornwall county. But lest the visitor be misled, the county offers much more. The parishes of Westmoreland and St Elizabeth also feature mountains, swamps, the island's longest river, an avenue lined with bamboo, major agricultural and industrial areas, and important historical sites.

Chances are you'll start your wanderings at **Negril's** famous 7-mile (11-km) beach, Jamaica's westernmost escape – a home for hedonism and bacchanalia, a nook for nude bathing, sun and sin.

But Negril is not restricted to swinging singles and hippies. More than any other resort area in Jamaica, accommodation here ranges over all levels of price and quality. Hotels stretch along the full length of the lovely beach, interspersed with local homes, fishermen's huts, patches of indigenous flora,

stretches of coconut trees and even some deserted sand. Local residents mix with the tourist population in a manner not possible elsewhere.

Food shops are almost infinite in number and variety, ranging from small "supper shops" selling hot pepper-fried fish and hard-dough bread, to establishments like "Miss Brown's" specializing in psilocybin (hallucinogenic) mushroom omelets; to higher-class seafood restaurants. Clothing varies as well, from none at all (a not-uncommon sight on Negril Beach), to shapeless, unisex flourbag pants and tops, to sophisticated dress in the resort's better hotels and eating spots.

There are many fascinating places to dine and sleep. Rita Hojan's **Sundowner Inn** is a quiet hideout to which artist Norman Rockwell often fled. The **Rock House** consists of a series of thatch-roofed, clifftop bungalows with a birds-eye view of waves crashing against the rugged shoreline. The **Awaeemaway** offers water beds and hammocks, free bananas, a communal kitchen – but no

Preceding pages: diving near Negril. *Left*, pepper shrimp higglers from Middlequarters. *Below*, Negril beach boys.

electricity. At **Rick's Cafe**, diners come not only for the seafood – fish chowder, river perch, red snapper and lobster – but for spectacular sunsets and to see local youths diving 100 ft (30 meters) from the clifftop into the crystal water below. Beyond is the **Negril Lighthouse** near South Negril Point; west of here is nothing but 600 miles (970 km) of ocean to the Yucatan.

Negril's most famous inn is **Hedonism II**, which offers all-inclusive weeklong holidays at reasonable rates. Scuba diving and snorkeling, sailing and parasailing, windsurfing and waterskiing, volleyball and horseback riding are part of the daily activities.

Hedonism II (formerly the Negril Beach Village) is located on a 22-acre (9-hectare) resort fronting **Long Bay**. Next to it is the up-market **Grand Lido**, on **Bloody Bay**, where pirate "Calico Jack" Rackham and his colleagues Anne Bonney and Mary Read were captured in 1720. Bloody Bay was not named for the pirates, though. It got its name from passing whalers who disemboweled their catch here, leaving the waters red with blood.

One of the best ways to see Negril's waters is by Polynesian catamaran. The 40-ft *Reggae II* leaves the harbor daily at 4 pm for a sunset party cruise along Long Bay's beautiful cliffs. At the northern end of the bay, is **Booby Cay**, a small island used for filming scenes in the movie version of Jules Verne's *20,000 Leagues Under the Sea*. The awkward booby, a species of gannet, flies to these cays to breed.

On the east side of the Negril Beach road is the **Great Morass** of Westmoreland. It is the habitat of an interesting variety of rare birds and plants. Explore it by airboat: the *Swamp Dragon* skims across the bog between 9 am and 5 pm daily.

The Petroleum Corporation of Jamaica is conducting experiments in extracting peat from beneath the water of the Morass. More than 7,000 acres (2,800 hectares) of peat here form a potentially valuable asset for Jamaica's future. Scientists are concerned, however, that

Left, Rick's Cafe scene. **Below**, need an oil change?

unless the peat can be extracted without harming the swamp's valuable vegetation, the local ecology might be so severely damaged that the entire region could become a wasteland of stagnant water. At the moment, the Morass is like a giant sponge, holding water from the mountains to the east, releasing it a little at a time into the sea.

Through canefields to Savanna-la-Mar: The highway east from Negril crosses several miles of swampland before emerging onto the vast Westmoreland Plain with its miles of canefields and pastureland.

At **New Hope Estate**, note the fanciful 1920s oriental gateways. Then continue to **Little London**, which is nothing like its British namesake. In fact, many feel it would be best renamed "Little Southall" (an Indian-dominated area of west London) for the numbers of East Indians who make it their home. Descendants of indentured laborers who were transported from South Asia to Jamaica after the abolition of slavery in the mid-19th century, many of these

Indians still work in the sugar industry.

The capital and chief city of Westmoreland parish is **Savanna-la-Mar**, best known as "Sav-la-Mar" or just "Sav" meaning literally "the plain by the sea." That plain has not always been kind to the town. Since its establishment in 1703, it has been devastated by hurricanes in 1748 and 1912, and by a tidal wave in 1780. The 20th-century storm left a schooner stranded in the middle of **Great George Street** – with the crew still aboard.

Great George Street is the longest city street in Jamaica. At its seaward end is the **Old Fort**, the surviving stone walls of which form a swimming and bathing pool for locals. Further up the same street is the **Courthouse**, with its ornate cast-iron drinking fountain dating from the 19th century. Note the admonition on all four sides of the fountain to "keep the pavement dry."

Savanna-la-Mar was established as a sugar port, and that is still its most important function. The bustling wharf is near the end of Great George Street,

Hot limbo at Hedonism II.

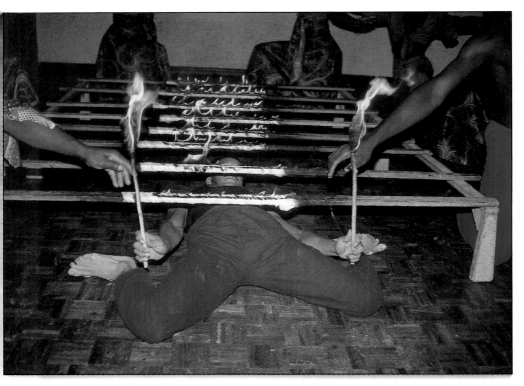

next to the Old Fort. Watch as raw brown sugar is loaded onto barges and carried to ships, to be transported to refineries abroad.

Most of the sugar comes from factories around **Frome**, 6 miles (10 km) north of Sav-la-Mar on Route B9 toward Lucea. The **Frome Central Sugar Factory** processes cane from estates throughout Westmoreland and Hanover parishes.

Sugar-coated riots: Sugar cane is in fact a type of grass that grows to 10 ft (3 meters) or more in height. Inside the hard rind of its stalk is a soft sugary fiber. Between mid-November and June, this cane is harvested and transported by truck or rail to the mill. Here, a double series of rollers crushes out the juice, containing about 13 percent pure sugar. At first a cloudy green in color, this cane juice is then clarified, evaporated and separated in centrifugal machines into golden sugar crystals and cane molasses. One of the eventual end products of the molasses, of course, is Jamaica's famed rum.

In 1938, Frome was the site of riots which led to the rise of Alexander Bustamante as a national labor leader. The sugar mill, then the largest West Indies Sugar Company plant in the country, had just been built. Thousands of unemployed Jamaicans converged on Frome hoping to find work, but were turned away. Police were called in to quell the property destruction and canefield burning that ensued. The disorder spread to other parts of Jamaica, and led to the formation of the island's first lasting unions and political parties linked with those unions.

Not far from Frome, at the Shrewsbury Estate, is the source of the **Roaring River**. Seemingly from nowhere, the river emerges in full flow from a subterranean course. Swimmers, spelunkers and picnickers enjoy the strange phenomenon and its beautiful surroundings.

East of Savanna-la-Mar, Route A2 meanders cross-country for 123 miles (198 km) before reaching its terminus in Spanish Town. Five miles (8 km) from

Seaford Town inhabitants.

Sav-la-Mar, at **Ferris Cross**, is **Paradise Park**, a 1,000-acre (400-hectare) 18th-century plantation. Book a week in advance, and take a horseback tour of the jungle, cattle ranch, tropical farm, bird sanctuary and botanical garden.

The inland route: Ferris Cross is the junction of Route B8 to Montego Bay. It is also the starting point for an interesting inland tour.

At the hamlet of **Whithorn**, turn right (east) toward **Darliston**. The winding 5-mile (8-km) climb up **Frame Hill** offers grand views across the sugar plains. Darliston itself is a tobacco-growing center where cheap local cigars are a popular purchase.

At **Struie** is a roadside landmark called the **Soldier Stone**. The inscription is almost illegible, but local folklore tells of an infantryman named Obediah Bell Chambers who rode out on muleback to do battle with rebellious slaves and had his head severed. Struie residents returning from market at night often claim to hear the clash of steel as they pass the Soldier Stone.

After passing through another village with the unlikely name of **Rat Trap**, you'll enter **Seaford Town**, the island's best-known German-descended community. In fact, although many of the residents have fair skins, blue eyes and German surnames, they have disappointingly preserved virtually no other traces of their European language or culture. Instead, this is a sadly inbred group of "poor whites."

The Roman Catholic priest of Seaford Town, Father Francis Friesen, will tell you the town's history if you visit his home across the street from the old stone **Sacred Heart Catholic Church**. Friesen, a Dutchman who is compiling a comprehensive history of the town, displays some of the memorabilia he has collected at the **Historical Museum** next to the church.

Seaford Town was founded in 1835 by peasant farmers from northern Germany. Their economy depended at first on sugar cultivation, and later on bananas. As late as the 1960s, the population was close to 500; today it is nearer

Black River market.

200, many have emigrated to Canada.

From Seaford Town, Route B6 continues to Mandeville via Maggotty. There are also easy routes north to Montego Bay and east to the Cockpit Country.

Pirates and fishermen: The route now reverts to Ferris Cross and follows A2 down the south coast to **Bluefields Bay**. It was from this wide curving bay, today popular as a swimming area, that Henry Morgan sailed in 1670 to sack Panama. No remains have been found, but this is believed to have been the site of the early Spanish settlement of Oristan.

At **Bluefields House**, near the Bluefields police station, naturalist Philip Gosse gathered materials for two classic reference books: *Birds of Jamaica* and *A Naturalist's Sojourn in Jamaica*. He lived here for 18 months in 1844 and 1845. A breadfruit tree on the lawn of the house is reputed to be the oldest in Jamaica; Captain Bligh may have anchored his *Providence* in the bay in 1793.

Auchindown Farm has its entrance on the north side of A2 just above Banister Bay. A working pimento property, its grounds include a fascinating ruined castle which rumor says was built to house the deposed Emperor Napoleon. That claim is disputed. The castle was certainly built early in the 19th century by Archibald Campbell, a descendant of the noted Campbell clan of Argyll, Scotland. An underground passage running to the castle from pimento barbecues at Orange Grove may have been used by smugglers.

The main road passes through **Whitehouse** village. Most of the north coast hotels get their supplies of seafood here. Every morning, weather permitting, local fishermen sell their previous night's catch on the beach. It is both cheap and fresh, having been kept overnight on ice taken to sea in the boats.

At **Black River**, you enter the first sizeable town since leaving Sav-la-Mar. The capital of St Elizabeth, it is nevertheless a sleepy settlement strung along the shore of Black River Bay at the

Black River, about 1830.

river's mouth. Many Georgian-style buildings remain from days long past when logwood and fustic – both dye-producing trees – and the ubiquitous sugar gave a strong base to the local economy.

Around the turn of the 20th century, Black River was a bustling port. In 1893, it became the first community on the island to have electric light, generated and sold by two local merchants, the Leyden brothers: and in 1903 there were already motor cars being driven on the streets of town. The **Parish Church of St John the Evangelist** was founded in 1837. The famous **Black River Spa** just outside town has not been maintained, in spite of the therapeutic value of its water; at present, it is little more than a watering hole for animals.

The Black River itself is the longest in Jamaica. It follows a winding course of 44 miles (71 km) from the mountains of southern Trelawny parish. There is good fishing for both freshwater and sea fish on the broadwater which is about a mile from the mouth.

Much of the Black River's lower course takes it through the Great Morass, a huge freshwater swamp that constitutes the largest remaining crocodile refuge in Jamaica. Slaughter by sportsmen and farmers has reduced the croc population to a fraction of what it once was. Two rival companies offer tours of the river, with guides knowledgeable about the flora and fauna.

At the upper end of the Morass, 8 miles (13 km) from Black River, is the little village of **Middlequarters**. If you stop your vehicle here, you'll be set upon by women vendors urging you to try the savory local shrimp. Hot and peppery, these morsels should be taken with some hard-dough bread and a bottle of beer lest the unsuspecting visitor's throat be set on fire.

Close to where A2 crosses the oddly labeled **Y S River** (whose name may have been adapted from the Welsh word *wyess* for "winding"), the **Holland Estate** and sugar factory stand just off the roadside. This small mill, no longer in operation, was once owned by John

Black River "gingerbread" house.

Gladstone, father of the famous Victorian prime minister of Great Britain. Gladstone made his fortune in the colonies, trading out of Liverpool. At Holland a dirt road, left, leads to the starting point of a tractor-drawn jitney ride to the spectacular Y. S. Falls. There are landscaped picnic grounds and stairs cut into the path leading to several levels of the falls. Lifeguards are stationed at all the swimming holes.

A 3-mile (5-km) stretch of road between Holland Estate and Lacovia is known as **Bamboo Avenue**. One of the most-photographed locations in Jamaica, it is easy to see why it is so well-known and loved. Entering the avenue is like walking into a giant cathedral whose nave disappears in the distance. Bamboo was planted on both sides of the road in the 19th century by local landowners appreciative of the shade as they traveled the road. The Hope Botanical Gardens now maintains the bamboo, assisted by local citizens who are swift to raise the alarm if anyone is discovered interfering with the plants.

At the eastern end of Bamboo Avenue is **Lacovia**, one of the longest villages in Jamaica. Divided into West Lacovia, East Lacovia and Lacovia Tombstone, it sprawls along A2 for some 2 miles (3 km) on either side of the Black River bridge. Originally a Jewish settlement, it was an inland port for the shipping of sugar, logwood and fustic downriver.

Logwood and fustic dyes were so important in days before the development of synthetic dyes that even the ermine robes of English Lords were stained in logwood. Although Jamaica's dye factories closed down in the 1950s, recent discoveries indicate that natural dyes are in fact brighter and longer lasting than synthetic ones.

Today, Lacovia is a center for the growing of cashew nuts.

Lacovia Tombstone is so named for two tombs in the middle of the road. Beneath are the bones of two young men, one of them just 15, who died following a tavern brawl in 1723. Tombstone is the junction for a road leading inland to **Maggotty**, where it connects

A bouncy ride down Bamboo Avenue.

with Route B6. Cecil Baugh, one of Jamaica's leading pottery artisans, maintains his workshop in Maggotty, a 7-mile (11-km) excursion.

Reynolds Jamaica Mines have established their **Revere Works** bauxite operation a short distance north of the town. From Maggotty, there is a road heading north to the Maroon village of Accompong in the Cockpit Country. Route B6 heads west to Seaford Town and east through Appleton and Siloah to Mandeville.

Rum and Ganja: Appleton is best known as the home of Jamaica's most famous and popular rum. The **Appleton Sugar Factory and Distillery** is picturesquely located alongside the Black River in a lovely green valley, surrounded by canefields and framed by mountains. It was founded in the 19th Century by a former St Ann wheelwright named John Wray, who acquired his plantation after perfecting his blend of rum in a small shop on a site next to Kingston's Ward Theater.

Route A2, meanwhile, proceeds

Storm clouds over Lover's Leap.

through Lacovia to **Santa Cruz**, St Elizabeth's bustling market center. Traditionally an area of horses and livestock, Santa Cruz once provided mules for all of the British army's garrison troops, as well as for parish councils and public works departments throughout the island. **Gilnock Hall**, just outside the town, still has a polo field in use. Next to the hall is **St Andrew's Church**, an Anglican house of worship built in the 1840s by Duncan Robertson, chief of the Scottish Clan Robertson of Struan.

The **Braes River**, **Elim** and **Barton Isles** districts northeast of Santa Cruz are noted for their prolific ganja farms. Rice and cattle farming, for beef and for dairy products, are more legitimate economic mainstays.

It is another 7 miles (11 km) on A2 from Wilton to Gutters at the Middlesex county line, and another 14 miles (22 km) into Mandeville. At **Goshen**, the Ministry of Agriculture has established a **Dairy Industry Training Center**. In addition to dairy cattle, a special ovine breed known as the St Elizabeth Sheep has been developed here. It lambs twice a year, and while its coat is too hairy to be wool and too woolly to be hair, it may someday form the basis of an unusual new fabric.

A jewel of a beach: Those looking for a south coast beach would be best advised to head for **Treasure Beach**. This out-of-the-way but lovely stretch of sand is an "in" spot for young Jamaicans. It can be reached from Black River via Fullerswood or from Mandeville via Downs, but the most direct approach is from Santa Cruz.

The route is extremely picturesque. It first winds uphill to **Malvern**, an old resort town 2,400 ft (732 meters) up in the Santa Cruz Mountains. The climate is cool – seldom over 80°F (27°C) – and dry. Today it is a quiet village. Its continued existence is due largely to the three fine schools located within a few miles of one another along the ridge. These are the **Munro School** for boys, the **Hampton School** for girls, and the Moravians' **Bethlehem Training College for Women**. Ten miles (16 km) to the south you will find **Lover's Leap**.

INSIGHT GUIDES
Travel Tips

FOR THOSE
WITH MORE THAN
A PASSING INTEREST
IN TIME...

Before you put your name down for a Patek Philippe watch *fig. 1*, there are a few basic things you might like to know, without knowing exactly whom to ask. In addressing such issues as accuracy, reliability and value for money, we would like to demonstrate why the watch we will make for you will be quite unlike any other watch currently produced.

"Punctuality", Louis XVIII was fond of saying, "is the politeness of kings."

We believe that in the matter of punctuality, we can rise to the occasion by making you a mechanical timepiece that will keep its rendezvous with the Gregorian calendar at the end of every century, omitting the leap-years in 2100, 2200 and 2300 and recording them in 2000 and 2400 *fig. 2*. Nevertheless, such a watch does need the occasional adjustment. Every 3333 years and 122 days you should remember to set it forward one day to the true time of the celestial clock. We suspect, however, that you are simply content to observe the politeness of kings. Be assured, therefore, that when you order your watch, we will be exploring for you the physical—if not the metaphysical—limits of precision.

Does everything have to depend on how much?

Consider, if you will, the motives of collectors who set record prices at auction to acquire a Patek Philippe. They may be paying for rarity, for looks or for micromechanical ingenuity. But we believe that behind each $500,000-plus

bid is the conviction that a Patek Philippe, even if 50 years old or older, can be expected to work perfectly for future generations.

In case your ambitions to own a Patek Philippe are somewhat discouraged by the scale of the sacrifice involved, may we hasten to point out that the watch we will make for you today will certainly be a technical improvement on the Pateks bought at auction? In keeping with our tradition of inventing new mechanical solutions for greater reliability and better time-keeping, we will bring to your watch innovations *fig. 3* inconceivable to our watchmakers who created the supreme wristwatches of 50 years ago *fig. 4*. At the same time, we will of course do our utmost to avoid placing undue strain on your financial resources.

Can it really be mine?

May we turn your thoughts to the day you take delivery of your watch? Sealed within its case is your watchmaker's tribute to the mysterious process of time. He has decorated each wheel with a chamfer carved into its hub and polished into a shining circle. Delicate ribbing flows over the plates and bridges of gold and rare alloys. Millimetric surfaces are bevelled and burnished to exactitudes measured in microns. Rubies are transformed into jewels that triumph over friction. And after many months—or even years—of work, your watchmaker stamps a small badge into the mainbridge of your watch. The Geneva Seal—the highest possible attestation of fine watchmaking *fig. 5*.

Looks that speak of inner grace *fig. 6.*

When you order your watch, you will no doubt like its outward appearance to reflect the harmony and elegance of the movement within. You may therefore find it helpful to know that we are uniquely able to cater for any special decorative needs you might like to express. For example, our engravers will delight in conjuring a subtle play of light and shadow on the gold case-back of one of our rare pocket-watches *fig. 7*. If you bring us your favourite picture, our enamellers will reproduce it in a brilliant miniature of hair-breadth detail *fig. 8*. The perfect execution of a double hobnail pattern on the bezel of a wristwatch is the pride of our casemakers and the satisfaction of our designers, while our chainsmiths will weave for you a rich brocade in gold *figs. 9 & 10*. May we also recommend the artistry of our goldsmiths and the experience of our lapidaries in the selection and setting of the finest gemstones? *figs. 11 & 12*.

How to enjoy your watch before you own it.

As you will appreciate, the very nature of our watches imposes a limit on the number we can make available. (The four Calibre 89 time-pieces we are now making will take up to nine years to complete). We cannot therefore promise instant gratification, but while you look forward to the day on which you take delivery of your Patek Philippe *fig. 13*, you will have the pleasure of reflecting that time is a universal and everlasting commodity, freely available to be enjoyed by all.

Should you require information on any particular Patek Philippe watch, or even on watchmaking in general, we would be delighted to reply to your letter of enquiry. And if you send u

fig. 1: The classic face of Patek Philippe.

fig. 4: Complicated wristwatches circa 1930 (left) and 1990. The golden age of watchmaking will always be with us.

fig. 2: One of the 33 complications of the Calibre 89 astronomical clock-watch is a satellite wheel that completes one revolution every 400 years.

fig. 5: The Geneva Seal is awarded only to watches which achieve the standards of horological purity laid down in the laws of Geneva. These rules define the supreme quality of watchmaking.

fig. 3: Recognized as the most advanced mechanical regulating device to date, Patek Philippe's Gyromax balance wheel demonstrates the equivalence of simplicity and precision.

fig. 6: Your pleasure in owning a Patek Philippe is the purpose of those who made it for you.

fig. 7: Arabesques come to life on a gold case-back.

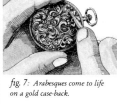

fig. 8: An artist working six hours a day takes about four months to complete a miniature in enamel on the case of a pocket-watch.

fig. 9: Harmony of design is executed in a work of simplicity and perfection in a lady's Calatrava wristwatch.

fig. 10: The chainsmith's hands impart strength and delicacy to a tracery of gold.

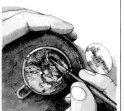

fig. 11: Circles in gold: symbols of perfection in the making.

fig. 12: The test of a master lapidary is his ability to express the splendour of precious gemstones.

PATEK PHILIPPE
GENEVE

fig. 13: The discreet sign of those who value their time.

your card marked "book catalogue" we shall post you a catalogue of our publications. Patek Philippe, 41 rue du Rhône, 1204 Geneva, Switzerland, Tel. +41 22/310 03 66.

You close your laptop and adjust your footrest. A taste of Brie. A sip of Bordeaux. You lean back and hope you won't be arriving too soon.

That depends on how far you're going.

The fact that Lufthansa flies to 220 global destinations comes as a surprise to some. Perhaps we've been too busy with our award-winning service to tell everybody that we are one of the world's largest airline networks. A network that can offer you fast and convenient connections to anywhere. A network that offers rewards with Miles and More, one of the world's leading frequent flyer programmes. And above all, a network that makes you feel at home, however far you're going. So call Lufthansa on 0345 252 252 and we'll tell you the full story.

 Lufthansa

Getting Acquainted

The Place 274
Climate 274
Government........................... 275
Economy 275
Culture & Customs 275

Planning the Trip

What to Wear........................ 275
Entry Regulations 275
Health 275
Money.................................. 276
Public Holidays 276
Getting There 276
Specialist Holidays................ 277
Foreign Investment 277
Useful Addresses 277

Practical Tips

Tipping 277
Business Hours 277
Media 277
Postal Services 278
Telephone & Fax 278
Tourist Information 278
Embassies
& Consulates 278
Emergencies 278

Getting Around

Public Transportation 279
Private Transportation 279

Where to Stay

Accommodation 280
Hotels 280
Villas 282

Eating Out

What to Eat 284
Where to Eat 283

Attractions

Culture 283
Nightlife 284

Sport & Leisure

Participant Sport 284

Shopping

What to Buy........................... 285
Shopping Areas 285

Further Reading

History & Politics 285
People 286
Arts & Culture 286
Natural History 286
Photography 287
Sports 287
Religion 287
Fiction 287
General 287
Other Insight Guides 287

Art/Photo Credits 288
Index 289

Getting Acquainted

The Place

Area: 4,244 sq. miles (10,992 sq. km), 90 miles (145 km) south of Cuba and 100 miles (161 km) west of Haiti.
Capital: Kingston
Highest mountain: Blue Mountain Peak (7,402 ft/2,256 meters)
Population: 2.5 million
Language: English
Religion: 60 percent Protestant, 18 percent non-religious and 10 percent other religions.
Time zone: Eastern Standard Time, five hours behind GMT, one hour behind the Eastern Caribbean.
Currency: Jamaican dollar (J$), sometimes the US dollar (US$) is accepted with change given in J$.
Electricity: 110 volts, 220 volts in some of the larger hotels.
International dialing code: 809

Climate

So many North Americans and Europeans winter in Jamaica because there is no winter. The average temperatures along the coast and plains range between 80°F and 90°F (27°C–32°C) year-round. In the hills, it's a bit cooler, dropping to the 70s and even the high 60s (about 20°C–25°C), while at the top of Blue Mountain Peak, the island's highest point, temperatures have been known to drop below 50°F (10°C) on rare occasions. The coolest months are November through April.

The rainiest times are May–June and September–October. Rain averages 77 inches (196 cm) annually, although some parts of the island, notably the north coast of Surrey, can get three times that amount.

There is more variance between daytime and night-time temperatures. Day breezes blow off the sea to cool the land; night breezes come in from the mountains, making conditions a bit chillier.

Hurricanes

When they talk about hurricanes in Jamaica they think of this jingle:

"June, too soon. July, stand by. August, prepare you must. September remember. October all over."

August is certainly the worst month for these tropical storms. But the official hurricane season begins on June 1 and continues into October. Throughout this period, you must be prepared for the possibility of a hurricane if you are visiting the island of Jamaica.

The most devastating hurricane to strike Jamaica this century was Hurricane Gilbert on September 12, 1988. Gilbert ravaged the entire island, but saved its worst blows for Kingston and the eastern parishes. The banana, coconut, coffee and chicken industries were damaged to the tune of millions of dollars.

Before Gilbert, there had been 37 years of comparative peace. On August 17, 1951, Hurricane Charlie was rated "the most powerful hurricane of the 20th century". Charlie scored a direct hit on the island, claiming 150 lives and wreaking the worst damage in Kingston and Port Royal.

In between Charlie and Gilbert, Jamaica received glancing blows from Hurricanes Flora in the 1960s, Edith and David in the 1970s, and was thankful to have been spared a direct hit from Allen. The latter crossed the eastern tip of the island on August 6, 1980, with winds of 175 miles (282 km) per hour. It did much damage to the agricultural, fishing and tourism industries of Portland, as well as destroying much of the infrastructure.

The number of hurricanes that forms in a given year has ranged from as few as 2 to as many as 20, but most years swing into Jamaica. Still, the US National Hurricane Center in Miami, Florida, tracks each of the massive storms carefully with sophisticated radar detection equipment, satellites and reconnaissance planes. It issues warnings throughout the Caribbean region in a spirit of international cooperation. In Jamaica, the Office of Disaster Preparedness and Emergency Relief Coordination (ODIPERC) was established in 1980.

A hurricane forms when wind rushes toward a low-pressure area and takes on a distinctive swirling motion.

It begins as a tropical disturbance and evolves through stages until it is classified as a hurricane when winds reach 74 miles (120 km) per hour. The size of such storms can range from 60 miles (100 km) in diameter to monsters more than 1,000 miles (1,600 km) wide. Despite improved technology, their patterns and routes remain difficult to predict.

Jamaica residents are well versed on precautions that should be taken when a hurricane approaches. Newspapers and magazines publish special sections on the subject at the beginning of each season. Most coastal communities publish information on evacuation planes and routes.

Needless to say, tourists caught in Jamaica during an impending hurricane should drop plans to work on suntans or visit tourist attractions and follow ODIPERC advisories, television directives and common sense in riding the storm out.

Above all, do not take a hurricane warning lightly by inviting friends over for a "hurricane party". The deadly forces of wind, rain and tides that accompany a hurricane are not cause for celebration.

HURRICANE DEVELOPMENTS

Tropical disturbance: This phase in a hurricane's development has no strong winds. But it may feature a weak counter-clockwise circulation of wind. Disturbances of this sort are common throughout the tropics in summer months.

Tropical depression: A small low-pressure system develops and the counter-clockwise rotation of air increases to speeds under 39 miles (63 km) per hour.

Tropical storm: By now, the low pressure system has developed speeds ranging from 39–73 miles (63–117 km) per hour and can be accompanied by heavy rains.

Hurricane: The low-pressure system has intensified to the point where strong winds of more than 74 miles (119 km) per hour rotate in a counter-clockwise direction around an area of calm called the "eye." Storm tides may rise as much as 15 ft (5 meters) above normal and can surge as much as 6 ft (2 meters) in minutes.

Wherever you're going we'll be there.

From Alice Springs to Zimbabwe, you can be sure Hertz will be at your service.

With over 500,000 cars in more than 150 countries, and 5,000 rental locations with 2,000 at airports, you can always rely on Hertz to offer the car you want, when you want it, and at the right price.

And wherever you go you'll always find the same friendly quality service that is second to none.

It's not surprising then that our combination of unbelievable prices and unbeatable service has made us the world's #1 car rental company.

Simply call your local travel agent, or Hertz direct for further information.

Highest Quality. Low, Low Prices.

Hertz

Government

Jamaica is a constitutional monarchy with a Governor-General who represents the Head of State, the British monarch. A two-party system operates with the Prime Minister leading the Government. The judicial system runs on the British model.

Economy

Jamaica is the world's third largest producer of bauxite, which accounts for around two-thirds of merchandise exports from the island. Agriculture contributes less to GDP, but because of the labor intensive systems used, employs more people than the bauxite mining companies. Sugar is the most important crop followed by bananas, coffee and cocoa.

Tourism is on the increase, so much so that it has become the second largest producer of foreign exchange.

Culture & Customs
Etiquette

There are only a few ironclad rules of etiquette the traveler should be concerned with in Jamaica. No 1: don't refer to Jamaicans as "natives," ignoring their cherished nationality. No 2: don't expect continued quality service without occasionally saying the words "thank you" or "please." No 3: always acknowledge a greeting like "hello", "good morning", "good afternoon" and "good evening" with a greeting in return, it is considered impolite to do otherwise. And No 4: don't shove a camera in a person's face and begin snapping away without asking permission first.

Soon Come

The bustling activity evident in most of Jamaica's larger cities often belies a laidback, unruffled attitude many Jamaicans adopt. It's an attitude that almost functions as a defense mechanism for the inevitable breakdowns and delays in electricity, mail, water, telephone service, train schedules, etc., that often occur. Since howls of protest and insistent demands for service generally yield few results, it's best to adopt the Jamaican approach and with a shrug of the shoulders patiently utter, "Soon come."

Photography

While you'll want to capture the character-rich visages found in Jamaica, it's easier to find a receptive subject if you offer the right incentive. A few people will accept money, while others will accept a picture of their own – which makes a Polaroid a handy item to carry along with your 35mm camera. It's a good idea to shoot most of your pictures during the early morning or late afternoon, because the midday sun tends to bleach out color shots.

Planning the Trip
What to Wear

Lightweight tropical clothing is best throughout the year. A light sweater is suggested for evenings, especially in the winter or for excursions into the hills. If you're climbing into the Blue Mountains, carry a warmer jacket and wear good walking shoes.

On the beaches, you can keep cool and comfortable in swimwear, but don't wear the same minimal cover in the business districts of the cities – particularly not in Kingston.

Entry Regulations
Visas & Passports

A passport is the ideal international calling card, and is recommended. Although in the past US and Canadian citizens have been known to get by with a birth certificate or voter's registration card, re-entry into North America is virtually impossible without a passport. All other visitors must show a passport and in some cases a visa, with the same rules applying to children. Check with authorities in your own country for specifics.

Anyone arriving from a Western country usually can bypass the health clearance in the airports. But all passengers must stop at the immigration checkpoint to submit proof of citizenship and flash a return ticket.

Airport officials also stamp the immigration card you fill out on the plane and ask for your Jamaican address. Save the card. It's required for your departure trip, which must be taken within the next six months.

Cruise-ship passengers skip this process under blanket ship clearance.

Customs

Jamaican officials pride themselves on extending a cordial welcome to visitors. One way they show off is by speeding up the customs process with a brief but thorough luggage inspection. Regulations prohibit anyone from bringing flowers, plants and fruits or any uncanned meats and vegetables into the country. Jamaican law also bans the transport of firearms or ammunition into the country. Simply put, you can bring in personal belongings, 25 cigars, 200 cigarettes, one pint of liquor (excluding rum), a half-pound of tobacco and one quart of wine.

It's what you can take out, though, that can become rather complicated. The first thing to remember is, most questions can be answered by calling Norman Manley International Airport in Kingston, tel: 924-8320 or Sangster International Airport in Montego Bay, tel: 952-2850.

General guidelines for US citizens: allow $600 worth of duty-free goods after a 48-hour stay. If you're worried about overstepping the limit, you can mail an unlimited number of gifts worth up to $10 each back to the States – provided one person doesn't get more than $25 worth in a day. Such gifts cannot include perfume, cigars, cigarettes or liquor.

Jamaica is rabies free and has very stringent rules about pets entering the country. Only animals born and bred in the United Kingdom are allowed entry.

A departure tax is levied on everyone leaving the island. This is currently J$400, but the amount is subject to change from time to time, depending on the stability of the Jamaican dollar.

Health

Tropical diseases like smallpox and yellow fever have been stamped out in Jamaica, all tap water is chlorinated and filtered by modern methods. But even the strongest constitution might not be ready for the spicy island food, so take along an effective antacid.

Sunbathing: First and last rule for sunworshipping; don't overdo it. Yes, the sun is shining; yes, the beach is inviting; yes, the water is sparkling; and yes, the breeze is refreshing. But in your eagerness to purchase that healthy, glowing look, you might emerge looking more like a boiled lobster than a bronzed deity. No matter what the skin color, first apply a sunscreen and then gradually follow up with tanning oil.

Pests: There are two kinds of pests in Jamaica: the human kind and the insect kind. The human kind quickly sum up your tourist status and barrage you with offers of straw goods, wood carvings, cocaine and ganja for sale. The insect kind organize into mosquito squads bent on attacking your blood system. Deal with the mortal nuisances with a polite, but firm "thank you, but no." Mount a counter-offensive on the thirsty bloodsuckers with a strong dose of insect repellent spray and a burning mosquito coil.

Money

You can bring in as much of your own money as you please. To make island purchases easier, exchange your own currency for Jamaican dollars at one of the banks, hotels or international airports. You will be given a receipt which you will have to present at the end of your stay if you want to re-convert back to your own currency. Do not, however, convert all your money at once because you can only redeem a portion (around J$200) when you leave. US dollars are widely accepted.

The exchange rate is subject to fluctuations and Jamaican law strictly forbids foreign currency exchanges with anyone other than an authorized dealer. Despite the government's best efforts to stamp it out, there are two major snags to black-market dealing: you will not be able to re-convert any unspent Jamaican dollars, and you may end up with counterfeit money.

Most credit cards are accepted and traveler's checks can be used throughout the island. In banks you will be asked for identification; your passport or travel document will suffice. Most commercial banks offer cash advances on credit cards. You can also get cash through any Western Union office (toll free: 991-2057).

For lost or stolen traveler's checks or credit cards contact:
American Express. Tel: 800-327-1267, to report loss or request replacement. Local representatives: Kingston, tel: 929-3077; Montego Bay, tel: 929-2586.
Visa. Tel: 800-8722-881 (AT&T operator), then place a collect call to tel: 415-574-7700.
MasterCard. Tel: 800-8722-881 (AT&T operator), then place a collect call to tel: 314-275-6690.

Public Holidays

Out of all the holidays celebrated in Jamaica, Christmas holidays and Jamaican Independence Day (first Monday in August) rank as the most festive occasions. Independence Day celebrations are marked by colorful parades, street dances, music, festivals and a rip-roarin' good time.

Other holidays when businesses are closed include:

New Year's Day	January 1
Ash Wednesday	variable
Good Friday	variable
Easter Monday	variable
Labor Day	May 23
National Heroes Day	third Monday in October
Christmas Day	December 25
Boxing Day	December 26

Getting There

By Air

Most travelers enter Jamaica through one of the two international airports Donald Sangster International, Montego Bay, or Norman Manley International, Kingston. Several international airlines serve the island, including Air Jamaica, and numerous charters which originate from North America and Europe.

At either airport, it's common to see Jamaicans loaded down with bulging handbags. Why? Because they're bringing in goods from other countries priced considerably cheaper than their Jamaican counterparts. Visitors, however, should keep their carry-on luggage to a minimum in preparation for the lengthy hike between the plane and the immigration and customs checkpoints. And if your plane lands during one of the many passenger waves that often descend on the airports, expect a prolonged check-in wait. In the Montego Bay airport, you can fill up the time spent waiting for your luggage by stopping by the Visitor Services booth or sipping the Jamaican rum offered at the Appleton Rum booth. The Kingston traveler should concentrate on nabbing one of the elusive baggage carts.

Some of the airlines which serve Jamaica are:
Aeroflot. Tel: 929-2251 (Kingston).
Air Canada. Tel: 924-8211 (Kingston); tel: 952-4300 (Montego Bay).
Air Jamaica. Tel: 929-4661 (Kingston); tel: 952-4300 (Montego Bay).
American Airlines. Tel: 924-8305 (Kingston); tel: 952-5950 (Montego Bay).
Antillean Airlines. Tel: 926-1762 (Kingston).
British Airways. Tel: 929-9020 (Kingston); tel: 952-3771 (Montego Bay).
British West Indies Airlines Intl Ltd (BWIA). Tel: 929-3771/3 (Kingston); tel: 952-4100.
Cayman Airways. Tel: 926-1762 (Kingston).
Cubana Airlines. Tel: 978-3406 (Kingston).
Northwest Airlines. Tel: 952-4033 (Montego Bay).

By Sea

The seaworthy traveler who prefers a leisurely ride coupled with a short stay can select from several cruise ships which include Jamaica on their itineraries. Ocho Rios in the middle of the north coast is the most popular port of entry, followed by Montego Bay to the north-west and Port Antonio in the north-east.

The main drawback to taking the sea route is the hassle involved in extending your stay beyond the ships' one-to-two-day docking time. Most cruise tickets are sold for round-trip voyages and you'll probably want to avoid the logistical manoeuvering involved in a change. Ensure your ship stops in Jamaica, cruise lines that include the island on their schedule are:
Carnival Cruises (Mardi Gras). Tel: 800-327-9501.
Commodore Cruises (Boheme). Tel: 305-529-3000.
Costa Cruises (Daphne). Tel: 212-682-3505.
Hapag Lloyd Cruises (Europa). Tel: 312-332-0090.

PRIMA SUPER 135 38-135 MM

PRIMA SUPER 115 38-115 MM

YOUR TRAVEL COMPANION FOR THOSE PRICELESS MOMENTS

PRIMA SUPER 28V 28-70 MM

PRIMA ZOOM 70F 35-70 MM

There's no better way to capture life's most cherished moments than with a Canon Prima Zoom camera. All Prima Zoom cameras are durable and light and come with easy-to-use features like an intelligent Automatic Focusing system, and a special feature that reduces the undesirable "red-eye" effect. Buying a Canon Prima Zoom also means you're getting Canon's reputation for optical excellence. It's your guarantee for breathtaking pictures, every time.

Canon
PRIMA ZOOM

Canon Europa N.V., P.O. Box 2262, 1180 EG Amstelveen, the Netherlands

PRIMA ZOOM SHOT 38-60 MM

HOLIDAY MAKER

Holland America (*Veendam, Volendam*). Tel: 800-223-6655.
Home Lines (*Atlantic*). Tel: 800-221-4041.
K-Lines/Hellenic (*Constellation*). Tel: 800-223-7880.
Norwegian Caribbean (*Southward*). Tel: 800-327-7030.
Paguet Line (*Rhapsody*). Tel: 800-221-2160/2490.
Royal Caribbean Line (*Nordic Prince, Song of Norway, Sun Viking*). Tel: 800-327-6700.
Royal Cruise Lines (*Royal Odyssey*). Tel: 415-788-0610.
Royal Viking Line (*Royal Viking Sea, Royal Viking Sky*). Tel: 800-227-4246.
Sitmar Cruises (*Fairwind*), no number available.
Sun Line (*Stella Solaris*). Tel: 800-223-5760.

Specialist Holidays
Wedding Bells

Always popular as a honeymoon destination, Jamaica also beckons as an idyllic spot for the wedding itself. Couples can apply for a license as soon as they arrive and should bring along birth certificates and, where appropriate, divorce papers.

In Kingston, licenses are dispensed at the Registrar's Office, The Ministry of National Security and Justice, 12 Ocean Blvd., Kingston, tel: 922-0080, 8.30am–5pm Monday through Thursday and 8.30am–4pm Friday. The Montego Bay office is open from 8.30am–4.30pm weekdays and from 8.30am to noon Saturday. Any priest, marriage officer or registrar can perform the ceremony.

Foreign Investment

The Jamaican Government encourages overseas investments and joint ventures, particularly those with export potential such as agriculture, agro-industries, mining, manufacturing (in the Free Zone), and tourism (hotels and resort cottages). There are liberal tax and non-tax incentives.

Potential foreign investors should obtain all information and assistance from Jamaica Promotions Corporation (JAMPRO) at 35 Trafalgar Road, Kingston 10, tel: 929-9450/6. This is the central agency which expedites the process of registration and can assist with a wide range of problem solving.

Interested prospective overseas investors may contact the agency's office in New York, or the Jamaican Trade Commissioners in London, Belgium, Germany, Canada and Trinidad.

Useful Addresses
Tourist Offices Abroad

Canada: 1 Eglington Avenue East, Suite 616, Toronto, tel: 416-482-7850.
United Kingdom: 1–2 Prince Consort Road, London SW7 2BZ, tel: 0171-224-0505; fax: 0171-224-0551.

USA

Boston: 21 Merchants Row, 5th Floor, Boston, tel: 617-248-5811/2.
Chicago: Suite 1210, 36 South Wabash Avenue, Chicago 60603, Illinois, tel: 312-346-1546.
Los Angeles: 3440 Wilshire Blvd Suite 1207, Los Angeles, Ca. 90010, tel: 213-384-1123.
Miami: 1320 South Dixie Highway, Suite 1100 Coral Gables, Fla. 33146, tel: 305-665-0557. This office represents Miami and Latin America.
New York: 866 Second Avenue, New York 10017, tel: 212-688-7650.

Embassies & Consulates

United Kingdom: 2 Prince Consort Road, London SW7 2BZ, tel: 0171 823 9911.
USA: 1520 New Hamshire Ave NW, Washington, DC 20008–1210, tel: 202-452-0660.

Practical Tips
Tipping

Tipping is definitely allowed and encouraged in Jamaica, which depends heavily on the largesse of visitors. The standard 10–15 percent gratuity is the norm in most areas, but make sure the tip hasn't already been added to the hotel or restaurant bill.

Business Hours

The majority of business offices operate from 8.30am until 4.30pm Monday through Friday, with few open on Saturday. Banks are open Monday through Thursday from 9am–2pm, and Friday from 9am to noon and 2.30pm–5pm. The main offices of some major banks include:
Bank of Commerce, 121 Harbour St (Kingston); 59 St James St (Montego Bay).
Citibank, 63-67 Knutsford Blvd (Kingston).
National Commercial Bank, 77 King St (Kingston); 41 St James St (Montego Bay).
Royal Bank Jamaica Ltd., 37 Duke St (Kingston); Sam Sharpe Square (Montego Bay).
Scotiabank Jamaica, Duke & Port Royal streets (Kingston); Sam Sharpe Square (Montego Bay).

Media
Newspapers

Two daily newspapers are published in Kingston and distributed throughout the island: *The Daily Gleaner* and *The Jamaica Herald*. *The Star*, owned by the Gleaner Company, is a daily afternoon tabloid. *The Observer* is a bi-weekly paper appearing on Wednesday and Friday. The Press Association of Jamaica is based in Kingston.

In Montego Bay, *The Western Mirror* is a bi-weekly appearing Wednesday and Saturday. Publications for visitors include the *Tourist Guide*, published by the Gleaner Company, *The Visitor*, *Vacation Guide* and *Destination Jamaica*, published by the Jamaica Hotel & Tourist Association (JHTA).

Foreign newspapers are available at hotels, book stores and better pharmacies in airmail editions. They include the *New York Times*, the *Financial Times*, *Miami Herald*, *The Times* of London, *Le Monde* and *Die Welt*.

Television & Radio

There are two television stations, JBC-TV and CVM, both based in Kingston, and 9 radio stations: RJR and its FM station FAME, JBC 1 and 2, Power 106 and Love FM are all based in Kingston; KLAS-FM (Mandeville), IRIE FM (Ocho Rios), and Radio Waves (Montego Bay).

Books & Magazines

The largest concentration of book stores is in Kingston. Sangster's have four branches in Kingston: 97 Harbour Street and 33 King Street (both downtown), The Mall Plaza on Constant Spring Road, and on the lower floor of the Sovereign Shopping Center, 106 Hope Road. There is also a branch of Sangster's in the Westgate Shopping Center, Montego Bay.

Other book stores include The Bookshop at The Springs Plaza, Constant Spring Road; their outlets include one in the Spanish Town Shopping Center, Spanish Town; 29 Main Street, Mandeville. Kingston Bookshop Limited has two outlets at: 70b King Street (downtown) and The Pavillion Shopping Center, Constant Spring Road.

The bookstores carry a variety of books including those on all aspects of Jamaican life. They also carry foreign and locally-written novels, and the centrally located outlets carry magazines and newspapers.

In addition to the above named stores, there are a number of specialty book stores listed in the Yellow Pages of the local directory, mostly dotted around Kingston. Pharmacies usually carry a selection of foreign and local newspapers and magazines, as well as paperback novels.

Postal Services

Every town in Jamaica has a post office, and there are postal agencies in smaller villages. Your hotel will handle your mail for you or will be able to give you the current postal rates.

Telephone & Fax

Jamaica's telephone network is controlled by Telecommunications of Jamaica (TOJ), a joint venture between the government and Cable and Wireless. High-speed satellite services to the US are provided by Jamaica Digiport International, which operates a teleport in Montego Bay. Lines are open 24 hours and it is possible to access almost anywhere in the world, 24 hours a day.

You can make collect calls to the United States, notably through AT&T Direct, tel: 800-872-2881; MCI "CALL

USA", tel: 800-674-7000, or to Canada through Teleglobe "Canada Direct", tel: 800-222-0016.

You may bring your cellular phone with you if you wish, but you will be charged a fee by customs at the airport. The fee is refundable on departure. TOJ also offers cellular service to visitors with a modest charge per minute for airtime. A full list of their offices is in the telephone directory. Another company called Boatphone offers rentals to visitors at competitive prices. Tel: 968-4000-1; 997-4832.

Jamaica is also linked to the rest of the world by facsimile and cable services, available through TOJ or your hotel. TOJ's offices are at 15 North Street, Kingston, tel: 922-6031; 52 Grenada Crescent, New Kingston, tel: 926-4201; 36 Fort Street, Montego Bay, tel: 952-4400.

Tourist Information

An estimated 552,000 people don't just descend on one country during the course of a year. Some organization must apply a method to the madness of such a mass influx. And in Jamaica, that organization is the Jamaican Tourist Board.

The board answers your questions before and after you arrive, issues maps and brochures on the places you want to see, and can even help you find a Jamaican who shares your interests. It is that last function that has garnered much of the attention since the late 1960s with the success of the "Meet the People" program, linking island visitors with Jamaicans. For more information, you can contact the board's local and/or overseas offices. Besides the board, embassies and high commissions of 24 countries have found a home in Kingston.

Tourist Offices in Jamaica

Kingston: ICWI Building, 2 St Lucia Avenue, Kingston 5, tel: 929-9200.
Negril: Shop 20 Villa de Negril, tel: 957-4243; Shop 9 Adrija Plaza, tel: 957-4489.
Ocho Rios: Top Floor, Ocean Village Shopping Center, tel: 974-2570.
Port Antonio: Top Floor, City Center Plaza, tel: 993-3051; Rafters Rest, St Margarets Bay, tel: 993-2778.

Embassies & Consulates
Kingston

British High Commission: 26 Trafalgar Road, tel: 926-9050/4, 926-1020/3.
Canadian High Commission: 30 Knutsford Blvd, tel: 926-1500/926-1701.
Cuban Embassy: 9 Trafalgar Road, tel: 978-0931.
Indian High Commission: 4 Retreat Avenue, tel: 927-0486, 927-4270.
Trinidad and Tobago High Commission: 60 Knutsford Blvd, tel: 926-5730/926-5739.
United States Embassy: 2 Oxford Road, tel: 929-4850/926-5679.

Security & Crime
Common Sense

Don't leave home without it. Just because you're on vacation doesn't mean you should shed all normal precautions. Place your jewelry and other valuables in the hotel safe until they're needed. When walking in crowds, women should clutch their handbags close to their bodies and men should transfer their wallets to front pockets. Carefully scrutinize the goods of all sellers proferring "fantastic" deals, and never forget that ganja and cocaine are illegal even though they may be freely offered to you.

Emergencies
Medical Services

For minor illnesses, cuts and bruises, most hotels employ nurses to treat guests and there is a doctor on call. Major illnesses can be handled by specialists, most based in Kingston.

All major towns have medical facilities. Large specialist hospitals are located in Kingston and Montego Bay:
Andrews Memorial Hospital, 27 Hope Road, Kingston, tel: 926-7401/2 (daytime); tel: 926-7403 (9pm–8am). Private.
Bustamante Hospital for Children, Arthur Wint Drive, Kingston, tel: 926-5721/5. Public.
Cornwall Regional Hospital, Mount Salem, Montego Bay, tel: 952-5100. Public.
Kingston Public Hospital, North St, Kingston, tel: 922-0210; 922-0530/1.
Medical Associates Hospital, 18 Tangerine Place, Kingston, tel: 926-1400. Private.

National Chest Hospital, Liguanea, Kingston, tel: 927-7121/927-6421.

Nuttall Memorial Hospital, 6 Caledonia Ave., Kingston, tel: 926-2139. Private.

St Joseph's Hospital, Deanery Road, Kingston, tel: 928-4955. Private.

University Hospital of the West Indies (UHWI), Mona, Kingston, tel: 927-1620; **The Tony Thwaites Wing** of UHWI (private patients), tel: 927-6520/927-6555.

AMBULANCE SERVICE

Wings (Ja) Ltd Air Ambulance (local & overseas), tel: 923-5416, 24-hour service.

Karvinair Air Ambulance, tel: 978-4913.

Medical Associates Ambulance, tel: 929-5531.

In addition, all parish capitals have their own infirmaries.

Antibiotics, tranquilizers and certain other drugs can be bought only on a doctor's prescription. Many other medications can be purchased at pharmacies located in all major towns.

EMERGENCY PHONE NUMBERS

Air-Sea Rescue	119
Ambulance	110
Fire	110
Police	119

Getting Around

Public Transportation

By Air

For short jaunts across the island, Trans Jamaican Airlines flies to the major cities and provides connections for flights at the two international airports. Domestic airports are at Tinson Pen, Kingston; Montego Bay; Negril; Boscobel, Ocho Rios; and Port Antonio. Trans Jamaican have also launched a direct service to other Caribbean destinations.

For schedules and information, tel: 923-8680/923-6664, Tinson Pen, Kingston; Norman Manley International Airport, tel: 924-8850, Montego Bay, tel: 952-5401/3; Boscobel aerodrome, Ocho Rios, 975-3254; Port Antonio, tel: 993-2405; and Negril, tel: 957-4251.

Several companies offer charter flights, priced according to destination: **Wings (Ja) Ltd**, Tinson Pen Aerodrome, Kingston, tel: 923-5416/923-6573.

Airways International Ltd, Tinson Pen Aerodrome, Kingston, tel: 923-8557/923-0371.

Karvinair, 1 Roosevelt Ave, Kingston, tel: 978-4913. Offer Lear jet charters and Air Ambulance service

Helitours (Ja) Ltd, 120 Main St, Ocho Rios, tel: 974-2265. Offer helicopter tours of the country as well as charter services.

By Bus

The rural areas are served by minibuses that crisscross the back and main roads, making impromptu stops as well as scheduled ones. Since no central agency handles the bus schedules, the only way to find out where the buses are going is to ask the driver. Fares are low, but there is not much elbow room and the music is loud. Because of the haphazard routes and crowded conditions, few tourists are bold enough to try to tackle the country system.

In the major population centers like Kingston and Montego Bay, the bus system isn't much better for the uninitiated. Here, too, mini-buses have taken over, traveling on the regular routes once used by the now vanished Jamaica Omnibus Service. Frequency is erratic, and the best way to travel is with someone who knows the system.

By Taxi

All licensed taxicabs carry red Public Passenger Vehicle (PPV) license plates, but they are not metered and the fares printed on the doors or elsewhere have not been applicable for years. Before embarking, you should first state your destination, ask the cost of the trip and whether the fare quoted is in Jamaican or US dollars. If in doubt, feel free to strike up a few rounds of bargaining with the driver.

Taxis are summoned either by a telephone call – most are radio controlled – or by the more common method of flagging them down on the street.

Private Transportation

Car Rentals

You'll probably find the Jamaican driving experience somewhat akin to a demolition derby as you steer to avoid potholes, animals, pedestrians and seemingly crazed oncoming drivers. But not to worry, the most important driving rule you need to remember while traveling around the country is to stay on the left side of the road. It is also useful to note that gas stations accept only cash.

"U-Drive" or rental-car operations in Jamaica include such big-name agencies as Avis, Budget Rent-A-Car, Hertz, and National Car Rental. Try to reserve a car before you arrive on the island to avoid the frequent surges in demand. Once you arrive, you should look for agency representatives at the two international airports, tourist centers and special desks in the hotels.

To rent a car, you must be at least 21 years old with a valid driver's licence from any country. Anyone between 21 and 25 will be required to post a bond to meet insurance regulations and all payment must be made in either foreign currency or with a major credit card.

Always check the car over thoroughly before signing the rental agreement. Report any knocks or bumps and insist that they are noted down, or you may lose some or all of your deposit.

Motorcycles & Scooters

You can also rent motorcycles, mopeds and bicycles. Inquire at your hotel reception desk.

Where to Stay

Accommodation

To accommodate the hundreds of thousands of visitors to Jamaica, dozens of hotels, inns and guest houses have sprung up. They dot the island, with more along the coast in resort areas and fewer as one moves inland. But there is always somewhere to rest your head.

Quality and price vary greatly. For those who want to live in the lap of luxury, there are many ultra-modern, all-inclusive packages available in resorts which provide food, drink and entertainment for a pre-arranged price. There are also tiny guesthouses and villas for those who are happy with the comforts of home – and less.

Following is a listing of hotels, which give an idea of what is on offer. Their facilities and charges are, of course, always subject to change.

Hotels

Surrey

KINGSTON & ST ANDREW

Expensive
Jamaica Pegasus, P.O. Box 333, tel: 926-3690/9; fax: 929-5855. 350 rooms with air-conditioning, telephone and private bath/shower; golf; tennis; swimming; nightclub/disco; restaurant; shops. Children welcome.
Morgan's Harbour, Port Royal, tel: 924-8464/5. 45 rooms with air-conditioning, private bath/shower; private beach; watersports. Children welcome.
Terra Nova, 17 Waterloo Road, tel: 926-2211; 926-9334; fax: 929-4933. 35 rooms with air-conditioning, telephone, private bath/shower; private beach; swimming pool; nightclub/disco; restaurant; shops. Children welcome.
Wyndham New Kingston, 77 Knutsford Blvd, P.O. Box 112, Kingston 5, tel: 926-5430; fax: 9297439. 315 rooms with air-conditioning, tel-

ephone and private bath/shower; golf; tennis; swimming pool; nightclub/disco; restaurant; shops. Children welcome.

Moderate
The Courtleigh, 31 Trafalgar Road, tel: 926-8174/8; fax: 926-7801. 40 rooms with air-conditioning, telephone, private bath/shower; swimming pool; nightclub/disco; restaurant. Children welcome.
Hotel Four Seasons, P.O. Box 190, tel: 926-8805/926-0682. 39 rooms with air-conditioning, private bath/shower; restaurant. Children welcome.
Medallion Hall, 53 Hope Road, tel: 927-5721/927-5866. 13 rooms with air-conditioning, private bath/shower; restaurant. Children welcome.

Inexpensive
Indies Hotel, 5 Holborn Road, tel: 926-2952/926-0989. 16 rooms with air-conditioning, private bath/shower.
Mayfair, P.O. Box 163, 4 West Kings House Close, Kingston 10, tel: 926-1610/2; fax: 296-7741. 32 rooms, some with air-conditioning, private bath/shower; swimming pool. Children welcome.
Pine Grove Guest House, Content Gap, St Andrew, tel: 922-8705. 20 rooms, some with air-conditioning, private bath/shower; cottages; restaurant. Children welcome.
Sandhurst Guest House, 10 Sandhurst Crescent, Kingston 6, tel: 927-7239; fax: 926-8443. 40 rooms, some with air-conditioning, private bath/shower; swimming pool; restaurant. Children welcome.
Sutton Place, 11 Ruthven Road, tel: 926-2297. 67 rooms; with air-conditioning, telephone, private bath/shower; swimming pool; restaurant. Children welcome.

PORT ANTONIO & EAST COAST

Luxury
Trident Villas, P.O. Box 227, tel: 993-2602; fax: 993-2705. 26 rooms with air-conditioning, telephone, private bath/shower; private beach; swimming pool; watersports; tennis; horse riding; cottages; nightclub/disco; restaurant; shops. Children welcome.

Expensive
Dragon Bay Villas, Dragon Bay, P.O. Box 176, tel: 993-3281. 100 rooms

with air-conditioning, telephone, private bath/shower; private beach; swimming pool; watersports; tennis; horse riding; cottages; nightclub/disco; restaurant; shops. Children welcome.
Goblin Hill Villas, P.O. Box 26, tel: 993-3286. 44 rooms with air-conditioning, telephone, private bath/shower; private beach; swimming pool; watersports; tennis; horse riding; cottages; nightclub/disco; restaurant; shops. Children welcome.

Moderate
Bonnie View, P.O. Box 82, Richmond Hill, tel: 993-2752; fax: 993-2862. 20 rooms with air-conditioning, telephone, private bath/shower; private beach; swimming pool; tennis; cottages; nightclub/disco; restaurant; shops. Children welcome.
Hotel Mocking Bird Hill, P.O. Box 254, Port Antonio, tel: 993-3370. 10 double rooms. Small friendly hotel; restaurant; craft workshops; tours and art gallery.

Inexpensive
De Montevin Lodge, 21 Fort George St, tel: 993-2604. 15 rooms with private bath/shower; restaurant; foreign languages spoken. Children welcome.

Middlesex

OCHO RIOS & SURROUNDINGS

Luxury
Jamaica Inn, P.O. Box 1, Main Street, tel: 974-2514; fax: 974-2449. 45 rooms with air-conditioning, telephone, private bath/shower; private beach; swimming pool; watersports; tennis; golf; horse riding; orchestra; restaurant; foreign languages spoken. Children welcome.
Sans Souci Hotel and Spa, P.O. Box 103, tel: 974-2353; fax: 974-2544. 111 rooms with air-conditioning, telephone, private bath/shower; private beach; pool; tennis; golf; orchestra; restaurant. Children welcome.

Expensive
Couples, Tower Isle P.O.; St Mary, tel: 974-4271/5. 172 rooms with air-conditioning, telephone, private bath/shower; private beach; swimming pool; watersports; tennis; horse riding; nightclub/disco; restaurant; shops. All-inclusive. No children.

Jamaica Grande, P.O. Box 100, Ocho Rios, tel: 974-2201; (800) 228-9898 (Resv.). 720 rooms with air-conditioning, telephone, private bath/shower; private beach; pool; watersports; tennis; supervised childrens program; nightclub/disco; restaurant; shops. All-inclusive available.

Plantation Inn, P.O. Box 2, tel: 974-5601; fax: 974-5912. 78 rooms with air-conditioning, telephone, private bath/shower; private beach; swimming pool; watersports; tennis; golf; restaurant; shops; foreign languages spoken.

Sandals Dunn's River, Mammee Bay, P.O. Box 51, tel: 972-2382/972-2300. 256 rooms with air-conditioning, private bath/shower; private beach; swimming pool; tennis; golf; gym/jacuzzi; nightclub/disco; restaurant; shops; couples only. All-inclusive.

Shaw Park Beach Hotel, P.O. Box 17, Cutlass Bay, tel: 974-2552/4; fax: 974-5042. 118 rooms with air-conditioning, telephone, private bath/shower; private beach; swimming pool; watersports; tennis; nightclub/disco; orchestra; restaurant; shops.

Turtle Beach Apartments Hotel, P.O. Box 73, tel: 974-2801/5. 130 rooms with air-conditioning, telephone, private bath/shower; swimming pool; watersports; tennis; restaurant; shops. Children welcome.

Moderate

Silver Seas, P.O. Box 81, tel: 974-2755/974-5005. 83 rooms with air-conditioning, telephone, private bath/shower; private beach; swimming pool; watersports; tennis; squash; nightclub/disco; restaurant; shops. Children welcome.

Tower Cloisters Condominiums, Tower Isle PO, tel: 975-4360. 30 rooms, some with air-conditioning, private bath/shower; swimming pool; restaurant; nightclub/disco. Children.

Inexpensive

Casa Maria, P.O. Box 10, Port Maria, tel: 994-2323/4. 30 rooms some with air-conditioning, telephone, private bath/shower; private beach; cottages; swimming pool; tennis; restaurant; shops. Children welcome.

Hibiscus Lodge, P.O. Box 52, Main Street, tel: 974-2676. 25 rooms with private bath/shower; private beach; restaurant. Children welcome.

Pineapple Penthouse Hotel, Pineapple Place, P.O. Box 263, tel: 974-2727. 23 rooms with air-conditioning, bath/shower; swimming pool; restaurant.

DISCOVERY BAY & RUNAWAY BAY

Expensive

Eaton Hall Hotel & Villas, P.O. Box 112, tel: 973-3404. 52 rooms. All-inclusive.

Jamaica Jamaica, P.O. Box 58, tel: 973-2436. 238 rooms. All-inclusive.

Moderate

Club Caribbean, P.O. Box 65, tel: 973-3507/9; fax: 973-3509. 128 rooms some with air-conditioning, private bath/shower; private beach; swimming pool; cottages; watersports; tennis; golf; horse riding; nightclub/disco; orchestra; restaurant; shops. Children welcome.

Inexpensive

Ambiance/Jamaica, P.O. Box 20, tel: 973-2066/7; fax: 973-2067. 80 rooms with air-conditioning, telephone, private bath/shower; private beach; swimming pool; fishing; tennis; golf; nightclub/disco; orchestra; restaurant; shops; bed & breakfast. Children welcome.

Caribbean Isle Hotel, P.O. Box 119, tel: 973-2364; fax: 974-1706. 23 rooms with air-conditioning, private bath/shower; swimming pool; nightclub/disco; restaurant. Children welcome.

H.E.A.R.T Runaway Country Club, Cardiff Hall, tel: 973-2671/4; fax: 973-2692. 20 rooms with fans, telephone, television, private bath/shower; golf; restaurant. Children welcome.

MANDEVILLE

Moderate

Astra Country Inn, P.O. Box 60, 62 Ward Ave, tel: 962-3265/962-3377; fax: 962-1461. 22 rooms with telephone, private bath/shower; private beach; swimming pool; fishing; golf; horse riding; tennis; restaurant. Children welcome.

Mandeville Hotel, P.O. Box 78, 4 Hotel Street, tel: 962-2460; fax: 962-0700. 60 rooms with air-conditioning, telephone, private bath/shower; swimming pool; golf; tennis; horse riding; restaurant. Children welcome.

Cornwall

MONTEGO BAY

Luxury

Half Moon Club, P.O. Box 80, Rose Hall, tel: 953-2211; fax: 953-2558. 209 rooms with air-conditioning, telephone, private bath/shower; private beach; swimming pool; cottages; watersports; tennis; squash; horse riding; orchestra; nightclub/disco; restaurant; shops. Children welcome.

Jack Tar Village, P.O. Box 144, tel: 952-4340; 952-1558. 128 rooms. All-inclusive.

The Palms, Rose Hall, P.O. Box 186, tel: 953-2160. 18 rooms with air-conditioning, private bath/shower; swimming pool; cottages; tennis; nightclub/disco; restaurant. Children welcome.

Round Hill, P.O. Box 64, tel: 952-5150/5; fax: 952-2505. 101 rooms some with air-conditioning, telephone, private bath/shower; private beach; swimming pool; cottages; tennis; golf; watersports; horse riding; nightclub/disco; orchestra; shops. Children welcome.

Sandals Royal Caribbean, P.O. Box 167, tel: 953-2231; fax: 953-2788. 190 rooms. Luxurious accommodation. All-inclusive.

Tryall Golf & Beach Club, Sandy Bay, PO, Hanover, tel: 952-5110. 54 rooms and 45 villas with air-conditioning, telephone, private bath/shower; swimming pool; watersports; tennis; golf; horse riding; nightclub/disco; restaurant; shops. Children welcome.

Wyndham-Rose Hall Beach Hotel, P.O. Box 999, tel: 953-2650; fax: 953-2617. 508 rooms with air-conditioning, telephone, private bath/shower; swimming pool; private beach; orchestra; watersports; tennis; golf; horse riding; nightclub/disco; restaurant; shops. Children welcome.

Expensive

Holiday Inn, P.O. Box 480, tel: 953-2485; fax: 953-2840. 558 rooms with air-conditioning, telephone, private bath/shower; swimming pool; private beach; golf; tennis; horse riding; watersports; nightclub/disco; orchestra; restaurant; shops. Children welcome.

Sandals Montego Bay, P.O. Box 100, tel: 952-5510; fax: 952-0816. 243 rooms. All-inclusive.

Trelawny Beach Hotel, P.O. Box 54, Falmouth, tel: 954-2450; fax: 954-2173. 350 rooms some with air-conditioning, telephone, private bath/shower; swimming pool; private beach; cottages; tennis; horse riding; watersports; nightclub; orchestra; restaurant. Children welcome.

Moderate

Buccaneer Inn, P.O. Box 469, tel: 952-2694. 18 rooms with air-conditioning, telephone, private bath/shower; swimming pool; nightclub/disco; cottages; orchestra; restaurant; shops. Children welcome.

Carlyle Beach, P.O. Box 412, tel: 952-4140. 52 rooms with air-conditioning, telephone; private bath/shower; swimming pool; restaurant. Children.

Club Paradise, P.O. Box 300, tel: 952-4780/1. 110 rooms with air-conditioning, private bath/shower; swimming pool; private beach; watersports; tennis; nightclub/disco; orchestra; restaurant; shops. Children welcome.

Coral Cliff, P.O. Box 253, 165 Gloucester Ave, tel: 952-4130/1; fax: 952-6532. 32 rooms with air-conditioning, telephone; private bath/shower; swimming pool; tennis; restaurant. Children welcome.

Doctor's Cave Beach, P.O. Box 94, tel: 952-4355; fax: 952-5204. 80 rooms, 10 apts with air-conditioning, telephone, private bath/shower; swimming pool; private beach; watersports; horse riding; tennis; squash; golf; nightclub/disco; orchestra; restaurant; shops. Children.

Fantasy, P.O. Box 161, tel: 952-4150. 120 rooms with air-conditioning, telephone; private bath/shower; swimming pool; private beach; cottages; tennis; nightclub/disco; restaurant; shops. Children welcome.

Hotel Montego, P.O. Box 74, Federal Ave, tel: 952-3286/7; fax: 979-0351. 35 rooms with air-conditioning, telephone, private bath/shower; swimming pool; restaurant. Children welcome.

Montego Bay Racquet Club, P.O. Box 245, Sewell Ave, tel: 952-0200; fax: 921-5335. 25 rooms, 16 villas with air-conditioning, telephone, private bath/shower; swimming pool; cottages; tennis; restaurant. Children welcome.

Richmond Hill Inn, P.O. Box 362, tel: 952-3859; fax: 952-6106. 23 rooms

with air-conditioning, private bath/shower; swimming pool; private beach; watersports; orchestra; restaurant. Children welcome.

Seawind Beach Resort, P.O. Box 69, Montego Freeport, tel: 952-4874/952-4070/3. 452 rooms with air-conditioning, telephone, private bath/shower; swimming pool; private beach; cottages; watersports; tennis; horse riding; nightclub/disco; restaurant; shops. Children welcome.

Wexford Court, P.O. Box 239, tel: 952-3679/952-2854. 16 rooms with air-conditioning, telephone, private bath/shower; swimming pool; restaurant. Children welcome.

Inexpensive

Beach View, P.O. Box 86, tel: 952-4420/2. 54 rooms with air-conditioning, telephone, private bath/shower; swimming pool; private beach; restaurant. Children welcome.

Blue Harbour, P.O. Box 212, Sewell Ave, tel: 952-5445; fax: 952-8930. 22 rooms with air-conditioning, private bath/shower; swimming pool; restaurant. Children welcome.

Chalet Caribe, P.O. Box 365, tel: 952-1365. 28 rooms with air-conditioning, private bath/shower; swimming pool; private beach; watersports; restaurant. Children welcome.

Harmony House, P.O. Box 55, tel: 952-5710. 21 rooms with air-conditioning, telephone; private bath/shower; swimming pool; restaurant. Children welcome.

Lady Diane's, P.O. Box 55, tel: 952-4415. 16 rooms with air-conditioning, private bath/shower; swimming pool; restaurant. Children welcome.

Ocean View Guest House, P.O. Box 210, 26 Sunset Blvd., tel: 952-2662. 12 rooms with air-conditioning, private bath/shower; swimming pool; restaurant. Children welcome.

Royal Court, P.O. Box 195, tel: 952-4531; fax: 952-4532. 22 rooms with air-conditioning, telephone, private bath/shower; swimming pool; nightclub/disco; restaurant. Children welcome.

Verney House, P.O. Box 18, tel: 952-4845/952-2875. 26 rooms some with air-conditioning, telephone, private bath/shower; swimming pool; private beach; restaurant. Children welcome.

NEGRIL & SOUTHWEST COAST

Luxury

Grand Lido, Negril, P.O. Box 88, tel: 957-4010. 200 rooms with air-conditioning, private bath/shower; swimming pool; private beach; watersports; tennis; nightclub/disco; orchestra; restaurant; shops. All-inclusive.

Sandals Negril, P.O. Box 12, tel: 957-4216. 199 rooms. All-inclusive.

Swept Away, Negril, P.O. Box 77, tel: 957-4040. Exclusive hotel set in a lush 10-acre (4-hectare) tropical garden. Good sports facilities.

Expensive

Hedonism II, P.O. Box 25, tel: 957-4200. 280 rooms. All-inclusive.

Sundowner, P.O. Box 5, tel: 957-4225. 26 rooms with air-conditioning, private bath/shower; swimming pool; private beach; restaurant; shops.

Moderate

Charela Inn, P.O. Box 33, tel: 957-4277; fax: 957-4414. 39 rooms with air-conditioning, private bath/shower; swimming pool; private beach; restaurant.

Negril Beach Club, P.O. Box 7, tel: 957-4220/1; fax: 957-4364. 100 rooms with air-conditioning, private bath/shower; swimming pool; private beach; watersports; tennis; horse riding; nightclub/disco; restaurant; shops. Children welcome.

T-Water Cottages, P.O. Box 11, tel: 957-4270/1. 73 rooms with air-conditioning, private bath/shower; private beach; restaurant; shops.

Wilton House, P.O. Box 20, tel: 955-2852. 4 rooms with private bath/shower; watersports; horse riding; restaurant. Children welcome.

Villas

You're basking in nature's generous gifts. An unending supply of clean fresh air fills your lungs with each breath you take, the sun is strong enough to bronze your back as you lounge under it, and the sea stretches for miles to the horizon and beyond. Nearby, stands the villa to which you've come to be "far from the madding crowd."

There are over 350 such villas and cottages available for year-round rental in Jamaica. These are not cluttered together; far from being an international holiday ground, they are sprinkled all over the island. You will find villas in Negril, Tryall, Rose Hall, Reading, Ironshore, just outside Montego Bay, Mammee Bay, Ocho Rios, Oracabessa, Port Antonio, and even more out-of-the-way places. Some rise dramatically out of a long stretch of beach; others are set away in secluded hills; still others are built on the sea with balconied, second-story windows overlooking cliffs or sandy coves.

A constant attraction common to all these homes is the opportunity to live entirely at your own pace, doing what you want to do when you want; of having the privacy and convenience of a home together with the promise of romance, luxury and solace conjured up by such names as East of Eden, Idle Hours and Come What May.

The homes are all fully equipped with linen, towels, cutlery and dishes. Most have private swimming pools and a bathroom adjoining each bedroom. Qualified full-time household staff take over the drudgery of housekeeping; they will tidy up the place and (if requested) prepare exotic meals and make sure larders are replenished with food. (Usually villas are stocked with enough food and liquor to last two days for each new group of visitors.) Guests may alternatively opt for the experience of shopping in the fresh food markets for calalloo (Jamaican spinach), ackees, red peas, sugar cane, orantiques, sweetsops and otaheiti apples.

Reservations can be made through most travel agents or the Jamaican Tourist Board, **Just Jamaica** in the UK, Suite 607, Langham House, 302–308 Regent Street, London W1 5AL, tel: (0171) 436-9292 or the Jamaican Association of Villas and Apartments (**JAVA**) in Jamaica at Pineapple Place, P.O. Box 298, Ocho Rios, tel: 974-2508.

Eating Out

What to Eat

There are tastes to please every palate in Jamaica's restaurants. Sophisticated hotel restaurants serve international cuisine, while cozy inns and roadside stands offer home-cooked local dishes. In the major towns, you can find everything from Kentucky Fried Chicken to excellent Chinese food, the latter a legacy of the island's large population.

The list of eating houses below, while by no means exhaustive, offers a sampling of the various types of food available to the connoisseur.

Where to Eat

Surrey

KINGSTON

Blue Mountain Inn, Gordon Town Road, tel: 927-1700. Continental and Jamaican cuisine.
Devon House, 26 Hope Road, tel: 926-3580. Good food and great for afternoon tea. Excellent ice cream.
Dynasty, 20 Constant Spring Road, tel: 926-4037. Chinese cuisine.
Golden Dragon, 9 Mona Plaza, tel: 927-0809. Chinese cuisine.
Gordons Restaurant, 36 Trafalgar Road, tel: 929-1390. Korean cuisine.
Hotel Four Seasons, 18 Ruthven Road, tel: 926-8805 or 926-0682.
Jade Garden Restaurant, Sovereign Shopping Center, tel: 978-3476.
Just Us, Holborn Road, tel: 929-1222. Mexican cuisine.
Mayfair Hotel, tel: 926-1610. Jamaican and Continental cuisine.
Mother Earth Vegetarian Restaurant, 13 Oxford Terrace, tel: 926-2575.
Restaurant Sutton Plaza, 11 Ruthven Road, tel: 929-2790. Jamaican and Continental cuisine.
Ristorante d'Amore, Wyndham-New Kingston Hotel, tel: 926-5430/9. Italian cuisine.
Royal Garden Restaurant, 15 Village Plaza, tel: 962-8863. Chinese cuisine.

Sea Witch, Knutsford Blvd, tel: 929-4386/7. Seafood.
Talk of the Town, Jamaican Pegasus Hotel, Knutsford Blvd, tel: 926-3690.
Terra Nova, 17 Waterloo Road, tel: 926-2211. Continental cuisine.
The Plantation Terrace, The Courtleigh, 31 Trafalgar Road, tel: 926-8174/8.
The Restaurant, Temple Hall Estate, Stony Hill, tel: 942-2340. Contemporary Caribbean cuisine.
Three Little Bears, 6a Holborn Road, tel: 926-5567.

PORT ANTONIO

Bonnie View Hotel, Bonnie View Street, tel: 993-2752.
Trident Hotel, Anchovy, tel: 993-2602. Russian and Viennese cuisine.

Middlesex

OCHO RIOS

Almond Tree, The Hibiscus Lodge, Main Street, tel: 977-2813. Jamaican cuisine.
Carib Inn, Main Street, tel: 974-2445. Seafood and Continental cuisine.
Evita's Italian Restaurant, Eden Bower Road, tel: 974-2333.
Moxon's of Boscobel, on main road to Couples, tel: 974-3234. Continental cuisine.
Nuccio's, DaCosta Drive, tel: 974-2333. Italian cuisine.
The Ruins Restaurant, DaCosta Drive, tel: 974-2789.

RUNAWAY BAY

Eaton Hall Great House, tel: 973-3404. Jamaican and Continental cuisine.
Runaway Bay H.E.A.R.T Academy & Country Club, tel: 973-2671.

Cornwall

MONTEGO BAY

Brigadoon, Queen's Drive, tel: 952-1723. Seafood.
Calabash, Queen's Drive, tel: 952-3891. Jamaican cuisine.
Casa Blanca, Gloucester Avenue, tel: 952-0720. Italian cuisine.
Cat Cay Brasserie, Wyndham-Rose Hall Hotel, tel: 953-2650. Continental cuisine.
Club House Grill, Half Moon Golf Club, Rose Hall, tel: 953-2314.
Diplomat, Queen's Drive, tel: 952-3353/4.

Fountain Terrace, Seawind Resort, Montego Freeport, tel: 952-4874.

Front Porch, Wexford Court, Gloucester Avenue, tel: 952-2854. Jamaican cuisine.

Georgian House, Union and Orange streets, tel: 952-0632. Jamaican and Continental cuisine.

Harmony House, Gloucester Avenue, tel: 952-5710. Jamaican cuisine.

House of Lords, Holiday Village, Rose Hall, tel: 953-2113/4. Seafood.

Le Papillon, Ironshore Golf Course, tel: 953-2710. French, Continental and Jamaican cuisine.

Marguerite's, Gloucester Avenue, tel: 952-4777. Seafood.

Pelican Grill, Gloucester Avenue, tel: 952-3171.

Richmond Hill Inn, Union Street, tel: 952-3859.

Sandals Royal Caribbean Hotel, Mahoe Bay, tel: 953-2231.

The Ambrosia, Wyndham-Rose Hall Hotel, tel: 953-2650. North Italian cuisine.

Town House, Church Street, tel: 952-2660. Seafood Jamaican style.

NEGRIL

Charela Inn Hotel, tel: 957-4277. Jamaican and French cuisine.

Country Restaurant, Negril Beach, tel: 957-4273. Tasty Jamaican vegetarian cuisine.

Negril Tree House Club, Negril Beach, tel: 957-4287. Jamaican and Continental cuisine.

Rick's Cafe, West End Road, tel: 957-4335. Seafood. The best place to watch the sunset.

Attractions

Museums

A country as rich in history as Jamaica requires several museums to house the exhibits which relate to her arts and crafts, archaeology, antiques and much more.

In Kingston alone, there is the Institute of Jamaica which has a **Science**

Museum and library; the **Coin & Note Museum** further downtown at the Bank of Jamaica; an **Archaeological Museum** and a **Maritime Museum**, among others. Three museums located in Spanish Town are the **Jamaica People's Museum of Craft and Technology**, the **Archaeological Museum**, and the **White Marl Arawak Museum**.

Art Galleries

Jamaican artists' works are on display in a large number of galleries. **The National Gallery** is the repository of the finest works of art produced on the island. Other exhibitions can be seen at the **Bolivar Gallery**, the **Olympia International Art Center**, the **Contemporary Arts Center**, **Gallery Makonde**, and the **Mutual Life Gallery**, all in Kingston. Further north in Montego Bay, galleries well worth visiting include **The Georgian Gallery**, the **Gallery of West Indian Art**, the **Budhai Gallery** and **Harmony Hall** in Ocho Rios.

Theater, Dance & Music

Jamaica's lively tradition of performing arts – theater, dance and music – is surveyed in the feature section of this book. In Kingston, the cultural center, be sure to see the **National Pantomime** at the **Ward Theater** between December and March or April. **The National Dance Theater Company** and the **Jamaica Folk Singers** stage important mini-seasons at **Kingston's Little Theater**; the dancers in December and the singers in March-April. Many smaller theaters also have regular seasons for stage plays; consult the daily newspaper for full details.

For classical and popular music, keep an ear out for performances by the **School of Music (Institute of Jamaica)**, the **Jamaica Philharmonic Symphony Orchestra**, and the **National Chorale** during the early summer and early winter months. And consult the University of the West Indies for performances by and for students.

Jamaicans are movie fans, too. Going to the cinema is an interactive experience, so don't be surprised if the audience is rather vocal during the film. American-made films are the most popular. The small but thriving local movie industry has tremendous support. Consult the local newspaper or your hotel for details.

Many young visitors come to Jamaica with reggae music on their minds. They've brought along their dancing shoes. Night clubs, bars, discotheques, open-air theaters and concert halls throughout the island offer a regular fare of this rhythmic music. And a variety of other musical genres will please everyone's ear.

In Kingston, the most popular night spots include **Illusion**, **Turntable**, **24K**, **Godfathers**, **Carlos** and **Chasers**. The **Jonkanoo Lounge** is at the Wyndham Hotel, New Kingston.

Montego Bay is the nightlife center of Jamaica. The **Witch's Hideaway** at the Holiday Inn has been established longer than any other club. Also in the Rose Hall area, try **Disco Inferno** at Holiday Village. On MoBay's Strip, look for the **Fantasy disco** in the Casa Montego. **Walter's Bar & Grill** and **Pier 1** are also popular. At Montego Freeport, check out **The Cave in the Seawind**. For less flamboyant action, there's a nightly piano bar at the **Doctor's Cave Beach Hotel**.

The most popular clubs in Ocho Rios are **The Ruins**, **The Little Pub** and **Acropolis** among the local crowds and **Silks** (at the Shaw Park Beach Hotel). You might also drop by **Footprints** in the Coconut Grove Shopping Centre, **Jamaca'NMeCrazy**, Jamaica Grande Hotel and **Bananas**. In Runaway Bay, look for **Jaws** at Club Caribbean.

Sport & Leisure

A perfect tropical climate with bright skies and warm weather year-round have spawned a breed of sports enthusiasts. Visitors to the island will therefore find plenty of facilities provided at hotels, sports associations and health clubs.

Traditional sports for watching and participating range from very-British cricket to conventional badminton and universal horse racing at **Caymanas Park**. The list below serves as a brief guide to some of the popular spots.

Golf: Caymanas Golf Club, Kingston; Constant Spring Golf Club, Kingston; Tryall Golf Course, Montego Bay; Ironshore, Montego Bay; Runaway Bay Golf Club, Runaway Bay; Sandals Golf & Country Club, Ocho Rios; Manchester Club, Mandeville; Half Moon Golf Club, Montego Bay.

Tennis: Liguanea Club, Kingston; Pegasus Hotel, Kingston; Dragon Bay, Port Antonio; Montego Bay Racquet Club, Montego Bay; Manchester Club, Mandeville; Negril Beach Club, Negril.

Horse Riding: Chukka Cove Farm, Runaway Bay; Errol Flynn's Plantation, Port Antonio; Prospect Plantation, Ocho Rios; Dunn's River Stables, Ocho Rios; Hotel Astra, Mandeville; Seawind, Montego Freeport; Double A. Ranch, Montego Bay; White Witch Stables, Montego Bay.

Water Skiing: Morgan's Harbour Club, Kingston; Royal Jamaica Yacht Club, Kingston; Club Caribbean, Ocho Rios; Jamaica Grande, Ocho Rios; Sandals Dunn's River and Sandals Ocho Rios; Ray's Parasailing, Negril; Coconut Cove Hotel, Negril; Montego Bay Yacht Club, Montego Freeport; Water Whirl, Montego Bay.

Sailing: Sandals Dunn's River; Negril Beach Club, Negril; Dragon Bay, Port Antonio; Half Moon Club, Montego Bay.

Yachting and Boating: Half Moon Club, Montego Bay; Sandals Dunn's River; Morgan's Harbour Club, Kingston; Royal Jamaica Yacht Club, Kingston.

Scuba and Snorkeling: Sea Jamaica Aquatic Club, Ocho Rios; Island Dive Shop, Priory, St Ann, Ocho Rios; Dive Shop, Rick's Cafe, Negril; Sea Crab, Chatham Cottages, Montego Bay; Jamaica Reef Divers, Montego Bay.

Wind Surfing: Jamaica, Jamaica! Hotel, Runaway Bay; Shaw Park Beach, Ocho Rios; Negril Beach Club, Negril; Dragon Bay, Port Antonio.

Jet Skiing: Jamaica Grande, Ocho Rios; Montego Bay Yacht Club, Montego Freeport.

Parasailing: Ray's Parasailing, Sundowner, Negril; Negril Beach Club, Negril; Jamaica Grande, Ocho Rios.

Deep Sea Diving: Aqua Sports, Negril; Ruddy's Water Sports, Shaw Park Beach, Ocho Rios. See Jamaica Aquatic Club, Ocho Rios.

Shopping

All over the island, there is a multitude of shopping possibilities. Many shops, offering a large variety of merchandise, at "in-bond" or duty-free prices, spell a paradise for shoppers. The vogue is shopping plazas and complexes which make it possible to do all your buying under one roof.

To trigger reminiscences of your visit to the island, look for Jamaica's renowned hand-crafted items. These include Annabella boxes made of wood to serve as cigarette boxes and tiny trinket boxes; pimento-filled Spanish jars; beautiful hand-embroidered linens with motifs of birds and flora; silk and cotton batiked in daring colors. There are good crafts shops at the pier in Port Antonio on 'Cruise-Ship' day; at **City Center**; the craft market on Main Street, Ocho Rios; also at Pineapple Place. **Harmony Hall** has a good selection of the best crafts the island has to offer. Look for straw goods, woodcarvings and bead work at local markets and roadside craft stalls throughout the islands.

Another home product, a must for visitors either to bring home or to savor across the counters, are Jamaica's famous rums and liqueurs. Take your pick from internationally known names like Appleton, Coruba, Gold Label, Rumona, Tia Maria and Sangster's Old Jamaican.

Shopping Areas

Those who have an eye for intricately delicate jewelry, and a bulging wallet to pay for it, can find a first-class selection at major shopping areas in north coast resorts and in Kingston. Those with less money in their pockets should study the workmanship and ingenuity in the semi-precious stones set by Blue Mountain Gems, and Jamaican black coral jewelry. The highly fashionable shell jewelry created by former Miss World, Cindy Breakspeare, and colleague Donna Coore can be bought at the **Italcraft**, their Kingston boutique.

Jamaica is a treasure trove of fineries like bone china and crystal. These are some of the better buys as they are priced at far less than they would be in the United States. You can make your selection at shops like **L.A. Henriques** (in Montego Bay, Ocho Rios and Kingston), **Americans** (in Ocho Rios) and **San-Hing's** (in Port Antonio).

The fashion conscious can browse through the boutiques strung along the **Gloucester Avenue** hotel strip in Montego Bay, and in shopping malls like **Beachview Arcade** and **Casa Montego Arcade**.

Further Reading

History & Politics

Barrett, Lloyd. *The Constitutional Law of Jamaica*. London: Oxford University Press, 1977.

Black, Clinton V. *History of Jamaica*. London: Collins, 1976. *The Story of Jamaica*. London: Collins, 1965. *Tales of Old Jamaica*. Kingston: Sangster, 1979.

Bridges, George W. *The Annals of Jamaica*. 2 vols. London: Murray, 1828.

Carley, Mary Manning. *Jamaica: The Old and The New*. London: George Allen and Unwin, 1963.

Clerk, James Otway. *An Abridged History of Jamaica*. Falmouth, Jamaica, 1859.

Cundall, Frank. *Chronological Outlines of Jamaica History 1492–1926*. Kingston: 1927.

Cundall, Frank, and Pietersz, Joseph L. *Jamaica Under the Spaniards*. Kingston: Institute of Jamaica, 1919.

Dallas, R.C. *The History of the Maroons*. 2 vols. London: 1803.

Dennis, Colin. *The Road not Taken*. Kingston: Kingston Publishers, 1985.

Dillion, J.T. *A Century of Progress: 1838–1933*. Kingston: 1933.

Earle, Stafford. *Basic Jamaica History*. Kingston: Earle Publishing, 1978.

Esquemeling, John. *Buccaneers of America*. London: 1684.

Foot, Hugh. *A Start in Freedom*. London: Hodder and Stoughton, 1964.

Gardner, William James. *A History of Jamaica From Its Discovery by Christopher Columbus to the Present Times*. London: E. Stock, 1873.

Graham, Tom. *Kingston 100: 1872–1972*. Kingston, Tom Graham, 1972.

Hall, Douglas. *Free Jamaica, 1838–1865: An Economic History*. New Haven: Yale University Press, 1951.

Hill, Richard. *Eight Chapters in the History of Jamaica*. Kingston: De Cordova, McDougall and Company, 1868; *Light and Shadows of Jamaica History*. Kingston: Ford and Gall, 1859.

Hurwitz, Samuel J. *Jamaica: A Historical Portrait*. London: Pall Mall Press, 1971.

Ingram, Kenneth E. *Sources of Jamaican History, 1655–1838*. 2 vols. London: Inter Documentation Co., 1976. A bibliographical survey.

Lacey, Terry. *Violence and Politics in Jamaica 1960–70*. Manchester: Manchester University Press, 1977.

Leslie, Charles. *A New History of Jamaica*. Printed for J. Hodges at the Lookingglass on London Bridge, 1740.

Long, Edward. *The History of Jamaica*. 3 vols. London: Frank Class, 1774.

Manley, Michael Norman. *The Politics of Change: A Jamaican Testament*. London: Andre Deutsch, 1974.

Nugent, Maria Lady. *Lady Nugent's Journal: Jamaica 150 Years Ago*. London: 1939.

Olivier, Lord. *Jamaica the Blessed Island*. London: Faber & Faber, 1934.

Post, Ken. *Arise ye Starvelings*. The Hague: Martinus Nijhoff, 1978.

Robinson, Carey. *The Fighting Maroons of Jamaica*. London: Collins/Sangster, 1969.

Stone, Carl, and Brown, Aggrey. *Essays on Power and Change in Jamaica*. Kingston: Jamaica Publishing House, 1977.

Van Sertima, Ivan. *They Came Before Columbus: The African Presence in Ancient America*. New York: Random House, 1976.

Wright, Richardson. *Revels in Jamaica, 1682–1838*. New York: Dodd, Mead, 1937.

People

Barrett, Leonard E. *The Rastafarians: The Dread-locks of Jamaica*. London: Heinemann, 1977.

Bennett, Louise, et al. *Anancy Stories and Dialect Verse*. Kingston: Pioneer Press, 1950.

Brathwaite, Edward. *The Development of Creole Society in Jamaica 1770–1820*. Oxford: Clarendon Press, 1971.

Brown, Aggrey. *Colour, Class and Politics in Jamaica*. New Jersey: Transaction Books, 1979.

Cassidy, Frederic G. *Jamaica Talk*. London: Macmillan, 1971.

Clarke, Edith. *My Mother Who Fathered Me*. London: Allen and Unwin, 1966 edition.

Cumper, George E. *The Social Structure of Jamaica*. Mona: University College of the West Indies, 1949.

Jekyl, Walter. *Jamaica Song and Story*. New York: Dover, 1966.

Kerr, Madeline. *Personality and Conflict in Jamaica*. Liverpool: University Press, 1952.

LePage, R.B., and David de Camp. *Jamaican Creole*. London: Macmillian 1960.

Mbiti, John S. *African Religions and philosophy*. London: Heinemann, 1969.

Owens, Joseph. *Dread: The Rastafarians of Jamaica*. Kingston: Sangsters, 1976.

Wynter, Sylvia. *Jamaica National Heroes*. Kingston: Jamaica National Press Commission, 1971.

Arts & Culture

Baxter, Ivy. *The Arts of an Island*. Metuchen, N.J.: Scarecrow Press, 1970.

Beckwith, Martha. *Jamaican Proverbs*. New York: Negro University Press, 1970.

Boot, Adrian, and Thomas, Michael. *Jamaica: Babylon on a Thin Wire*. London: Thames and Hudson, 1976.

Clerk, Asley, *Music and Musical Instruments of Jamaica*. Kingston: 1916.

Cundall, Frank. *Sculpture in Jamaica*. London: William Clowes and Sons.

Dalrymple, Henderson. *Bob Marley: Music, Myth and the Rastas*. London: Carib-Arawak, 1976.

Davis, Stephen. *Reggae Bloodlines: In Search of the Music and Culture of Jamaica*. New York: Anchor Press/Double Day, 1977.

Ekwene, Laz E.N. *African Sources in New World Black Music*. Toronto: 1972.

Green, Jonathan. *Bob Marley and the Wailers*. London: Wise Publications, 1977.

Lewin, Olive. *Brown Gal in de Ring: 12 Folk Songs from Jamaica*. London: Oxford University Press, 1974.

Manley, Edna. *Focus: An Anthology of Contemporary Jamaican Writing*. Mona: University College of the West Indies, 1956.

McFarlane, J.E. Clare. *A Literature in the Making*. Kingston: Pioneer Press, 1956; *A Treasury of Jamaican Poetry*. London: University of London Press, 1949.

Murray, Tom. *Folk Songs of Jamaica: 32 Songs With Words and Music*. London: University Press, 1952.

Nettleford, Rex. *Caribbean Cultural Identity: The Case of Jamaica*. Kingston: Institute of Jamaica, 1979; *Roots and Rhythms: Jamaica's National Dance Theatre*. London: Andre Deutsch, 1970; *Dance Jamaica*. London: Grove Press, 1985.

Tanna, Laura. *Jamaican Folk Tales and Oral Histories*. Kingston: Institute of Jamaica Publications, 1985.

Whitney, Malika Lee and Dermott Hussey. *Bob Marley: Reggae King of the World*. Kingston: Kingston Publishers 1984.

Natural History

Adams, C. Dennis. *Flowering Plants of Jamaica*. Mona: University of the West Indies, 1972.

Bond, James, *Birds of the West Indies*. London: Collins, 1960 edition.

Grosse, Philip Henry. *Illustrations of the Birds of Jamaica*. London: Van Voorst, 1849.

Gosse, Philip Henry and Hill, Richard. *A Naturalist's Sojourn in Jamaica*. London: 1851.

Kaye, W.J. *Butterflies of Jamaica*. Transactions of the Entomological Society of London, 1926.

Lack, David. *Island Biology Illustrated by the Land of Birds of Jamaica*.

Berkeley & Los Angeles: University of California Press, 1976.

Sloane, Sir Hans. *A Voyage to the Islands Madeira, Barbados, Nieves, St Christophers and Jamaica, with the Natural History of the...last of those islands.* 2 vols. London: 1707, 1725.

Stewart, D.B. (ed.) *Gosse's Jamaica 1844–45.* Kingston: Institute of Jamaica Publications, 1985.

Storer, Dorothy. *Familiar Trees and Cultivated Plants of Jamaica.* London: Macmillan for the Institute of Jamaica, 1958.

Swabey, Christopher. *The Principal Timbers of Jamaica.* Kingston: Dept. of Agriculture, 1941.

Photography

Blake, Evon. *Beautiful Jamaica*, 4th Edition. Jamaica: Vista Publications, 1980.

Canetti, Nicolai. *The People and Places of Jamaica.* London: Peebles Press International, 1976.

Chen, Ray. *Jamaica.* Montreal: Ray Chen, 1985.

Duperly, Adolphe. *Daguerian Excursions in Jamaica.* Kingston: A Duperly, 1844.

Egan, Anne. *Jamaica: Story of a People, A Legend and A Legacy.* Kingston: Rose Hall Ltd., 1973.

Yeager, Bunny. *Camera in Jamaica.* Cranbury, N.J.: A.S. Barnes & Co., 1967.

Sports

Carnegie, James A. *The Jamaican Tradition of Greatness in Sports.* Kingston: Agency for Public Information, 1977.

Dacosta, Eugene. *Sixty Years of Horseracing in Jamaica.* Jamaica, 1934.

Hannau, Michael P. *Fishing in Jamaica.* Hamilton: Buccaneer Publishing House. 1964.

Smith, Lloyd S. *Public Life and Sport: Trinidad, Jamaica and Grenada.* Spain, 1941.

Religion

Banbury, R. Thomas. *Jamaican Superstitions.* Jamaica: Mortimer C. DeSouza, 1849.

Beckwith, Martha. *Jamaica Forklore.* New York: American Forklore Society, 1928.

Buchner, J.H. *The Moravians in Jamaica.* London: Longman Brown & Co., 1854.

Coleman, Stanley J. Douglas, *Isle of Man: The Forklore Academy.* 1960.

Cumper, George E. *The Potential of Rastafarianism as a Modern National Religion.* New Delhi: Recorder Press, 1979.

Hogg, Donald W. *Jamaica Religions: A Study in Variations.* Michigan: Theses Yale University Phd., 1967.

Mullings, Bing. *The 1860 Spiritual Awakening in Jamaica.* Kingston: Jamaica Theological Seminary, 1972.

Seaga, Edward. *Revival Cults in Jamaica.* Kingston: Institute of Jamaica, 1982.

Fiction

Delisser, Herberts G. *The White Witch of Rose Hall.* London: Ernert Benn, 1929.

Duffus, Lee R. *The Cuban Jamaican Connection.* Kingston: Kingston Publishers, 1983.

Hearne, John. *Voices under the Windows.* London: Faber and Faber, 1956. *Land of the Living.* London: Faber and Faber, 1956. *The Sure Salvation.* London: Faber and Faber, 1983.

Hymann, Esther. *Study in Bronze.* London: Constable, 1928.

Mais, Roger. *Brother Man.* London: Jonathan Cape, 1954.

Marr, N.J. *Nigger Brown.* London: Museum Press, 1953.

Ogden, David. *Jones, 38.* Kingston: Kingston Publishers, 1985.

Patterson, H.O. *Children of Sisyphus.* London: Hutchinson, 1964.

Reid, Mayne. *The Maroon.* London: Hurst and Blackett, 1862.

Reid, Victor Stafford. *The Leopard.* New York: Viking Press, 1958.

Salkey, Andrew. *Escape to an Autumn Pavement.* London: Hutchinson, 1960.

Winkler, Anthony. *The Painted Canoe.* Kingston: Kingston Publishers, 1985.

General

Beckford, William. *A Descriptive Account of the Island of Jamaica.* 2 vols. London: 1796.

Black, Clinton V. *Spanish Town: The Old Capital.* Glasgow: Macclehose, 1960.

Cargill, Morris ed. *Ian Fleming Introduces Jamaica.* London: Andre Deutsch, 1965.

Cassidy, Frederic G. and R.B. LePage. *Dictionary of Jamaican English, 2nd Edition.* Cambridge: Cambridge University Press, 1980.

Henriques, Fernando. *Jamaica: Land of Wood and Water.* London: MacGibbon & Lee, 1957.

Henry, Mike. *Caribbean Cocktails and Mixed Drinks.* Kingston: Kingston Publishers, 1980.

Kuper, Adam. *Changing Jamaica.* London: Routledge & Kegan Paul, 1976.

Macmillan, Mona. *The Land of Look Behind: A Study of Jamaica.* London: Faber, 1957.

Miller, Elsa. *Caribbean Cooking and Menus.* Kingston: Kingston Publishers, 1983.

Senior, Olive. *A to Z of the Jamaican Heritage.* Kingston: Heinemann, 1984.

Sibley, Inez. *Place Names of Jamaica.* Kingston: Institute of Jamaica, 1979.

Wright, Philip and Paul F. White. *Exploring Jamaica: A Guide for Motorists.* London: Andre Deutsch, 1968.

Other Insight Guides

There are nearly 190 Insight Guides including several to the Caribbean. Titles include *Insight Guide: Caribbean, Trinidad and Tobago, Bahamas, Bermuda, Cuba* and *Puerto Rico.*

Apa Publications has two other series of guidebooks. *Insight Pocket Guides* feature the author's suggestions for tours and daytrips, with a full-size pull out map. *Insight Compact Guides* are handy mini-encyclopedias.

Index

A

Accompong 86, 259
ackee 141, 144, 224
airports 185, 247
Alexandria 228
Alley 234
Alligator Pond 238
aluminum industry 235, 237 *see also* bauxite
Anansi the Spiderman 53, 92, 126
animals 22
animism 98
Annotto Bay 198
Appleton 144, 271
Arawak Indians 26–27, 30, 85, 97–98, 130–31, 199, 238, 246
Museum 26, 231
athletics 138
Auchindown Farm 268

B

"Back-to-Africa" 101
Baker, Captain Lorenzo Dow 202
Balcarres, Earl of 55
bamboo 22, 270
Bamboo Avenue 148–49, 270
Bamboo Lodge 194
bananas 22, 30, 60, 201–04, 256
Barrett family 251, 253
bars 144, 182
Barton Isles 271
basketball 138
Bath Spa 211–12
bats 22
bauxite 62, 69, 75, 227, 233, 235, 236–37, 271
Beckford, Theophilus 112–13
beer 144
Belafonte, Harry 109
Belancita 194
Benbow, Admiral John 42
Bengal Bridge 227
Berrydale 199
birds 22, 193, 254, 264
Black River 142, 268–69
Blackwell, Chris 117
Blenheim 256
Bloody Bay 264
Blue Hole 208
Blue Mountain coffee 190, 192–93, 194
Blue Mountain Inn 182, 189
Blue Mountain National Park 193
Blue Mountain Peak 21, 166, 194
Blue Mountains 87, 144, 150–51, 161, 189–94

Bluefields Bay 268
bobsleigh 138
Bodles Agricultural Station 233–34
Bog Walk 233
Bogle, Paul 56, 211
Bonney, Anne 40, 43
Bonnie View Hotel 204–05
Booby Cay 264
Boston Bay 209
botanical gardens 189–90, 191–92, 197, 211, 212
Bowden 210
boxing 138
Braes River 271
Brimmer Hall 223–24
British conquest 33–34
Brown's Town 228
buccaneers 39–41, 184
Bull Bay 212
Bump Grave 205
Bustamante, Sir William Alexander 61, 62, 64, 194, 256, 266

C

Caguaya 30, 31, 33
Cane River Falls 212
Canoe People 85
Canoe Valley 238
Carib Indians 26, 85
Carlisle Bay 41
carnivals 120, 156
cashew nuts 270
Castleton Gardens 197
cattle 35, 234, 271
cave paintings 27, 130–31
cave systems 21–22, 208, 226–27, 259
Cave Valley 234–35
Chapelton 234
Charlottenburg House 190–91
Chinese 89
Christiana 237
Ciboney Indians 85
Cinchona Botanical Gardens 191–92
Cinnamon Great House 253
citrus fruits 22, 30, 234, 236
Cliff, Jimmy 114, 117
climate 22, 161, 193
Clydesdale 191
Cockpit Country 21, 86, 243, 259
coconuts 22
coffee industry 35, 73, 191, 192–93, 194
Colbeck Castle 233
color prejudice 73, 74, 89, 90–91
Columbus, Christopher 26, 27, 29–30, 85, 227, 245–46
Columbus Park 227
Constantine, Learie 137
Content Gap 190
Copacabana Beach 212
Cornwall 243–71
Coromantees 49, 53, 54
cotton 27
Coward, Noel 223
Craighton Great House 194
cricket 135–38

crime 75
crocodiles 22, 234, 269
Cromwell, Oliver 32, 33
Cuba 29, 30, 69, 85
Cudjoe 49, 50, 86
Cudjoe Day 86, 259
cuisine 141–44
"curry goat" 142, 157, 224, 238

D

D'Oyley, Col. Edward 34, 35
Daily Gleaner 174
dance 125–26, 176
Dancehall 119–20
Darliston 267
de Grasse, Count 44
DeMontevin Lodge 201
Discovery Bay 227
Dodd, Clement (Coxonne) 112, 113, 115
Dominican Republic 42
drinking 143–44
Drummond, Don 112, 113
du Casse, Admiral Jean 41, 42
Dunkley, John 129
Dunn's River Falls 220–21
dye 198, 270

E

earthquakes 41, 60, 168, 184
East, Hinton 189
economy 35, 65, 66, 67, 68–69, 75, 76, 92
Edinburgh Castle 225
education 73, 74, 76
Eleven Miles 212
Elfin Woodland 194
Elim 271
emigration 62, 66, 73, 92
Espeut, William Bancroft 198
Esquivel, Juan de 30
Ethiopia 65, 103, 104
ethnic composition 21, 85, 89, 90
Ewarton 233

F

Falmouth 253–54
Fern Gully 218, 219
Festival! 125–26
Firefly 223
First Maroon War 49
flag 61
Flat Bridge 232–33
Fleming, Ian 223
flowering plants 22, 189–90, 194, 197
Flynn, Errol 21, 199, 200, 205
Flynn, Patrice 205, 206, 209
food 141–44
Fort Charles 44, 185
Fort George 200
French invasions 41–42, 45
Frenchman's Cove 206, 207, 208
Friendship Farm 219
Frome 60, 266

G

ganja 77, 103, 102, 104, 271
Garvey, Marcus 101–103, 225, 226
geography 21
geology 21, 198
Germans 86, 89, 267
Goat Islands 234
God's Well 238
Goldeneye 223
golf courses 226, 235, 236, 250
Gordon, George William 56, 90, 173, 211
Gordon Town 189
Goshen 271
Grant, Sir John Peter 60
Great Houses 51, 189, 190, 192, 194, 222, 235, 240–41, 251, 253, 255
Great Morass 264–65, 269
Green Grotto 226–27
Green Island 256
Greenwood Great House 253
Guava Ridge 190
Gutters 238

H

Haile Selassie 65, 67, 101, 104
Haiti 42, 54, 130
Halse Hall 235
Headley, George 134, 137
Hedonism II 264
Hellshire Hills 166, 182
Hibbert, Frederick 'Toots' 114–15
higglers 165, 174, 250
Hispaniola 33, 39, 42
Holland Estate 269–70
Hope Bay 198
horse racing 175–76, 178
hurricanes 42, 69, 198, 265

I

immigration 89
independence 62
Indians 89, 265
Industry 189
Irish Town 189, 194
Iron Bridge 231
Island Records 117

J

Jamaica Defence Force 66, 87, 90, 194
Jenkins, Robert 43
jerk cooking 142–43, 209
Jews 56, 91, 173
JLP 61, 62, 65, 66, 67, 68
John Canoe (Junkanoo) dances 53, 124, 126, 131, 169
John Crow Mountain National Park 193

K

Kenilworth Estate 255–56
Kingston 35, 41, 60, 75–76, 119, 161, 165–82
  Bob Marley Museum 180
  Carib Theater 178
  Coin and Note Museum 172
  Coke Church 170–71
  Craft Market 171
  Cultural Training Center 133, 174, 178
  Devon House 133, 180
  Duke Street 173
  Gleaner Building 174
  Gordon House 173
  Half Way Tree 179
  Headquarters House 174
  Holy Trinity Cathedral 174–75
  Hope Gardens 180–81
  Institute of Jamaica 174
  King Street 173
  Kings House 167, 180
  Little Theater 125, 126, 178
  Mico College 176–77
  National Gallery 133, 172
  National Heroes Park 176
  National Library of Jamaica 174
  National Stadium 179
  Parade 168–69, 171
  Parish Church 167
  Port Bustamante 171, 173
  Sabina Park 135, 138
  St Andrew Parish Church 179
  St Andrew Scots Kirk 173
  Synagogue 173
  Tivoli Gardens 129, 175
  Tom Redcam Drive 178
  Trench Town 175
  University of the West Indies 181–82
  Up Park Camp 178
  Vale Royal 177–78
  Ward Theater 168
  Waterfront 171, 172
  Wolmer's School 176
Kirkvine Works 236
kumina 98–99, 161, 205, 210

L

Lacovia 270
"Land of Look Behind" 86, 259
language 146–47
las Casas, Bartolomé de 97–98
Lee, Byron 109, 120, 121
lignum vitae 177
Linstead 233
liqueurs 144, 145, 190
Little London 265
logging 35
logwood 270
Lucea 256

M

Maggotty 271
Malvern 271
manatees 22, 238
Mandeville 21, 236
Manley, Edna 56, 129, 132–33
Manley, Michael 61, 65–66, 67, 68, 69
Manley, Norman Washington 60, 61, 62
mannish water 142
marijuana see ganja
markets 171, 204, 250
Marley, Bob 66–67, 68, 103, 104, 109, 110, 114, 115–18, 180, 228
Maroon Town 259
Maroons 34, 49–50, 53, 54–55, 85–87, 143, 200, 205, 209, 243
Mavis Bank 190, 194
May Pen 234
measurements 147
Melrose Hill 236
mento 109, 111
Middlequarters 269
Middlesex 217–37
Milk River Bath 235
Modyford, Sir Thomas 39, 41, 50
mongooses 198
Monkey Island 208
Montego Bay 29, 55, 119, 242, 243, 245–50
  Canterbury 248
  Church Street 248
  Crafts Market 249–50
  Doctor's Cave Beach 242, 246
  Fort Montego 247
  Half-Moon Club 250
  Harbour Street 249
  Jarrett Park 249
  Richmond Hill Hotel 248
  Sam Sharpe Square 247
  Sandals Montego Bay 250
  Slave Ring 247
  St James Parish Church 248
  The Cage 247
Montpelier 254
Moore Town 205
Morant Bay 210–11, 212
Morant Bay Rebellion 56
Morant Point Lighthouse 209–10
Morgan, Captain Henry 38, 40–41, 268
Mount Diablo 218
Mount Horeb 193
music 109–20, 127, 175, 249
myal cult 98–99
mythology 27

N

Naipaul, V S 208
Nanny Town 49, 87, 205
National Dance Theater Company of Jamaica 125
Navy Island 200
Negril 243, 263–64
Nelson, Horatio 44, 184–85
Newcastle 190, 192, 195, 193–94
Nonsuch Caves 208
Norman Manley International Airport 185
nudism 263

O

obeah 98
Ocho Rios 154–55, 218, 219–21
  Couples 222
  Harmony Hall 222
  Prospect Estate 222
  Shaw Park Gardens 220
  Turtle Beach 221
  White River 221
Old Harbour 233

Oracabessa 223
Orange Bay 198
Orange Valley Estate 228
Oristan 30, 268

P–Q

painting 129–33
Palisadoes 184, 185
pantomime 126–27, 168
Paradise Park 267
parishes 65, 161, 243
Parliament 65, 173
Passage Fort 30, 31, 33, 182
patois 146–47
"pens" 177
Perry, Lee 116
Pickapepper sauce 237
Pine Grove Hotel 190
pirates 31, 42
PNP 60, 65, 67, 69
Pocomania 99, 100, 101
political parties 60–61, 62
politics 60–61, 67–68, 69
polo 224, 226, 271
population figures 21, 73, 75, 167
Port Antonio 30, 197, 199–201, 202,
    204, 206
    Christ Church 206
    Folly 206
Port Esquivel 234
Port Maria 223
Port Morant 210
Port Royal 40, 41, 184–85
    Archaeological Museum 184
    Fort Charles 44, 185
    Giddy House 184, 185
Portland 143, 161, 197–209
Portmore 182
Porus 235–36
Queen Nanny 49, 87, 205

R

Rackham, Jack ("Calico Jack") 42–43,
    264
rafting 199, 254
Rastafarianism 65, 101–04, 113, 147,
    175
Reach Falls 209, 213
Read, Mary 40, 43
Reagan, Ronald 68
reggae 103, 109, 114–20, 175
Reggae Sunfest 243
Reggae Sunsplash 23–24, 119, 182,
    249
Reid, Duke 112
religion 97–104, 161
"renting a tile" 113–14
Retreat 222
rhythm-and-blues 111–12
Rio Bueno 227–28
Rio Grande 198, 199
Rio Nuevo 34, 222
roads 161, 189, 197
Roaring River 266
Rock 254
"Rock Steady" 113–14

Rocklands bird sanctuary 254
Rocky Point 234
Rodney, Admiral George 44, 45
Rose Hall Great House 240–41, 251
Round Hill Hotel 255
"Rude Bwoys" 115–16
rum 144, 190, 254, 271
    distilleries 190, 254, 271
Runaway Bay 226
Runaway Caves 226–27

S

Salt River 234
Santa Cruz 271
Santo Domingo 54
Savanna-la-Mar 30, 44, 265–66
seafood 142, 264, 268
Seaford Town 86, 89, 266, 267–68
Seaga, Edward 62, 66, 67, 68, 69, 175
Second Maroon War 54–55
Sevilla la Nueva 30, 131, 224, 225–26
Seville Estate 224
Sharpe, "Daddy" Sam 56
Shearer, Hugh 61, 62
Shirley, Sir Anthony 31
Shooter's Hill 237
Silver Hill Coffee Factory 192–93
Sir Donald Sangster International Airport
    247
ska 112–13, 114
Skatalites 113
slave rebellions 51, 53–54, 56
slave trade 30, 42, 50, 51–52, 85
slaves 30, 50, 51–54, 56, 109, 247
Sobers, Gary 138
soca 120
Somerset Falls 198
Spaldings 235
Spanish 30–31, 42, 85
Spanish Town 30, 33, 35, 60, 231–32
    Cathedral Church of St James 232
    Court House 231
    Jamaican People's Museum 231
    King's House 31, 231
    Parish Council Office 231
    Records Office 232
    Rodney Memorial 232
    Town Square 231–32
sport 135–38
Spring Garden 189–90, 198
St Ann's Bay 29, 30, 224–25
St James parish 246
St Thomas parish 161, 209–12
Stewart Castle 254
Stokes Hall 210
Stony Hill 197
Struie 267
sugar cane 22, 228, 266
sugar industry 22, 35, 50–51, 74, 201,
    255–56, 266
Surrey 161–212
"Syrians" 89

T

Tacky 53–54, 223
Tacky's Rebellion 53–54
Teach, Edward ("Blackbeard") 42
television 75
theater 125, 126, 127, 168, 178
Three-Fingered Jack 39, 44, 212
Titchfield 201
tobacco 27, 267
Top Mountain 191
Tortuga 39
Treasure Beach 271
trees 22, 192, 193
Trelawny Town 50, 55, 259
Trident Hotel 206
Trinidad 109, 111, 120, 126, 137
Trout Hall 234
Tryall 255

U–V

ugli fruit 234
Vane, Captain Charles 42
Vernon, Admiral ("Old Grog") 43–44

W

Wag Water River 197
Walderston 237
Walker's Wood 219
War of Jenkins' Ear 43–44
White Marl Arawak Museum 26, 231
Whitehouse 268
Whitfield Hall 194
Wickle Wackie 212
Wilberforce, William 55, 56
Windsor Cave 259
Windward Maroons 49, 87, 205
World's End 190

Y

Y S Falls 270
Yallahs Ponds 212
Yallahs River 190, 212
Ysassi, Governor Cristobal Arnaldo de 34,
    222

A
B
C
D
E
F
G
H
I
J
a
b
c
d
e
f
g
h
i
j
k
l

The Insight Approach

The book you are holding is part of the world's largest range of guidebooks. Its purpose is to help you have the most valuable travel experience possible, and we try to achieve this by providing not only information about countries, regions and cities but also genuine insight into their history, culture, institutions and people.

Since the first Insight Guide – to Bali – was published in 1970, the series has been dedicated to the proposition that, with insight into a country's people and culture, visitors can both enhance their own experience and be accepted more easily by their hosts. Now, in a world where ethnic hostilities and nationalist conflicts are all too common, such attempts to increase understanding between peoples are more important than ever.

Insight Guides:
Essentials for understanding

Because a nation's past holds the key to its present, each Insight Guide kicks off with lively history chapters. These are followed by magazine-style essays on culture and daily life. This essential background information gives readers the necessary context for using the main Places section, with its comprehensive run-down on things worth seeing and doing. Finally, a listings section contains all the information you'll need on travel, hotels, restaurants and opening times.

As far as possible, we rely on local writers and specialists to ensure that the information is authoritative. The pictures, for which Insight Guides have become so celebrated, are just as important. Our photojournalistic approach aims not only to illustrate a destination but also to communicate visually and directly to readers life as it is lived by the locals.

Compact Guides
The "great little guides"

As invaluable as such background information is, it isn't always fun to carry an Insight Guide through a crowded souk or up a church tower. Could we, readers asked, distil the key reference material into a slim volume for on-the-spot use?

Our response was to design Compact Guides as an entirely new series, with original text carefully cross-referenced to detailed maps and more than 200 photographs. In essence, they're miniature encyclopedias, concise and comprehensive, displaying reliable and up-to-date information in an accessible way.

Pocket Guides:
A local host in book form

However wide-ranging the information in a book, human beings still value the personal touch. Our editors are often asked the same questions. Where do *you* go to eat? What do *you* think is the best beach? What would you recommend if I have only three days? We invited our local correspondents to act as "substitute hosts" by revealing their preferred walks and trips, listing the restaurants they go to and structuring a visit into a series of timed itineraries.

The result is our Pocket Guides, complete with full-size fold-out maps. These 100-plus titles help readers plan a trip precisely, particularly if their time is short.

Exploring with Insight:
A valuable travel experience

In conjunction with co-publishers all over the world, we print in up to 10 languages, from German to Chinese, from Danish to Russian. But our aim remains simple: to enhance your travel experience by combining our expertise in guidebook publishing with the on-the-spot knowledge of our correspondents.